A Teacher's Life

A Teacher's Life

Essays for Steven M. Cahn

EDITED BY
ROBERT B. TALISSE AND MAUREEN ECKERT

WIPF & STOCK · Eugene, Oregon

Wipf and Stock Publishers
199 W 8th Ave, Suite 3
Eugene, OR 97401

A Teacher's Life
Essays for Steven M. Cahn
By Talisse, Robert B. and Eckert, Maureen
Copyright © 2009 Lexington Books All rights reserved.
Softcover ISBN-13: 978-1-7252-8667-2
Publication date 8/25/2020
Previously published by Lexington Books, 2009

This edition is a scanned facsimile of the original edition published in 2009.

Contents

Introduction *Robert B. Talisse and Maureen Eckert*	vii
About Steven M. Cahn	xi
1. Lessons for Philosophers from Business Ethics: How Philosophy Can Get Its Groove Back *Norman Bowie*	1
2. Academic Standards and Constitutive Luck *Randall Curren*	13
3. Meaningful Lives *Alan Goldman*	33
4. The Relevance of Empirical Findings in Psychology to the Study of Philosophical Ethics *Tziporah Kasachkoff*	43
5. The Teaching Profession *Peter Markie*	61
6. Philosophy and Its Teaching *David M. Rosenthal*	67
7. Philosophical Humor, Lewis Carroll, and Introductory Philosophy *John O'Connor*	85
8. Shake 'Em Up: On Teaching Weird or Irrelevant Philosophical Views *David Shatz*	93
9. Global Norming: An Inconvenient Truth *George Sher*	107
10. Intercollegiate Athletics and Educational Values: A Case for Compatibility *Robert Simon*	113
11. How to Duck Out of Teaching *Douglas Stalker*	143
12. The Happy Immoralist *Christine Vitrano*	149
13. Mentoring: Lessons from Steven Cahn *Robert B. Talisse and Maureen Eckert*	155
Afterword *Steven M. Cahn*	163
Bibliography	165
Index	169

Introduction

Robert B. Talisse and Maureen Eckert

We present this collection of essays honoring Steven M. Cahn on the twenty-fifth anniversary at The Graduate School and University Center of The City University of New York Ph.D. Program in Philosophy. Our Festschrift is titled *A Teacher's Life* in the effort to express a unique aspect of Steve's multifaceted career. Steve is among the rare university scholars whose range of scholarly works have contributed to discipline-specific debates and also substantially contributed to the scholarship of teaching and pedagogical practice, as well as scholarship regarding the overall context of scholarship and teaching—the institutions of higher learning itself. His diverse scholarly interests are of a piece with his participation in university life throughout his career and the responsibilities he undertook as scholar, teacher, administrator, editor, and mentor. In an age where teaching is commonly understood as a burden and "load," very few university scholars are distinctive for their commitment to teaching and the institutional context that supports that mission. For Steve, a professor's life is "a good life," a life spent "working on what we love and sharing our satisfactions for the benefit of others."[1] Teaching, broadly understood, has informed Steve's vision of the good professorial life, exemplified in word and deed throughout his career.

The essays in this volume reflect the diversity of Steve's scholarly interests, and can be roughly organized into topics regarding Academic Ethics, Teaching Philosophy, and Steven M. Cahn's Scholarship. Writing on topics concerning Academic Ethics, we have contributions from Randall Curren, Peter Markie, George Sher, Douglas Stalker, and a co-authored piece by Robert Talisse and Maureen Eckert. Randall Curren contributes "Academic Standards and Constitutive Luck," in which he examines Steve's view of academic standards with respect to excellence and teaching effectiveness, developing puzzles that mirror those developed in Thomas Nagel's "Moral Luck," and ultimately determining the use of grades that is least encumbered by constitutive luck. Peter Markie contributes "The Teaching Profession," in which he examines the concept of professionalism and determines its consistency with college teaching as a profession. Although college teaching meets the criteria established as a professional practice, there is a failure to honor expectations with respect to training that are a part of professionalism. George Sher contributes "Global Norming: An Inconvenient Truth," in which he examines the moral dilemma involved in composing academic letters of recommendation for students that are not wholly and enthusiastically recommendable: On the one hand, there is a duty to tell the truth; on the other hand there is an obligation to promote one's students' best interests. Sher finds a compromise available that does not fall too far into inflation while meeting the obligation to assist one's students. Robert Simon contributes "Intercollegiate Athletics and Educational Values: A Case for Compatibility," in which he examines the role of intercollegiate athletics with respect to the academic mission of universities. Against the criticism that intercollegiate athletics are inconsistent with this mission, Simon argues that intercollegiate athletics (properly conducted) and academic inquiry and study (properly conducted) are mutually reinforcing, both being mutual quests for excellence through challenge. Douglas Stalker contributes a reprint of his satirical article "How to Duck Out of Teaching," a piece that warns against the use of technology and popular pedagogical strategies as crutches to avoid the intellectual labors and difficult decision making encountered in successful teaching. Robert Talisse and Maureen Eckert contribute "Mentoring: Lessons from Steven M. Cahn," in which they examine the role of an academic mentor, and present "Five Principles of Good Mentoring."

On the topic of Teaching Philosophy we have contributions from Norman Bowie, Tziporah Kasachkoff, John O'Connor, David Rosenthal and David Shatz. Norman Bowie contributes "Lessons for Philosophers from Business Ethics: How Philosophy Can Get Its Groove Back," in which he presents a case that business ethics can reinvigorate philosophy, utilizing theoretical support from other disciplines (in this case economics) and traditional philosophical argumentative methods in order to increase the scope of philosophical knowledge and its relation to other disciplines and worldly practices. Tziporah Kasachkoff contributes "The Relevance of Empirical Findings in Psychology to the Study of Philosophical Ethics," in which she assess and critiques the SIM "social intuitionist model" of moral reasoning which holds that moral reasoning itself is epiphenomenal to intuitive emotional reactions, and challenges the soundness of this research program. David Rosenthal contributes "Philosophy and Its Teaching," in which he examines the unusual position of philosophy with respect to teaching historical texts in contrast to other disciplines in the humanities and in the sciences. He asks, "Why study the history of philosophy?" Against the Historicist explanation, he defends a Scaffolds and Connections explanation, which values the interpretive skills and conceptual means needed to transcend the theoretical conflicts represented in classic philosophical systems. John O'Connor contributes a reprint of his essay "Philosophical Humor, Lewis Carroll, and Introductory Philosophy," in which he provides a model for utilizing the works of Lewis Carroll in topics-approach introduction to philosophy courses. Carroll's *Alice's Adventures in Wonderland* and *Through the Looking Glass* can be taught over the course of a semester alongside other philosophical works, assisting students' understanding of subtle philosophical distinctions and providing illustrations to problems found in classic philosophical works. Lewis Carroll's works are memorable for students, enjoyable to teach and, importantly, introduce philosophical humor through which philosophy can be better appreciated. David Shatz contributes "Shake 'Em Up: On Teaching Weird or Irrelevant Philosophical Views," in which he discusses the pedagogical virtues of presenting controversial philosophical views in the classroom, providing examples through which he determines more (and less) productive attitudes and exercises in utilizing counter-intuitive positions and materials.

On the topic of Cahn's Scholarship we have contributions from Alan Goldman and Christine Vitrano. Alan Goldman contributes "Meaningful Lives" in which he addresses and assesses Steven Cahn's critique of Susan Wolf's account of the meaningful life. While Cahn rejects Wolf's account of determining this meaning with respect to projects that have objective value, Goldman develops a middle ground, agreeing that while objective grounds cannot be in play, internal relations between activities can distinguish meaningful from non-meaningful life-projects. Christine Vitrano contributes "The Happy Immoralist," in which she examines a set of objections raised against Steven Cahn's article "The Happy Immoralist," and his thought experiment with Fred, a happy yet immoral figure. She diagnoses a main flaw in the objections—the temptation to keep happiness and morality closely linked and without conflict so as to insure that people find motivation to be moral. However, Vitrano argues that Cahn is correct: happiness and morality are not intrinsically linked and can conflict. Happiness can conflict with moral duty, it is rational to pursue happiness, and thus behaving immorally can be rational.

Douglas Stalker's contribution is reprinted with permission from *The Chronicle of Higher Education*. John O'Connor's contribution is reprinted with permission from the *APA Newsletter on Teaching Philosophy*. We thank Tyler Zimmer and D. Micah Hester for help in preparing the text. Finally, we thank all the contributors to this Festschrift honoring Steve. It has been an honor for us to edit this collection of essays inspired by his work.

Note

1. Steven M. Cahn, *From Student to Scholar: A Candid Guide to Becoming a Professor* (New York: Columbia University Press, 2008), 71.

About Steven M. Cahn

Steven M. Cahn was born in Springfield, Massachusetts in 1942. His early years were devoted to the piano, which he studied with Herbert Stessin of the Juilliard School and with the noted chamber music artist Artur Balsam. Dr. Cahn has continued to perform recitals with his brother, Victor L. Cahn: violinist, playwright, actor, critic, and Professor of English at Skidmore College.

Following his graduation from Woodmere Academy, where he was taught Latin by the celebrated poet and translator Rolfe Humphries, Dr. Cahn attended Columbia College and studied American history with James Shenton, music theory with William Mitchell, and philosophy with Ernest Nagel. After earning his A.B. in 1963, Dr. Cahn pursued doctoral studies in philosophy at Columbia University, where he worked closely with Richard Taylor and also was influenced by Charles Frankel.

Upon receiving his Ph.D. in 1966, he published his first book, *Fate, Logic, and Time*, with Yale University Press. Based on his doctoral dissertation, the work was the first full-length study of historical and contemporary arguments regarding the metaphysical problem of fatalism.

After serving as a Visiting Instructor at Dartmouth College, he spent two years as Assistant Professor at Vassar College, then joined the faculty at Washington Square College of New York University. During the next five years, he taught undergraduate and graduate courses while also fulfilling various administrative responsibilities, including departmental director of undergraduate studies, departmental director of graduate studies, and chair of the college-wide Educational Policy Committee. In 1971 he wrote *A New Introduction to Philosophy* and in 1973 *The Eclipse of Excellence*, an oft-cited critique of American higher education.

That year he became Chair of the Department of Philosophy at the University of Vermont, where over the next five years he led the successful effort to build a nationally ranked undergraduate program. In 1978 he took a leave of absence to become a program officer at the Exxon Education Foundation, and in 1979 published *Education and the Democratic Ideal*, a study in the philosophy of education. At that time he moved to the Rockefeller Foundation, where later he became Acting Director for Humanities. In 1982 he accepted the position as

Director of General Programs at the National Endowment for the Humanities in Washington, D.C.

In 1983 Dr. Cahn was appointed Professor of Philosophy and Dean of Graduate Studies at The City University of New York Graduate Center. A year later he was named Provost and Vice President for Academic Affairs, a position he held until 1991, when he served as Acting President. While overseeing the school's rise to national prominence, he taught graduate courses in philosophy, and regularly co-taught with Distinguished Professor of English Lillian Feder a seminar in classics of world literature, a course for dissertation-level students from all of the school's programs. His pioneering work *Saints and Scamps: Ethics in Academia* was published in 1986, laying the groundwork for the field of academic ethics. A collection of his essays, *Philosophical Explorations: Freedom, God, and Goodness*, appeared in 1989.

In 1992 he returned to full-time graduate teaching. A revised edition of *Saints & Scamps* was published in 1994, *Puzzles & Perplexities: Collected Essays* appeared in 2002 with a second edition five years later, and in 2006 Wadsworth/Thomson issued his *God, Reason, and Religion*, a provocative study in the philosophy of religion. His most recent book, *From Student to Scholar: A Candid Guide to Becoming a Professor*, which was brought out in 2008 by Columbia University Press, offers advice on traversing the thickets of academia.

For a decade Dr. Cahn has offered a colloquium on college teaching, open to doctoral students in any Graduate Center program, introducing them to the practices and responsibilities of faculty membership. In recent years, he has also taught a semester-long course he developed for doctoral students in philosophy who are seeking to enhance their skills in teaching undergraduates.

Since 1983 he has been President of the John Dewey Foundation and has also served five-year terms as Chair of the American Philosophical Association's standing committee on the teaching of philosophy and as the Association's delegate to the American Council of Learned Societies.

He has spoken frequently at colleges and universities throughout the United States, delivering among other addresses the first Naumberg Memorial Lecture at UCLA, the Minerva Lecture at Union College, the convocation address at Florida International University, and a keynote speech to the Kenan Convocation at the University of North Carolina at Chapel Hill. He has also lectured at meetings of numerous educational organizations, including the College Entrance Examination Board, New England Association of Schools and Colleges, American Association of State Colleges and Universities, National Association of Academic Affairs Administrators, and Northeastern and Midwestern Associations of Graduate Schools.

He has edited or co-edited more than thirty books, nearly half of which have been published by Oxford University Press, including *Political Philosophy: The Essential Texts*; *Exploring Philosophy: An Introductory Anthology*, now in its third edition; and *Ethics: History, Theory, and Contemporary Issues*, now in its fourth edition. His widely used anthology *Classics of Western Philosophy*, published by Hackett Publishing Company, is in its seventh edition. He has also been general editor of four multi-volume series: *Blackwell Philosophy Guides*

(21 books), *Blackwell Readings in Philosophy* (14 books), *Issues in Academic Ethics* (15 books), and *Critical Essays on the Classics* (20 books), the latter two published by Rowman & Littlefield.

His many articles have appeared in a broad spectrum of publications including *The Journal of Philosophy, The Chronicle of Higher Education, Shakespeare Quarterly, The American Journal of Medicine, The New Republic,* and *The New York Times.*

He resides in Old Greenwich, Connecticut with his wife, Dr. Marilyn Ross, a pediatrician, and continues to be active as a writer and teacher.

1. Lessons for Philosophers from Business Ethics: How Philosophy Can Get Its Groove Back[1]

Norman E. Bowie

Introduction

In the beginning philosophy constituted knowledge. By that I mean all branches of knowledge were considered a part of philosophy. The paradigm example of a philosopher who wrote on all branches of knowledge of the time is Aristotle. Even today persons earning doctorates in most academic disciplines receive doctor of philosophy degrees. As the centuries have gone by, one branch of knowledge after another has gained its independence from philosophy. First the natural sciences, then the biological sciences, then the social sciences and eventually cognitive science and linguistics gained their independence. By the beginning of the twenty-first century, there was not much for philosophers to do. There is the history of philosophy, of course. There is the free will problem, although much of that issue is now discussed in terms of cognitive science and evolutionary theory. And there is ethical theory and applied ethics. Since neither ethics nor applied ethics is scientific, other disciplines have been content either to leave normative ethics to the philosophers or to focus on ethical issues that can be studied scientifically.

In addition philosophy became more and more of an academic discipline and less connected to the lives of people outside the academy. It is important to remember that this withdrawal into the academy is a rather recent development in the history of the discipline. John Dewey, who lived until the middle of the twentieth century, wrote for the layperson as well as for professional philosophers. And even when he wrote for colleagues he wrote about subjects that had a great impact on ordinary people, the justification of democracy, the philosophy of education, the philosophy of art. A large portion of his book *Individualism: Old and New* incorporated articles Dewey had written for *The New Republic*. Dewey had no difficulty being both an academic philosopher and a public intellectual. Perhaps a few quotations from Dewey are appropriate here. In speaking of the reconstruction of philosophy Dewey said:

> From the position taken here, reconstruction can be nothing less than the work of developing, of forming, of producing (in the literal sense of that word) the intellectual instrumentalities which will progressively direct inquiry into the deeply and inclusively human—that is to say, moral—facts of the present scene and situation....One of the operations to be undertaken in a reconstructed philosophy is to assemble and present reasons why the separation once set up between theory and practice no longer exists.[2]

> The separation of morals from human nature leads to a separation of human nature in the moral aspects from the rest of nature and from ordinary social habits and endeavors which are found in business, civil life, the run of companionships and recreations....In short, the severance of morals from human nature ends by driving morals inwards from the public open out-of-doors air and light of day into the obscurities and privacies of an inner life.[3]

As we know, under the spell of logical positivism and its relatives, Dewey's insights as to the nature of philosophy became passé and what was considered philosophical became restricted. Ethics became meta-ethics—the study of the meaning of ethical terms and a debate about whether ethical claims could be objective. John Rawls is primarily responsible for reintroducing the normative. His classic work, *A Theory of Justice*, not only stimulated normative thinking in ethics, but it invigorated political philosophy and encouraged the development of applied ethics. Although Rawls' *A Theory of Justice* was hardly a book for the layperson, its subject matter was of great importance to lay people. Academics outside philosophy took an interest. One of Rawls' earliest appearances to explain and defend his work was before the American Economic Association.

Partly in response to changing intellectual fashion and partly in response to the employment crisis for philosophers that started in the 1970s and has continued to this day, professional philosophy as embedded in the American Philosophical Association changed. Philosophy and the American Philosophical Association have embraced—out of necessity more than love—a number of applied ethics disciplines: medical ethics, legal ethics, and thanks primarily to the work of Steven Cahn, ethics in education. Some recognition also has been given to Cahn's passion, the teaching of philosophy.

Despite the interdisciplinary interest in Rawls' work and the turn towards normative ethics and applied ethics, academic non philosophers have become less clear what philosophers do.[4] Or to put it another way, what is the methodology? This lack of knowledge became clear when a colleague at the University of Minnesota applied for a university grant. The review committee wrote the philosopher asking for a statement of methodology. My philosophy colleague was perplexed but finally responded by saying philosophers give arguments, consider objections to the arguments, and then improve upon the arguments. I have heard more than one economist say that no one should get tenure for doing that since any smart person—or at least any smart economist—could do that. In the early nineties I served on a review panel for the National Science Foundation. My chief task was to defend proposals by philosophers by explaining what they do and why it was important—their methodology, in other words. Our colleagues either do not know what we do or when they clearly realize what we do they think that any intelligent person can do it. This problem persists but professional philosophers and the American Philosophical Association largely ignore it. A studied intellectual arrogance and aloofness seem to be the preferred strategy.

Even more disconcerting to me is that business ethics has been almost completely ignored by professional philosophers. There is no American Philosophical Association newsletter on business ethics and the Board of Officers of the APA has made clear that there will not be. Neither is there a committee on business ethics. Philosophers interested in business ethics were forced to create their own society—the Society for Business Ethics. That society is flourishing, by the way. Most philosophers are deeply suspicious of capitalism and its values. To engage business is to sell out for money and/or to deal with the enemy. The future of the discipline may require the acceptance of some branches of applied ethics but not business ethics. That would be a step too far.

To his credit Steven Cahn never took this point of view. The teaching of philosophy was always a passion. He lectured us on the ethics or lack thereof of university professors (*The Eclipse of Excellence: A Critique of American Higher Education, Education and the Democratic Ideal*, and *Saints and Scamps: Ethics in Academia*). He has written about the philosophy of religion (*Freedom, God and Goodness*). He has an abiding interest in music and is an accomplished pianist. Steven has had major administrative appointments in the National Endowment for the Humanities, the Rockefeller Foundation and the Exxon Education Foundation. He also has served ably as a college administrator in a number of positions culminating in his being Acting President of the Graduate School and University Center of the City University of New York. Although he did not write on business ethics himself he was one of the few philosophers who considered it a legitimate activity. Thus in his series on Issues in Academic Ethics, he asked me to write a book in the series on university business partnerships. Steven has shown that you can be a philosopher's philosopher and still make philosophy relevant both to academics in other disciplines and to lay people.

As a tribute to Steven I will argue that business ethics has much to offer the profession. Most importantly it provides an opportunity to illustrate how philosophy once again can be at the center of knowledge. However, I will not argue that philosophy is the Queen of the Sciences. It isn't. Rather I will show how philosophy can integrate other knowledge in a way that makes normative arguments in ethics plausible and I will show how adapting a concern with ethics can improve knowledge and practice in other disciplines and in the world. If these arguments are successful, perhaps I can show how philosophy can get its groove back.

Using Knowledge from Economics to Make an Ethical Argument

Transaction Cost Economics[5]

My framework for the argument is transaction cost economics—a branch of economics developed by Oliver Williamson.[6] From the transaction cost perspective, the first and perhaps most important attribute for assessing a transaction is the degree to which individuals involved in the transaction must invest dedicated assets. Dedicated assets are transaction specific and have high asset specificity. Suppose a large retailer seeks a supplier to provide a product with specifications that are unique to that retailer. To provide the product, the supplier must invest in the resources that will enable it to meet the unique specifications of the retailer. Those resources would be dedicated assets and have high asset specificity. On the other hand, suppose a supplier provides products for a number of retailers all of whom have the same specifications. In these circumstances, the resources of the supplier can be used for any of the retailers; the resources are not specific to one retailer. In such cases we say that the resources have low asset specificity; they are not dedicated to one retailer.

The existence of assets that are highly specific can create moral problems. In the literature, transaction cost economists showed how suppliers with resources that were characterized by high asset specificity could be subject to what is called "the hold-up" problem. The supplier invests in the resources to make the specific product only to face demands by the retailer to lower prices. Since the supplier's resources are dedicated to that retailer, he has little choice but to lower the price. It is alleged that many of Wal-Mart's suppliers were subject to the hold-up problem. Let us see how the insights of transaction cost economics provide theoretical support for ethical claims.

Why Codes of Ethics Alone Are Not Effective

When people in the public arena speak of organizational ethics, one of the first questions is, "Does the organization have a code of ethics?" In the scholarly business ethics literature, there is a large literature on codes of ethics. People think that codes of ethics are important for maintaining organizational ethics. I disagree. Codes of ethics are not a good indicator of an organization's commitment to ethics. In addition, a code of ethics is only useful if the other factors that contribute to organizational ethics are present. To see why this is so, we need to return to our discussion of transaction cost economics and specifically consider the distinction between high and low asset specificity.

Codes of ethics have low asset specificity. They are easily copied. Enron had one of the best codes of ethics, yet the ethical climate at Enron was terrible even before the collapse. Thus a good code of ethics is not a good indicator as to whether an organization has high ethical standards or low ethical standards. For this reason, I do not consider codes of ethics to be an important factor in organizational ethics.

However, when a code of ethics is deeply embodied within a moral climate, it can be a useful device for guiding employee and even management conduct. Perhaps the best known example of a code of ethics that has made a difference in management decision-making and really does contribute to organizational integrity is Johnson and Johnson's Credo. The Johnson and Johnson Credo is not simply a document that all employees sign off on. It is a living document. The Credo is evaluated periodically to see if it still reflects the values and vision of the company and if it is still useful as a tool for helping resolve ethical issues or dilemmas the company might face. Thus there is a symbiotic relationship between the ethical climate at Johnson and Johnson and their credo.

Thus the insights from transaction cost economics enables the normative ethical theorist to conclude that a code of ethics by itself is an ineffective way to make business concerns ethical. Transaction cost economics provides a theoretical basis for that claim.

The Viability of an Ethical Climate

Unlike codes of ethics that have low asset specificity, I believe organizations with an ethical climate have an asset with high asset specificity and that such organizations thereby have a tremendous competitive advantage. An ethical climate involves ethical commitments that have the following characteristics: they are values based and the values are embodied in the character of the organizational members and in the organization's routines and incentive structures. Experience teaches us that ethical climates are difficult to copy.

What is the evidence of that? Both the scholarly literature and business experience speak to the fact that it is very difficult to change a corporate culture and an ethical climate, where it exists, is part of the corporate culture. One good example here is the contrast between Ashland Oil Company and Exxon-Mobil. When Ashland Oil was involved in an oil spill at its facility in Floreffe, Pennsylvania in 1988, the CEO John Hall and other corporate officers quickly went to the site of the spill, admitted fault and directed the clean-up. This action was wise from both an ethical and a business perspective. Ashland Oil had its fines reduced and suffered less litigation as a result of their behavior. They also gained respect as an ethically responsible company. Within two years Exxon, as it was known then, had the Exxon Valdez oil spill. Exxon had learned nothing from the Ashland Oil incident and thus was subjected to much litigation and a serious blow to its reputation. Corporate culture and specifically an ethical climate have high asset specificity and are not easily copied. Thus it should not come as a surprise that Exxon really did not learn anything from the Ashland Oil spell. The courts have awarded 287 million dollars for actual damages and (on appeal) punitive damages of 2.5 billion dollars.[7] Organizational learning or organizational sense making is intimately tied to and to a large extent constrained by its culture. Exxon Oil had a very different culture from Ashland Oil and Exxon's sensitivity to ethical issues (its ethical culture if you will) was different from Ashland Oil's.

You can observe the same phenomenon with respect to climate change. Both BP and Shell recognized that climate change was taking place and both were proactive in devising strategies, including a public relations strategy, for dealing with it. Exxon Mobil only recently has recognized the importance of climate change and its strategy, unlike BP's and Shell's, is limited to technological fixes. BP wants to be an energy company; its slogan Beyond Petroleum speaks to that. Exxon Mobil sees itself as an oil company.

Unlike codes of ethics, an ethical climate does contribute to making a business corporation ethical. Transaction cost economics provides a theoretical argument why that is so. The next step—future research if you will—is to determine both what a corporation ought to do (the philosophical question) and what kinds of organizational structure will contribute to a corporation's achieving its moral purpose (the social science question). Social science and organizational theory will also tell us what organizational structures will inhibit the achievement of a moral climate.

Why Companies Adopt Universal Ethical Norms

While teaching executive MBAs in Minnesota as well as teaching Polish executive MBAs at the Warsaw School of Economics, I discovered that multinational corporations sought to instill their core values across all their subsidiaries. Thus the 3M Corporation had a universal policy against bribery for example. 3M employees were not allowed to pay bribes anywhere—even in countries where bribery was commonplace. I was tempted to believe that this statement of commitment to policy might be just ethical window dressing. As we know from the argument above, a code of ethics divorced from an ethical culture may not mean much. However, my Polish students who worked for multinationals—US, German, and French—complained that these companies insisted on doing things the way they were done in their home countries. These Polish students could not understand why these multinationals did not attempt to adapt more to their host countries. In other words, why don't multinationals adopt more of a "When in Rome do as the Romans do" policy?

I want to limit the discussion here to the core ethical values of a multinational corporation (MNC). One reason that a MNC might give for making their core ethical values universal across all their operations is because it is the right thing to do. But I think there is another argument for doing that. This argument is limited to those MNCs that believe that their core ethical values are an essential part of their brand. In other words, being a socially responsible corporation is part of the Johnson and Johnson brand. Johnson and Johnson believes that its reputation as a socially ethical corporation gives it a competitive advantage. Companies like Johnson and Johnson could give the following argument for applying their core ethical values universally.

The Argument for Universal Ethical Values
1. Certain ethical values are believed by the management of a MNC to provide the MNC with a competitive advantage.
2. Those ethical values which provide a durable competitive advantage abroad will tend to be knowledge based, be embodied in individual employees or firm routines, and be characterized by high asset specificity.
3. Highly specific assets associated with high return should not be diluted.
4. If ethical values are such assets they should not be diluted.
5. If ethical values vary among subsidiaries, these assets will be diluted due to the phenomenon of cognitive dissonance.
6. Therefore a MNC should have common ethical values in all its subsidiaries.

Let's examine the argument in detail. The first premise limits the argument to those corporations that believe that their ethical values give them a competitive advantage. Premise 2 describes the nature of ethical values or perhaps more accurately of an ethical culture in the multinational corporation (MNC) that embodies those ethical values. Using the terminology of transaction cost economics, premise 2 asserts that the nature of an ethical climate is such that it has high asset specificity and thus cannot be easily copied. Given premises 1 and 2, we have MNCs that believe that their ethical values are a competitive advantage and if transaction cost economics theory is right, these MNCs have a competitive advantage that is hard to copy. For one doing corporate strategy, this is an ideal situation. A MNC like Johnson and Johnson has an asset that gives it a competitive advantage and it is an asset that is very difficult for its competitors to copy. Given that, it is easy to see why premise 3 is true. A MNC that has an asset that gives it a competitive advantage and cannot be copied has an asset that it does not want to dilute. Premise 4 simply identifies the asset in this argument as ethical values.

Suppose a MNC considers adopting the "when in Rome do as the Romans do" philosophy or ethical relativism with respect to ethical values. In other words if bribery is widely practiced in a country where it does business, the company policy would be that it is ok to bribe in those countries. However, employees could not bribe in countries where bribery was forbidden and not practiced. Since employees on track to be senior executives of a MNC do multiple postings abroad, in such an environment they would suffer from the psychological phenomenon of cognitive dissonance. Cognitive dissonance is a state of discomfort or tension that results when people hold or are asked to hold incompatible beliefs. In our example of the MNC that adopts ethical relativism with respect to bribery, up-and-coming managers are told that company policy with respect to bribery is that it is ok to bribe and it is not ok to bribe according to the circumstances. Strictly speaking there is no logical contradiction here since whether the employee should bribe or not bribe depends on the circumstances. However, as a matter of psychology there is a tension, because if people think that bribery is wrong (or right), they would tend to think that it is right or wrong universally. Most people cannot contextualize their core ethical values.

Adding the knowledge regarding cognitive dissonance to the knowledge about the nature of the competitive advantage of ethical values gives us the conclusion that a MNC of that type should impose its ethical values universally in all its subsidiaries. Transaction cost economics gives us an argument why a MNC like Johnson and Johnson should not bribe. Of course it is a prudential argument, but so what? What such a prudential argument does is show that any independent ethical argument for a corporation to do or not do something is buttressed by a prudential argument—at least for a certain type of corporation.

This argument can be pushed further. Suppose that premise 1 of the argument is true. By that I mean it is not only the case that certain multinationals believe that their core ethical values give them a competitive advantage, but it is also true that their core ethical values give them a competitive advantage. In other words, the beliefs of those MNCs are true beliefs. We could then rewrite premise 1 as follows:

1. Certain ethical values of a MNC provide the MNC with a competitive advantage.

What should the response be of a MNC that adopts the "when in Rome do as the Romans do" strategy? Such a MNC could hold to the strategy. However, other things being equal, economists would say that such stubbornness would have to end in failure. If the MNCs that do not have the "when in Rome do as the Romans do" strategy really do have a competitive advantage, then eventually those companies will win out in the competitive struggle, other things being equal. A company that has a "when in Rome do as the Romans do" strategy will eventually, other things being equal, go bankrupt. In that case, the wise strategy is to try to develop an ethical culture with ethical values that are adopted universally. In other words the appropriate strategy is to make a universal commitment to certain ethical values a part of the MNC's brand. This strategy is rational even though it is hard to achieve. It is hard to achieve because an ethical culture with universal ethical values is hard to copy. Nonetheless, the company strategy should be to try. And this is good news for the raising of international standards of business ethics. Here is the formal argument for that claim.

An Argument for Truly Universal Standards of Business Ethics
1. Certain ethical values are either necessary for the MNC's economic success or provide it with a competitive advantage.
2. Thus, other things being equal, MNCs will be driven by market forces to adopt those ethical values which are necessary for economic success or provide competitive advantage.
3. Thus other things being equal, market forces will favor the development of at least a common core of ethical standards. Thus all MNCs will ultimately tend to adopt nearly identical standards

whatever their beliefs of the competitive advantage of ethical commitments.

But what should these ethical commitments be? In part that is a task for moral philosophers. It is fairly easy to give ethical arguments against discrimination and against bribery. I will not make those arguments here. What is interesting from an interdisciplinary perspective is that economists can provide efficiency arguments against discrimination and against bribery. Moreover, empirical investigation shows that as a matter of fact discrimination against women is decreasing in most parts of the world and all international agreements on business ethics have a provision against bribery. Thus both ethical arguments and economic arguments can be provided against discrimination and bribery. Moreover, these arguments can influence policy. Action at the corporate level is developing in a way that both efficiency and normative ethics require.

These three arguments illustrate how a philosopher in business ethics who is familiar with another discipline can take the concepts of that other discipline as the centerpiece of arguments for a normative position. I can use a theoretical position that has validity in the social science to ground a normative position. Am I able to derive an "ought" from an "is"? Not quite. But I can show how insights in a social science support normative arguments.

How Concepts from Ethics Can Improve Business Decision Making

This process can work in reverse. I can use concepts from ethics to improve both business scholarship and decision-making in business itself.

Fairness as an Explanatory Variable in Economics and Management Theory

The possibility of using a norm of fairness owes much to the rise of behavioral economics. Herbert Simon is credited with the notion of bounded rationality. Bounded rationality reflects the fact that human beings have limited cognitive abilities that constrain human problem-solving. A less well known concept from behavioral economics is the notion of "bounded willpower." Bounded willpower reflects the fact that human beings make choices that are not in their self-interest. Once economists had a notion of bounded willpower, there was an opening for looking at the role of fairness in economics—an opening that has been brilliantly taken by the economist Robert Frank. Frank cites numerous economic phenomena that cannot be explained on what he calls the self-interest model. Among these phenomena are the facts that people tip in restaurants to which they will not return, that restaurants and barber shops do not charge more for meals or haircuts on weekends, that people who will consume a beer on the beach will pay more for the beer at a hotel than at a grocery, and that compensation is not simply a function of productivity but also of status. By that Frank means that low ranked workers receive more than productivity would justify and high ranked workers receive less. This phenomenon is explained, Frank argues, by fairness. Fairness explains the fact that low ranked workers are paid more to offset their lower status. Frank also points out that pay is higher in more profitable firms than less profitable ones. In an openly competitive market that should not be the case. But again fairness requires that firms with higher profits share some of those profits with the employees in the form of pay.

These insights, ironically by an economist rather than a philosopher, are helpful to those working in business ethics. Many professors in the business school wonder what ethics has to add to management training. I think it is easy to show that a philosopher who understands notions of fairness has much to contribute. Consider a Coca-Cola case concerning a newly invented Coke soft drink dispenser that can adjust the price of a Coke to temperature. Such a dispenser which actually was invented meant that Coca-Cola could charge more for a Coke on a hot day than on a cold day. To the standard marketing or finance student, this invention should be welcomed. A firm can usually increase profits if it can successfully differentiate markets. This new soft drink dispenser allows Coke to differentiate the hot day and cold day markets. However, this invention was never realized in the market, contrary to what one would expect.

The first public reference to Coca-Cola's invention was made in an offhand comment to the Brazilian press by Coca Cola's then Chief Executive Officer Douglas Ivester. That quotation was picked up by the New York Times. A huge public outcry followed. Charging more for a Coke on a hot day was perceived as unfair and the public let Coca-Cola know of their feelings. The chief competitor Pepsi piled on saying they would never use such a soft drink dispenser. An invention that would increase profits never saw the light of day. Why? It was perceived to be unfair.

Many of my MBA students are outraged at this turn of events. They accurately point out that differential pricing is often accepted and makes sense. What my students forgot were lessons about bounded rationality and bounded willpower and that perceptions of fairness matter in marketing.

The impact of notions of fairness in economic transactions is not culture bound. It is not limited to citizens of the United States. For example, I had the opportunity to teach a section on ethics to a number of Chinese executive MBA students in Minnesota's joint program with a university in China. I had given the following assignment to my Chinese students: Write up an example of an ethical issue in business in China. A number of students chose the same issue. They pointed out that during the SARS epidemic in 2003, a rumor circulated that vinegar would prevent SARS. The students pointed out that the price of vinegar rose precipitously and the students thought this was unfair.

Assume I am right in the claim that there are norms of fairness regarding pricing in all cultures. Of course, what price rises are considered unfair might vary from culture to culture. An interesting piece of research would be to discover the factors that lead some differential pricing decisions to be considered fair and others unfair. As a start it seems that large price increases in responding to so-called acts of God are considered unfair. Thus charging more for candles, water, or gasoline after a hurricane is considered unfair and in the U.S. such price increases are punished as price gouging. Are there other factors that are relevant? For example, how important is the fact that a person has no choice but to purchase an item in question?

Getting Philosophy's Groove Back

I hope the reader has found these arguments and the cases that support the arguments convincing. However, more is at stake here than the soundness of the arguments. Doing business ethics as described above is, I argue, doing philosophy in its traditional sense. That is, my methodology, if you will, is exactly what my colleague at Minnesota says it is: it is to make arguments, consider counter arguments, and revise arguments accordingly. However, the arguments need not come from philosophy as it is practiced today. The theoretical support can come from disciplines outside contemporary philosophy. However, what is outside philosophy comes inside. Thus in business ethics philosophy uses other branches of knowledge. The scope of philosophical knowledge is thus increased.

Moreover, concepts from normative ethics can, in business ethics, be used to improve both theory and practice in other disciplines. Thus by adding intuitions about fairness to current marketing theory, organizational theory, and finance theory, these disciplines can be placed on a stronger empirical footing. Moreover the insights are useful for business practice and for policy makers. Taking fairness into account can affect profitability.

In sum business ethics allows the theoretical concepts—theoretical concepts that have empirical support—to be incorporated into philosophical knowledge. Business ethics also provides philosophical normative ethical concepts to make other branches of knowledge more theoretically adequate. Finally business ethics done in this manner is of great relevance to business managers and to governments that regulate business. Business ethics done in this way is done in the spirit of John Dewey and Steven Cahn. Business ethics allows philosophy to gets its groove back.

Notes

1. Title inspired by the 1996 movie *How Stella Got Her Groove Back.*
2. John Dewey, *Reconstruction in Philosophy Enlarged Edition* (Boston: Beacon Press, 1948) xxvii, xli.
3. John Dewey, *Human Nature and Conduct* (New York: The Modern Library, 1957) 8-9.
4. The comments in this paragraph and the next are admittedly oversimplified but as statistical generalities, I think my claims are correct.
5. These arguments are adapted from my "Economics: Friend or Foe of Ethics" to be published in *Notizie di Politeia*, 2008.

6. See Oliver E. Williamson, *Markets and Hierarchies* (New York: The Free Press, 1975) and *The Economic Institutions of Capitalism* (New York: The Free Press, 1985).

7. This decision by the 9th U.S. Circuit Court of Appeals has been appealed by Exxon to the U.S. Supreme Court. In other words litigation on this case continues nearly 20 years after it occurred.

2. Academic Standards and Constitutive Luck

Randall Curren

Steven Cahn's *Education and the Democratic Ideal* was the first book I read in the fall of 1988 as I was orienting myself to the demands of a joint professorship in philosophy and education.[1] The choice was a fortuitous one in providing me with a clear-eyed vision of pedagogical practice, as well as a starting point for philosophical reflection on some important aspects of higher education. By the time I began teaching classes in the ethics of education three years later, Cahn's collection, *Morality, Responsibility, and the University,* had appeared, and the flourishing of academic ethics to which he's contributed so much was underway.[2] As series editor of Rowman & Littlefield's Issues in Academic Ethics series, Cahn has more or less invented the field of academic ethics and generated a rich foundation for teaching and further ethical inquiry.[3] One cannot teach academic ethics without feeling both gratitude and some measure of amazement.

1. Common Wisdom

Much of *Education and the Democratic Ideal (EDI)* is concerned with testing, grading, and academic standards, and its observations and practical guidance on these topics are sensible. Under the heading of *excellence*, Cahn affirms the educational importance of distinguishing the excellent from the adequate, the exceptional from the merely satisfactory. "Recognizing such distinctions depends upon an awareness of critical subtleties," he notes, "and each great teacher in his own distinctive ways leads his students to acquire and prize such insight."[4] Students only learn to appreciate and achieve excellence to the extent that they acquire the requisite sensitivity to subtleties, and Cahn observes that teachers cannot nurture such sensitivity unless they are "willing to judge fairly the efforts of those who are attempting to acquire mastery."[5] From there, he goes on to defend examinations and grades as instruments of evaluation, observing, first, that "an examination provides an opportunity for a student to discover the scope and depth of his knowledge," and, second, that "Students ... are not the only ones who are tested by an examination, for the second purpose examinations should serve is to provide an opportunity for a teacher to discover how effective his teaching has been."[6] This seems right, as does Cahn's observation that, "Ideally, a grade represents an expert's opinion of the quality of a student's work within a specified area of inquiry."[7] Combined with discursive comments, grades might reasonably be expected to serve a useful function by communicating judgments that are both reliably *informative* about the quality of a student's work, and *formative* of further advances in discernment and judgment as the student strives for excellence in the field of study.

This is a laudable ideal, and Cahn's concern in *EDI* was to defend conventional practices of student evaluation in the face of controversies that raged in the 1960s and 70s. Examinations and grades are still with us, and as instruments of student evaluation used by college faculty they excite little protest at present. What controversy there is pertains to grade inflation, the SAT and its use in college admissions, and the systems of evaluation known as "Outcomes Assessment."[8] I will comment on the significance of Outcomes Assessment for student evaluation in due course, grade inflation only in passing, and the SAT controversy not at all. My primary concern in this paper is not with any of these controversies, but with tensions just below the surface of Cahn's remarks. The articulation of those tensions will occupy the following three sections, and their resolution will occupy three beyond those.

2. Academic Standards and the Limits of Instruction

Consider Cahn's observation that examinations test the effectiveness of teaching and not just the knowledge of students. Now suppose an examination reveals that the unit tested was *not* taught effectively.[9] What then? If it is the teacher's *fault* that the students have done poorly, then it is the teacher who should *bear the responsibility* for that and not them.[10] If she were to grade them according to the normal standards on the basis of the work they have done, that would place the burden of failure on them and let her off the hook—assuming there are no mechanisms of accountability through which she would be penalized for her students' poor performance. That is not an ethically acceptable course, as most teachers will intuit. To the extent that a grade is an academic credential and expression of approval or disapproval, fairness could be achieved most easily by grading less stringently. One way to do this is simply to "throw out" test questions that were too hard, owing to deficiencies of instruction. Depending on what one takes grades to mean, this might even yield a more accurately informative grade. A teacher who agrees with Cahn that one should "judge fairly the *efforts*" of students, or who wants grades to reflect students' efforts and general ability in the subject, could argue that grades adjusted upward to compensate for deficiencies of teaching are not only more fair but also more accurate.

It is, of course, not entirely clear what grades mean, or that they always mean the same thing. In practice, they reflect the degree to which students have met the teacher's expectations for what is to be done, when it is to be done, and how it is to be done. Those expectations are designed, more or less thoughtfully, to organize students' efforts in ways that will enable them to acquire some measure of knowledge, understanding, and ability in the subject. Grades might be intended to report what students have learned, understand, and can do, but the role of meeting expectations in the assignment of grades entails a role for following instructions and adhering to schedules. Some variation in grades will reflect differences of compliance with teacher expectations that do not reflect any difference in knowledge, understanding, or ability. To some degree it will be true that cooperation and hard work will *yield* more learning, but to some extent they won't. Courses that demand hard work will to that extent assign grades that report how hard students work and how cooperative they are, and cannot be regarded as simply reporting what students have learned. This may be what much of the world is looking for in grades: reports of how students have *done* in school (i.e., the extent to which they have met a complex and intellectually challenging set of demands) as a basis for predicting how they *will do* (i.e., how well they will succeed) in other settings. From this point of view, it does not diminish the information value of grades if a teacher makes modest adjustments to her expectations of what students should be able to do, as she recognizes gaps between those expectations and the support she has provided students in meeting those expectations. If the adjustments are beyond modest, there might be truth in the complaint that a high grade misleadingly suggests success in satisfying a complex and intellectually challenging set of demands, when no such success had been achieved.

There may, of course, be conventions or specific institutional arrangements governing the levels of student achievement signified by different grades. It may be important that students learn some very specific things they will need to know for independently administered exams, in subsequent stages of their program, or in life. In that case, it won't do for the teacher to hold students immune from adverse grades by simply expecting less of them. She would have to interpret her responsibility in the circumstances as calling for at least a good faith attempt to compensate the students for the deficiencies of the instruction she provided. The best way to do that might be to "throw out" the test or a section of it, *re-teach* the offending material, and set a new assignment or retest. That would be a way to accept responsibility for the students' poor performance, while preserving a basis for maintaining the academic standards called for. This won't be possible in every case, however. There may simply not be enough time left in the session, or it might unreasonably burden students to expect them to come for extra sessions or give up the time they need for other subjects or units of the same course. In that case, there may be no good remedy, and any approach the teacher takes will in some way do some students an injustice.

Whatever remedy the instructor adopts, a question that should guide her deliberations is: How well did the students learn what they *could have been reasonably expected to learn*, given the limitations of the instruction they received?[11] She will accept a share of *responsibility* for the deficiencies evident in her students' work, whether through withholding punitive judgments of the students' work or by suspending judgment while providing further, compensatory instruction.

The possibility of flawed teaching provides an important illustration of the reality that students' academic performances are joint products of at least their own efforts and the efforts of their teachers. Grades for academic performances are ordinarily assigned to the students as if the work were entirely theirs, as indeed it is, in some sense. A student who conceives and composes a story on her own is the author or creator of that story, has full authorial rights in it, and would rightly regard the contributions of teachers and others as simply formative of the writer she's become. It's her story, not theirs. Some of its merits and deficiencies may, however, be traceable to the merits and deficiencies of teaching previously received. We've seen that when notable deficiencies of teaching descend directly through a lack of knowledge, understanding, or ability into a flawed academic product, it is appropriate for the teacher to accept responsibility for that and hold the student blameless. It is somewhat puzzling that this does not similarly apply to merits of teaching descending directly into student work. While the teacher may rightly claim responsibility, the responsibility claimed does not diminish the student's responsibility or claim to credit. If there is an asymmetry here, what explains it?

Assigning a grade is tantamount to holding a student responsible for an academic performance, while also recognizing the teacher's responsibility to conscientiously nurture the student's academic development within a specified domain. The teacher bears significant responsibility for the state of the student's understanding, knowledge, and ability—responsibility for academically salient aspects of how the student comes to be constituted. This is a kind of intergenerational *constitutive responsibility*, and I shall refer to it for the sake of simplicity as responsibility for the student's state of *intellectual virtue*.[12] It is analogous to the responsibility of adults to nurture the sound moral development of the young, or to promote their *moral virtue*. In both spheres, adults bear constitutive responsibility—formative responsibilities associated with observance of standards, academic or moral—and children may be lucky or unlucky in how they are taught and constituted; their natural endowments, the environmental factors that influence their development, and the formative efforts of others, are largely beyond their control. In the intellectual domain, as in the moral, it is fundamental to any conceivable social order that we would rely on judgments of individual responsibility (i.e., for good or bad intellectual products or morally good or bad conduct and outcomes), but equally fundamental that we would rely on elders to accept responsibility for the sound development of the young.

What is not clear is the logic through which these two forms of responsibility may be reconciled when credit is assigned and fault found. We have made some progress with regard to grades and inadequate teaching, but are left with a puzzle regarding good teaching. Nor can we say yet whether the reconciliation will share a common structure across the two domains, if indeed a coherent reconciliation is possible in both domains.

These remarks apply to teaching and grading both in schools and in colleges. It must be noted that at both levels the landscape of student evaluation is being altered by the arrival of Outcomes Assessment (OA). OA is rooted in a number of distinct and somewhat conflicting *purposes* (institutional accountability versus improvement of instruction), *methods of evaluation* (qualitative, such as observation of student performance, versus quantitative, in the form of standardized tests), and *units of evaluation* (individual student performance versus institutional or school district performance).[13] Broadly speaking, OA aims to determine what students are able to do, sometimes both before and after instruction occurs so as to measure the "value added" by instruction, and to use that to enforce academic standards and improve teaching and academic programs. To the extent that OA systems are implemented and effective, instances of ineffective teaching may decline and teachers may be constrained by more regimented grading schemes or penalized for deficiencies in student learning through external accountability schemes. I will return to this later, and simply note for now that it does not alter the fundamental moral logic of joint student-teacher responsibility for student performances.

3. Constitutive Luck and Constitutive Responsibility

Consider next the decidedly different attitude a teacher will have toward deficiencies in a student's prior education and upbringing. She should, and likely will, feel it improper to impose low grades when deficiencies of her own teaching are to blame for poor student performances, but she should, and likely will, feel it proper to ignore third-party contributions to a student's intellectual limitations when she assigns grades. This is a bit puzzling, since we surely want grades to be fair, and it seems just as unfair that a student should suffer from one bit of bad *constitutive luck* as another.

The language of *moral luck* seems appropriate here. "Where a significant aspect of what someone does depends on factors beyond his control, yet we continue to treat him in that respect as an object of moral judgment, it can be called moral luck," wrote Thomas Nagel, in a classic discourse on the topic.[14] Nagel distinguished four ways in which the objects of moral judgment are subject to luck, one of them being constitutive luck, or luck with regard to one's personal characteristics or the kind of person one is. Traits of temperament and inclination are determined largely by factors beyond a person's control, including aspects of one's upbringing and social circumstances, but they matter to how one acts and is morally judged. Intellectual traits are similarly determined largely by factors beyond a person's control, and matter to one's academic performance and grades.

Grades do not express moral judgments, of course, but to the extent that grades are rewards and penalties administered within a state sanctioned institutional framework, the judgments imposed through grades are morally significant. Concern with moral luck is explained by the thought that judgments of moral worth and responsibility should of all things be the most secure against luck, or matters beyond one's control. Perhaps that is so, but if our concern is a human justice we can work toward and not a cosmic justice beyond this world, the judgments of worth and responsibility imposed and sanctioned by institutions of government should concern us the most. Grades *are* judgments of worth and responsibility imposed and sanctioned by institutions of government, and fairness seems to require that the bases of such judgments be within the control of those judged.

For these reasons, constitutive luck with respect to intellectual virtue should matter in much the way that constitutive luck with respect to moral virtue matters. The constitutive luck entailed by upbringing and other formative factors beyond a student's control should matter to the fairness of grades. Yet, it doesn't seem to in the way that bad luck in the quality of the teaching at hand does. If teachers should mitigate the severity of grades in light of deficiencies in their own instructional practices, why should they not also adjust individual grades in light of information about formative deficiencies in their students' homes and communities—i.e., in light of intellectually formative bad constitutive luck outside of school? The teacher's responsibility matters to the fairness of grades, but other constitutive luck and the responsibility of others doesn't seem to, and this is puzzling. It's all equally a matter of luck from the student's point of view, isn't it? Indeed, it would seem to be, and this suggests that the idea of moral luck does not capture all that is at stake. There seems to be a problem of *constitutive responsibility* that does not reduce to a problem of *constitutive luck*.

4. Grades and Fair Equality of Opportunity

A further tension below the surface of common wisdom about academic standards and evaluation emerges when one considers the significance of constitutive luck for *fair equality of opportunity*. Fair equality of opportunity "is said to require not merely that public offices and social positions be open [to all, in accordance with talent] in the formal sense, but that all should have a fair chance to attain them.... Those who have the same level of [natural] talent and ability and the same willingness to use these gifts should have the same prospects of success regardless of their social class origin, the class into which they are born and develop until the age of reason," writes John Rawls.[15] And in order for those with the same level of native talent, ability, and ambition to have substantially equal opportunity in a market system, "Society must establish, among other things, equal opportunities of education for all regardless of family income."[16] Rawls recognizes that one's sense of self worth (hence motivation and "willingness to use [one's] gifts") is strongly influenced by education and other institutions, and he articulates a theory of justice which entails that societies have a responsibility to be equitable in their formative influences on their members' constitutions—their self-respect, moral powers, and ability to compete and flourish.[17] This *formative* or *constitutive* responsibility must be borne before children can justly be held responsible for the consequences of their choices.[18]

The ramifications of the constitutive responsibility associated with fair equality of opportunity are spelled out in some detail by Brian Barry. Barry, like others who dwell on what would be required to create "equal opportunities of education for all regardless of family income," concludes that:

> The first demand of social justice is to change the environments in which children are born and grow up so as to make them as equal as possible, and this includes (though it is by no means confined to) approximate material equality among families. The second demand—which is more pressing the further a society fails to meet the first—is that the entire system of social intervention, starting as early as is feasible, should be devoted to compensating as far as possible, for environmental disadvantages.[19]

The cumulative developmental disadvantages of poverty are simply too great to be overcome without substantially equalizing family resources, and in our current circumstances there can be little progress toward equalizing educational opportunity without aggressive interventions in the form of parent education, assistance, and "multidimensional high-quality child-care."[20]

Most important for our purposes are the academic consequences of children's choices, and the factors that shape their choices. How well they do in school is a function of both their abilities and their choices, but both are subject to luck or factors beyond their control; and children are in any case too immature to be made to suffer long-term consequences for making poor choices. A problem arises because the grades that report how well they do become part of a cumulative record, which has a powerful impact on their opportunities in life. This seems to place the burden of choices before "the age of reason" on the children themselves, violating the terms of fair equality of opportunity. This is the problem that I will elaborate now in more detail.

Grades should reflect the quality of school work, but in doing so they will ignore the role of constitutive luck that accounts for variations in academic performance and impairs quality of foresight, judgment, and capacity for disciplined follow-through and sacrifice.[21] In a society without social justice of the kind Barry describes, those variations in performance will be substantially attributable not simply to luck, but to institutional failures of constitutive responsibility. Grades, which are thus insensitive to constitutive luck, injustice, and the inappropriateness of holding children responsible for the consequences of their choices, will in turn become part of a cumulative record that will profoundly influence later opportunities. It matters a great deal, then, *when* one can ethically hold children responsible for, or expect them to bear the burden of, the poor choices they make, such as to neglect their studies, to be disruptive in class, or to choose easy classes which will not prepare them for college. Can we justly allow children's choices to influence the quality of education they receive, if the result is widely divergent opportunities for children of comparable native endowments? Barry holds,

> It is doubtful how far decisions taken even by older children can be said to be autonomous in a way that generates responsibility for outcomes. There is something very unrealistic about a model of choices from choice sets which abstracts from parental encouragement and discouragement, peer pressure and the attitudes of other children at school, for example.[22]

I would agree, but take the argument a step farther. A fundamental educational goal must be to enable children to develop good judgment and the ability to act from it, and until some meaningful threshold of such judgment and ability is achieved, impositions of responsibility must be guided by educational aims. The psychological evidence on maturity and independence of judgment is that the developmental bases of such judgment continue to develop through the late teens. There are thus reasons of more than administrative convenience for setting the threshold or "age of reason" at the conclusion of high school, provided schools are doing their part to nurture rational and informed judgment.[23] Accepting this, it follows that to the extent that grades in primary and secondary schools are intended to inform and motivate students, they have an acceptable function, but to the extent that they become external credentials or a basis for meritocratic allocations of subsequent educational resources, they violate the terms of fair equality of opportunity. Fair equality of opportunity requires that we not allow children to make educational choices that diminish their opportunities, but instead aim for "equal educational attainments at the age of 18."[24]

If this is the right way to understand fair equality of opportunity and assignments of responsibility to children, then there is an obvious tension between the requirements of justice and conventional uses of grades at the primary and secondary levels.

5. Fair Grades

In order to now address, and perhaps resolve, the tensions identified in the preceding sections, let's begin by distinguishing three aspects of grades. First, grades express or report *judgments of academic merit*: judgments of the quality of a specific academic product produced, of a level of accomplishment in a field of study, or of a degree of success in meeting expectations for learning a field of study. Second, when grades are communicated to students, they are perceived as *expressions of approval or disapproval*, and often inspire feelings of satisfaction or distress. Finally, grades function as rewards and penalties in the form of *credentials* within and beyond educational systems. In their role as credentials, grades can have a substantial impact on students' life chances, by serving as the basis for promotion, tracking, ability grouping, advanced placement opportunities, graduation, admission to selective higher education and graduate and professional school, and hiring.

As expressions of judgments of academic merit, grades should provide accurate and useful information to students and others who are entitled to it. Students need to know whether they are good at logic, whether they need to work harder to master the rules of indirect and conditional proof, and so on. Grades can communicate as much, though much more of what is essential to learning is communicated by the detailed correction of students' work that is usually the basis for a summary grade. Robert Paul Wolff refers to such correction and associated commentary as *criticism*, or "the analysis of a product or performance for the purpose of identifying and correcting its faults or reinforcing its excellences."[25] Criticism communicates *academic standards*, and is thus "at the very heart of education," whereas *evaluation* (against "an independent and objective standard") and *ranking* (against other students) are external to it and used to allocate scarce academic and professional goods, writes Wolff.[26] Fair equality of opportunity should govern the allocation of those goods, and this requires that to the extent grades are used as credentials in making those allocations, they should express sound evaluations and rankings, hence sound judgments of students' work. Otherwise, they cannot serve as a reliable basis for judging the "talents," or bona fide occupational qualifications, to which offices and positions are to be open. It seems, then, that in both their reporting and credentialing functions, grades should provide accurate and useful information. As we have seen, they must do this on terms that do not violate the responsibility strictures on fair equality of opportunity, and this makes it hard to see how grades accumulated in the course of primary and secondary schooling can legitimately function as credentials at all.

As rewards and penalties and expressions of approval and disapproval, grades should also be sensitive to considerations of *fairness*. This is self-evident, but opaque. Is it possible that fairness in grading may be nothing over and above accuracy? If fairness in grading is *not* simply a matter of accuracy, is it possible that fairness and accuracy might sometimes conflict in a way that undermines the information value of grades (as might happen when standards are adjusted to compensate for ineffective teaching)? If fairness is not reducible to accuracy, might it turn out, on the contrary, that an investigation of fairness, or failures of fairness, can serve to clarify the nature of the judgments expressed by grades, hence what it means for a grade to be accurate? It might.

Considered as rewards and penalties and expressions of approval and disapproval, it is evident that grades should first of all be *equitable*. Better performances should get better grades, worse performances should get worse grades, and indistinguishable performances should get the same grades. This implies that grading systems should "contain the maximum number of grade levels teachers can use consistently," a recommendation Cahn defends on the basis of the information value of grades.[27] To the extent that students absorb and accept the academic standards of the relevant field of study, they will justifiably detect unfairness in assignments of grades that do not recognize relevant discriminations of merit they can discern. This is a matter of equity, or consistency and adequate discrimination in arraying performances along a scale of merit, and it is basic to fairness.

A second, distinguishable aspect of fairness pertains to how one *anchors* that scale of merit. How good will a performance need to be to qualify for a passing grade? How good will it need to be to qualify for a low passing grade, or for the highest grade? The question at issue is the absolute severity of the grading scheme, or how harsh or generous it is.

The analytical utility of distinguishing equity and severity in much this way has been demonstrated in the context of criminal sentencing theory and the idea of a punishment that is deserved. Andrew von Hirsch has argued that

> It is essential to distinguish between *ordinal* and *cardinal* magnitudes of punishment, that is, between (1) the question of how crimes should be punished relative to each other, and (2) the question of what absolute levels of severity should be chosen to anchor the penalty scale.... Desert should be treated as a determining principle in deciding *ordinal* magnitudes. But it becomes only a limiting principle in deciding the system's *cardinal* dimensions of severity.... The intuitive reason why this is so is the greater difficulty of making cardinal desert judgments.[28]

Punishments should express censure commensurate with the relative moral gravity of crimes, but "how much censure is expressed through given levels of penal deprivation—is in part a convention," he goes on to explain.[29] This leaves room for other factors to enter into the determination of how severe penalties will be, including such practical ones as the availability of "penal resources"—how much prison space is available and how much it would cost to create more.[30]

How much approval is expressed by a "B" and how much disapproval is expressed by a "D" is similarly subject to evolving conventions, so by parity of reasoning there should be some room for legitimate consideration of circumstantial factors in anchoring grading scales.[31] The availability of spaces in the next course in a sequence, or the dependence of an institution's financial health on not failing too many students, could be legitimately considered *up to a point.*

Yet, whatever flexibility the matching of grades to performances may be subject to, there are surely circumstances that would lead us to agree that an assignment of grades, though equitable, is unfair because it is too harsh.

First, it might be so harsh as to fail to be equitable, in much the way that overly generous grading might entail a failure of equity, by failing to preserve the discriminating capacity to reflect significant differences of performances, so that recognizably better work would receive better grades and recognizably worse work would receive worse grades.[32]

Next, consider whether it would be fair to fail all or nearly all of the students who enter a course of study, if they are *trying*. Perhaps it could be, if the course of study is elective, and students enter the course of study knowing the odds and already mature enough to make morally significant life choices and bear responsibility for them. We could then say that they have voluntarily assumed the risk of failure. Perhaps we could imagine this in some advanced courses of study through which students attempt to achieve something extraordinary that cannot be reliably achieved through teaching and study, such as a fundamental breakthrough in theoretical physics, or some other achievement involving a high order of creativity. Yet often we can say no such thing. The conditions for voluntary assumption of risk are not present, and it seems reasonable to think of ordinary good teaching as a reliable method for bringing about the desired learning outcomes, albeit with some cooperation on the student's part. We could not justify requiring a population of children to attend school unless we thought teachers could reliably educate them or achieve something like a normal distribution of mostly passing outcomes. Yet if this is so, we will feel obligated to take students *as we find them*, having admitted them to a school and course of study, or having required the course of study, and we will gauge their progress and think it quite inappropriate to fail all of them, or even half. They won't all deserve to fail, because at least some of them will be exerting about as much effort as one could expect, and the limits of what they learn are largely determined by their prior intellectual constitution and the quality of instruction they receive.

In elective educational settings, an implied contract at the point of admission would set a limit to the severity of grades. Absent some indication to the contrary, it is commonly understood that incoming students are admitted on the strength of evidence that they are capable of doing passable work. Cases arise in which this understanding is breached, as sometimes happens in transitions. There may be no ethical objection to running a graduate program known for high standards and high attrition, but a strong basis for objecting to a program that changes the terms on which students well into their programs may graduate. If standards are raised dramatically and abruptly, so that all students fail their comprehensive exams one year (7 of 7 students, let's say) and only one passes the following year (1 of 11 students, let's say), we may regard this as not an ethically permissible exercise of institutional discretion.[33] In these circumstances, it seems unfair to fail such a high percentage of students, because there is, first of all, a breach of implied contract. If the institutional strategy is to *raise standards* and climb the rankings of graduate programs in this way, then the ethical failing might also be characterized as an instance of using at least some students who fail as mere means to an institutional end. This would seem to be the case if they could have passed and graduated under the standards prevailing when they were admitted, and can't—are not "good enough" to—pass and graduate under new ones imposed without their agreement.

Seen in this light, one can also discern a problem of constitutive luck. These students who are used as mere means to the institution's ends should not be made to suffer adverse fortune on account of limitations that could have been known at the point of admission to preclude graduation under standards of the sort later imposed. That is, they could only be admitted ethically on the strength of a judgment that their intellectual virtues at the point of admission were sufficient to make it reasonably likely they would be able to complete the program requirements and graduate. But this is just to say, in essence, that (in the absence of some overriding understanding) there should be coordination between admissions standards and grading standards, of such a kind as to ensure that most students who are admitted have the intellectual ability to successfully complete the requirements for graduation, and to ensure that no student who is admitted is known to lack such ability. The effect of such coordination is to forgive some measure of constitutional luck, whatever its origins, though not to adjust for luck in a way that would equalize the academic prospects of all admitted students. Those who are *not* admitted *may* be spared the prospect of enduring bad grades they have little capacity to raise, but being rejected does not offer them any broader immunity from bad luck, constitutive or otherwise, of course.

Does this tell us anything about the meaning or form of judgment expressed by grades, or only about fairness in grading? Perhaps it does reveal something about the form of judgment expressed, by qualifying the common understanding of grades identified in § 2. I said there that grades are commonly interpreted to be reports of how students have done in a class or in school (i.e., the extent to which they have met a complex and intellectually challenging set of demands). The qualification that can be added is that grades are implicitly norm-referenced to the population of students admitted to the school issuing the grades. An "A" says, in effect, "This student has done as well at this (assignment, class, program of study) as any student *at this institution* could be expected to."

This analysis yields at least a partial solution to the problem of constitutive responsibility posed in § 3. The academic standards that anchor grades reflect admissions standards (or an overriding voluntary assumption of risk by the student), and are thereby adjusted to *mitigate* prior constitutive luck, much as they should sometimes be adjusted to compensate for inadequate teaching. Variations in prior constitutive luck will account for some of the differences in performance between different students, but the scale will be anchored (re-anchored in the case of faulty teaching) in a way that gives the population of students as a whole a fair opportunity to succeed. This is compatible with the pattern identified in § 3, namely that teachers will not adjust the grades of individual students in light of constitutive luck. Teachers at the collegiate level would presumably be most tempted to do so if they suspect prior failures of equal educational opportunity. Those prior failures imply that it cannot be entirely fair that the students who are worse off through no fault of their own are at an academic disadvantage and get worse grades than they otherwise could have. Adjustments to grades as such would provide only the most problematic remedy for such unfairness, however. Compensatory instruction would be more helpful. Far better still would be to eliminate the inequities in constitutive investments that occur prior to college, a matter we will revisit in § 7. What we have seen in this section is that adjustments to mitigate constitutive luck *are* made, and that they are made not individually during the course of study, rather collectively in a way that coordinates academic standards with admissions standards. It falls to the next section to explain what remains distinctive about the compensatory responsibilities of teachers who discover their teaching has been ineffective. As I've noted, their constitutive responsibility cannot be fully understood through the idea of constitutive luck. I also noted that one aspect of understanding that constitutive responsibility is seeing how it can be reconciled with students' responsibility for the academic products they produce.

6. Reconciling Constitutive and Individual Responsibility

I will argue that judgments of individual responsibility can be reconciled with the developmental or constitutive responsibilities of adults, teachers, and just institutions, and that the reconciliation shares a common structure across the moral and intellectual domains. An important feature of the account I will outline is the proposition that failures of constitutive responsibility are problematic in a way that constitutive luck as such is not. I begin with an account of the nature of judgments of moral responsibility.

There is only space here to sketch in barest outline the account of moral responsibility I have developed elsewhere.[34] It is not uncommon for writers on the subject to equate judgments of responsibility with blame and license to punish, and to struggle with the question of whether people are free in a way that would directly license blame and punishment when they act badly and do harm to others. The approach seems misconceived on a number of grounds, beginning with the simple linguistic point that blaming is a form of speech act that is separable from conceiving and expressing a judgment of responsibility. A judgment of responsibility as such is simply a proposition expressing a kind of relationship between an actor and something the actor has done or produced. It is a form of *diagnostic* judgment, reflecting an often vital need to understand who and what we are dealing with. Having that understanding does not, however, entail any one form of response. One must still determine what form of response is most productive and ethically acceptable. An ethically acceptable response will honor the requirements of interpersonal respect, and will not, on the Socratic view I endorse, treat guilt as voiding those requirements. This view begins in a conception of respect for persons as rational beings, and infers a requirement to deal with others as much as possible through truthful and reasoned persuasion and instruction and only as a last resort through force and violence.[35] In the context of instruction, judgments of responsibility presented as praise and blame may be deployed with educational purpose, but harsh censure and punishment cannot be appropriate until educative efforts have run their course. Punishment might be justified when vital interests must be protected and educative measures have been exhausted, but it is conceivable that a system of restorative justice would be more successful in protecting those interests, more consistent with the requirements of respect for persons, or both.

A judgment of moral responsibility is on this account a kind of *causal* judgment: A is responsible for an act (under some description) iff A's state of character is the *intrinsic efficient* cause of the act (under that description).[36] The act must be traceable back to A's character, and the nature of the act must reflect A's (moral) character, being of a kind predictably produced and explained by such a state of character. Intuitively, A is morally responsible for something (an act, an intended outcome, an unfortunate consequence of a careless oversight, etc.) if A's state of moral character is its origin and cause. This basic account of moral responsibility can accommodate many features of ordinary judgments of responsibility, including the role of excusing conditions. Excuses that defeat judgments of moral responsibility do so by deflecting the causal and explanatory diagnosis away from the state of character, and toward an external explanation and cause.

"Free will" is not a presupposition of judgments of moral responsibility, since they treat a rational actor's state of character as an originating source and cause of conduct, but are compatible with the view that the development of character and a rational will is a social and political *responsibility*, largely beyond the actor's control.[37] It follows, clearly enough, that immunity from moral luck is not assumed. Aspects of natural endowment, upbringing, and formative circumstances beyond an actor's control will influence moral judgments of him. Isn't this terribly unfair? It's not unfair if a judgment of moral responsibility is a diagnostic judgment, and not a license to impose censure and punishment. What fairness demands is that we limit our use of judgments of responsibility by observing a principle of non-coercion: educational efforts are to be used first and as much as possible, and punitive measures used as little as possible.

Of course, the educative enterprise of character formation will require correction and coaching in moral self-awareness, and so some use of judgments of responsibility. We can follow Plato in distinguishing a gentle, educative use of these judgments from a harsh and punitive use of them.[38] The teacher will be free to use the former as needed, but not the latter. No one will use those except on the assumption that the duty to first educate has been conscientiously discharged. That is, a society's constitutive responsibilities to its members must be fulfilled before censure and penalties can be justly imposed. The fulfillment of constitutive responsibility is in this way a fundamental determinant of what can justly be imposed on a person, in a way that moral luck as such is not.

I would argue that intellectual virtue and the responsibility for intellectual products that flow from it are similar to moral virtue and moral responsibility, in the ways that concern us here. The judgments of academic merit expressed by grades reflect inferences from academic performances to states of mind—of knowledge, understanding, and ability—or states of intellectual virtue or deficiency, and are considered accurate only to the extent that the merits of performances or intellectual products really do reflect corresponding virtues of mind.[39] Conditions that defeat inferences from the merits of academic work to corresponding virtues of mind are called "cheating," and are grounds for voiding a favorable judgment and grade. Considerations that defeat inferences from deficiencies in academic work to corresponding deficiencies of mind are called "excuses," just as they are in the moral sphere. A much fuller investigation would be required to confirm the parallel structure of judgments in the two domains, but if the reconciliation of individual and constitutive responsibility I have suggested in the moral domain has a plausible analog in the academic domain, that will itself be a good start and perhaps sufficient to resolve the puzzles we began with, even if it turned out to be inadequate in the moral domain.

The account of responsibility I have outlined suggests that adequate teaching is assumed when we grade, much as adequate constitutive investments are assumed when we venture to censure and punish. When teaching is adequate, the student's intellectual virtues can be credited in part to the teacher. However, it follows from the nature of judgments of responsibility that academic performances and products generated from those virtues are ones for which the student is responsible and can claim credit, even if there is a form of serial responsibility running through the student's state of mind or intellectual virtue back to the teacher. The teacher's responsibility does not undercut the student's. When teaching is inadequate, the student will be similarly responsible for the flawed product if it is a product of his poor understanding or deficient ability. That too is a consequence of the nature of responsibility, but in this case the teacher will not only be responsible for the flaw in the product, but is furthermore *in no position* to express disapproval or impose any penalty on the student. The teacher's responsibility does not undercut the student's *responsibility* in this case either; it undercuts her *authority* or right to criticize or impose penalties. This is where the asymmetry noted in § 2 lies. The teacher can truly judge the work to be poor, but it would be unfair of her to impose a low grade since she cannot do so without communicating disapproval and imposing a penalty. In both the moral and intellectual domains, failures of constitutive responsibility can constitute a kind of *complicity* in failure, which undermines the right to blame and penalize. On the other hand, if the student has had every reasonable opportunity to learn, but "throws away" the opportunity and does poor work, then disapproval and penalties may be in order. A teacher's constitutive responsibility is thus compatible with a student's individual responsibility for academic performances in the way common experience suggests. *If* adequate teaching is taken for granted, teachers can credit students with their successes and failures, providing they do so in ways which do not violate the requirements of fair equality of opportunity. As we've noted and will soon revisit, those requirements have teeth at the primary and secondary school levels.

We can now see that constitutive responsibility has a distinctive status, not reducible to constitutive luck, because it stands in an important relationship to having authority. Neither in morality nor in student evaluation is luck in natural endowments eliminated, though in both there is reason to think that some form of global equity in constitutive *investments* is required.[40] Respect for persons as rational beings compels us to put instruction first, in both domains, before imposing responsibility in ways that may cause pain and diminish life prospects. In both cases, education is not uniformly and completely efficacious, however, and we may be compelled to secure vital public goods to some extent through other means. In the moral and criminal domain, we may need to deny liberties or compel compensation, and in the world of productive endeavor beyond schools and college, we need to inform, guide, and select on the basis of what people can and will do, in ways productive for them and for society. Some luck arising from differences of endowment will enter into this, but *luck egalitarians* can insist, as Rawls does, on a secondary principle of distributive justice which ensures that tolerance of unequal life outcomes will work to the advantage of the worst off.[41] That is perhaps as much immunization against constitutive luck as one can envision enacting as a matter of public policy. Accuracy in collegiate credentials will matter to fair and efficient allocations of society's offices and positions, and in a just society, as Rawls conceives it, those fair and efficient allocations will also yield mutual advantage, making bad constitutive luck not as unlucky as it might have been.

7. Equal Opportunity and Outcomes Assessment

The final puzzle to be addressed was framed in § 5: The responsibility stricture on fair equality of opportunity makes it hard to see how grades accumulated in the course of schooling can legitimately function as credentials or a basis for meritocratic allocations of subsequent educational resources at all. Fair equality of opportunity requires that we not allow children to make educational choices that diminish their opportunities, but instead aim for equal educational attainments, while an accumulating record of grades seems to be pervasively influenced by choices that have the potential to diminish opportunities.

One might dispute the conception of fair equality implicated in this puzzle, but I'm not inclined to myself. Allowing children to be burdened by the long-term consequences of immature and uninformed choices seems a most unacceptable form of constitutive luck, and it is hard to see how any system of distributions substantially controlled by such choices could be morally legitimate. Making such choices meaningful, and equally so (as they must be to bear any justifying weight in a scheme of just distributions), would itself require a globally equalizing education for autonomy up to some threshold of adequacy probably unattainable much before the age of 18. I will simply accept, then, that grades assigned in the course of schooling cannot legitimately function as external credentials or internal bases of meritocratic educational allocations. An essential corollary to this is that schools must be designed to minimize the impact of immature choices not only on grades, but on *learning*.

We're left, then, not with a puzzle, but with a problem that calls for educational reform. Grades should only be used in schools to promote learning and make decisions conducive to equal educational attainment, and not released for use as credentials. Assessments of talent for use in labor markets and admissions to higher education should not occur until the completion of high school, when the effort to produce equal educational attainments as a basis for fair equality of opportunity will have run its course. And to spare children the weight of responsibility for choices subject to countless matters of luck they can scarcely understand, care must be taken in motivating and supervising them.

An important aspect of the Aristotelian view of moral development and the constitutive responsibilities of adults is its emphasis on supervision to ensure that children do the right things so they can develop well. They won't be told, "These are your choices, and these are the consequences of making the wrong choice." Some children will simply follow their antecedent inclinations, do the wrong things, and get used to suffering the consequences. We can regard this as exactly what cannot be tolerated, if adults are to honor their developmental or constitutive responsibilities to children. Being too undeveloped as autonomous agents to properly bear the consequences of their choices, it is in any case wrong to let their developmental fate rest with those choices. And this applies as much to the development of intellectual virtue as moral virtue. We can't, in fairness, simply give children the choice to learn or not—to develop intellectually or not—then expect them to suffer the consequences if they weren't adequately motivated. We need, rather, to provide supervision and instruction that motivates and leaves little room for immature choices that curtail favorable development and opportunity.

Grades could be used to tailor the education of individual students pursuant to their own development and needs. A system that would tailor allocations of educational resources in this way would be egalitarian, not meritocratic, at least until a threshold of adequacy is reached—a threshold of intellectual efficacy and self-determination, including with respect to the efforts students make to learn and the quality of their judgments.[42]

Outcomes Assessment could support this conception of ethically appropriate evaluation policies, by encouraging productive and motivating supervision of students' intellectual development, and by providing exit exams or other forms of evaluation that could serve as credentials. It would need to have the right ends in view, and use the right kinds of measures of student learning, which are at present very far from existing in standardized test formats. OA might thereby serve the purposes of justice, but it will only do so if schools are *able* to rise to the demands of educating all students adequately. At its best, OA can create incentives to teach well and align teaching and evaluation with intended curricular outcomes. Used cleverly by schools as a tool of self-assessment, it can be a useful tool of educative capacity-building. It is no remedy for a fundamental failure to invest adequately in the intellectual formation of children, however, and at its worst, it might regiment and raise academic standards without enabling more children to achieve them.[43]

Notes

1. Steven Cahn, *Education and the Democratic Ideal* (Chicago: Nelson-Hall, 1979).
2. Steven Cahn, ed., *Morality, Responsibility, and the University: Studies in Academic Ethics* (Philadelphia: Temple University Press, 1990).

3. Scholarship in academic ethics was not unknown before Cahn, but what little there was had all but died out by the end of the 1970s. See, e.g., Sidney Hook, Paul Kurtz, and Miro Todorovich, eds., *The Ethics of Teaching and Scientific Research* (Buffalo, NY: Prometheus Books, 1977). The affirmative action debate, multiculturalism, and other developments have also inspired projects independent of Cahn's since 1990. See, e.g., M. S. N. Sellars, ed., *An Ethical Education: Community and Morality in the Multicultural University* (Oxford: Berg, 1994), Michael Davis, *Ethics and the University* (London: Routledge, 1999), and Robert Fullinwider and Judith Lichtenberg, *Leveling the Playing Field: Justice, Politics, and College Admissions* (Lanham, MD: Rowman & Littlefield, 2004). Nevertheless, Cahn's success in drawing an array of talented philosophers into sustained work on issues in academic ethics has had a singular impact on the field.

4. EDI, 38.

5. EDI, 39.

6. EDI, 43, 44.

7. EDI, 47.

8. On the myths and realities of grade inflation, see Valen E. Johnson, *Grade Inflation: A Crisis in College Education* (New York: Springer, 2003), and Harry Brighouse, "Grade Inflation and Grade Variation: What's all the Fuss About?" in Lester Hunt and Deborah Hunt, eds., *Academic Standards and Grade Inflation* (Albany, NY: SUNY Press, forthcoming). For a perceptive examination of the issues at stake in the SAT "wars," see Robert Fullinwider and Judith Lichtenberg, *Leveling the Playing Field*. On Outcomes Assessment, see Trudy Banta and Associates, *Building a Scholarship of Assessment* (San Francisco: Jossey-Bass, 2002), Lee Dunn, et al., *The Student Assessment Handbook* (London: Routledge Falmer, 2004), and (with specific reference to its role in collegiate philosophy instruction), the APA Statements on the Profession, Outcomes Assessment statement, available on-line at the American Philosophical Association website (http://www.apa.udel.edu/apa/governance/statements/outcomes.html).

9. In many instances it may be impossible to attribute failures to learn to deficiencies of instruction, but we can imagine circumstances in which independent aspects of the setting for an examination make this possible: Suppose Fran and Kim have students known on independent grounds to be comparable, have taught the same unit during the same session, have administered the very same examination, and made no attempt to prepare students for the exam apart from teaching the unit as well as they could. If Fran's students do significantly worse on one part of the exam, that provides reasonable (not to say conclusive) evidence that he did not teach the related sub-unit as well as Kim did. Supposing we could know that Kim taught it just adequately, we could reasonably infer that Fran taught it inadequately.

10. For the sake of simplicity, I will leave aside cases of teaching that could be more effective but are not so poor or deficient with respect to the level of student achievement expected as to warrant the judgment that the teacher is responsible for the students' poor performance.

11. How she will answer this question is a matter to be addressed in § 5.

12. "Intellectual virtue" may suggest too narrow a conception of the non-moral aspects of development promoted by education, but there is no convenient term that embraces the artistic, athletic, and other creative, productive, and social abilities we might want to include among the human goods properly promoted by education.

13. Trudy Banta & Associates, *Building a Scholarship of Assessment*, 3-11.

14. Thomas Nagel, "Moral Luck," in *Mortal Questions* (Cambridge: Cambridge University Press, 1979), 24-38, at 25.

15. John Rawls, *Justice as Fairness: A Restatement* (Cambridge, MA: Harvard University Press, 2001), 43-44. Cf., *A Theory of Justice* (Cambridge, MA: Harvard University Press, 1971), 73.
16. John Rawls, *Justice as Fairness*, 44.
17. See *A Theory of Justice* (Cambridge, MA: Harvard University Press, 1971), 101, 107, where Rawls emphasizes the value of education "in enriching the personal and social life of citizens" and "provid[ing] for each individual a secure sense of his own worth."
18. For a similar argument in which the language of responsibility is pivotal, see Harry Brighouse, "Educational Equality and Justice," in Randall Curren, ed., *A Companion to the Philosophy of Education* (Oxford: Blackwell Publishing Ltd., 2003), 471-486.
19. Brain Barry, *Why Social Justice Matters* (Cambridge: Polity, 2005), 58.
20. Brain Barry, *Why Social Justice Matters*, 60.
21. They will also ignore other forms of luck, such as the luck that contributes to how a particular student's project turns out, or luck pertaining to how well a particular student's abilities are matched to the demands of a particular assignment. In the next section, I will argue that in selective schooling and higher education the role of circumstantial luck, luck in the kinds of problems one faces, is mitigated by admissions standards. On the four forms of moral luck, see Nagel, "Moral Luck," 27.
22. Brian Barry, *Why Social Justice Matters*, 46.
23. See Laurence Steinberg and Elizabeth Cauffman, "Maturity of Judgment in Adolescence: Psychological Factors in Adolescent Decision Making," *Law and Human Behavior* 20 (1996): 249-72.
24. Brian Barry, *Why Social Justice Matters*, 47. Barry proposes that the demands of justice are met to the extent that equal educational attainments are achieved at this age. Equality of this kind is not strictly required if the burden is to ensure that the structure of society does not undermine equality of opportunity (as opposed to ensuring that all aspects of constitutive luck, or undeserved advantages and disadvantages, are eliminated), but it may—on some interpretation—be the most reasonable administrative target.
25. Robert Paul Wolff, "A Discourse on Grading," reprinted in Randall Curren, ed., *Philosophy of Education: An Anthology* (Oxford: Blackwell Publishing, Ltd., 2007), 459-464, at 459.
26. "A Discourse on Grading," 460, 461, 462.
27. EDI, 69.
28. *Past or Future Crimes: Deservedness and Dangerousness in the Sentencing of Criminals* (New Brunswick: Rutgers University Press, 1985), 39, 43.
29. *Past or Future Crimes*, 94.
30. *Past or Future Crimes*, 95 ff.
31. The claim that the meaning of grades, or the amount of praise or censure they express, is subject to evolving conventions suggests that grade inflation is not the problem it might seem. Harvey Mansfield insists, famously, that "everyone knows that C is an average grade, whereas B+ is next to the top. Mere recalibration [in one's mind, noting that B+ now means what C meant some years ago] does not address the real problem: the raising of grades way beyond what students deserve" (Harvey C. Mansfield, "Grade Inflation: It's Time to Face the Facts," *Chronicle of Higher Education* 4/6/2001, 47(30): B24). This simply denies the reality that if grade inflation occurs, it alters what the grades signify. More sensible is Mansfield's complaint that compression at the upper end of the grading scale might rob it of essential discriminatory capacity. In my terms, the problem would arise not from grades being too high, but from failures of equity—failures to as-

sign better grades to recognizably better work, and worse grades to recognizably worse work.

32. See the previous note.

33. Depending on the circumstances, this might also constitute a legally actionable breach of contract. The applicability of contract principles to standards for graduation at the collegiate level was established in Carr v. St. John's University, New York, 187 N.E.2d 18 (N.Y. 1962).

34. See Randall Curren, *Aristotle on the Necessity of Public Education* (ANPE)(Lanham, MD: Rowman & Littlefield, 2000), 160-174, and related background material at 21-34 and 43-62. For an application of the account to juvenile violent crime and the moral distinctiveness of childhood, see "Moral Education and Juvenile Crime," in Stephen Macedo and Yael Tamir (eds.), *NOMOS XLIII: Moral and Political Education* (New York: New York University Press, 2002), 359-380.

35. See ANPE, 21 ff.

36. ANPE, 167. "The intrinsic effect of an efficient cause is a result of the type that the causal power is productive of or that it naturally produces. This is what the causal power produces reliably or 'always or for the most part'" (Susan Sauvé Meyer, *Aristotle on Moral Responsibility* [Oxford: Basil Blackwell, 1993], 104).

37. I argue that this is a responsibility fundamental to establishing a rule of law. See ANPE, 150 ff., "Moral Education and Juvenile Crime," and "Public Education and the Demands of Fidelity to Reason," *The School Field* 13(1/2) (2002), 79-105, at 82-89.

38. See Plato, Laws IX 863, and ANPE, 53-62 and 172-173.

39. On the structure of inference from academic performances to states of mind, see Randall Curren, "Educational Measurement and Knowledge of Other Minds," *Theory and Research in Education* 2(3), (Nov. 2004), 235-253, and "Connected Learning and the Foundations of Psychometrics: A Rejoinder," *Journal of Philosophy of Education* 40(1), (Feb. 2006), 17-29.

40. See ANPE, 183-201. Global, as opposed to marginal, equity in such investments pertains not just to the distribution of such investments that happen to be controlled by schools, but to all such investments.

41. The reference here is to Rawls's difference principle: "Social and economic inequalities are to satisfy two conditions: first, they are to be attached to offices and positions open to all under conditions of fair equality of opportunity; and second, they are to be to the greatest benefit of the least-advantaged members of society (the difference principle)" (*Justice as Fairness*, 42-43).Being least-advantaged does not mean being least advantaged with respect to natural endowments, but one effect of the principle would nevertheless be to mitigate the disadvantages of bad luck in natural endowments. Whether this would be true even of people with severe cognitive impairments is a matter of dispute, but their fate will presumably not hinge on assignments of grades.

42. I discuss the promotion of intellectual self-determination as an aspect of student evaluation in "Coercion and the Ethics of Grading and Testing," *Educational Theory* 45, no. 4 (Fall 1995): 425-41.

43. I owe thanks to Dianne Gereluk, Lorella Terzi, Carrie Winstanley, and my students and audience at the PESGB International Graduate Philosophy of Education Summer School at Roehampton University, London, where I presented a version of this paper as an open seminar lecture, July 13, 2007. Research for this paper was supported by a stipend from the National Endowment for the Humanities, and later facilitated by the work of colleagues on the APA Committee on Teaching.

3. Meaningful Lives

Alan Goldman

In her well known paper, "Happiness and Meaning," Susan Wolf argues that meaningfulness is an element of a good life distinct from happiness. Meaningful lives according to her involve engagement with projects of real worth.[1] Worthy projects are objectively valuable. One can be engaged in activities and values that are shallow, and these do not lend meaning to life.[2] Furthermore, not all valuable or pleasurable activities contribute to a meaningful life: her examples of those that do not are riding roller coasters and writing checks to charities. The latter activity, while valuable, does not produce a sense of fulfillment reflective of activities that do make a life meaningful. Finally, we may be committed to activities that we find pleasurable and meaningful, but we may be mistaken about their being meaningful. Even if Sisyphus found his endlessly repetitive action of rolling a stone up a hill pleasurable and meaningful, a life of such endless repetition would still be a wasted, not a meaningful, life.[3]

The possibility of mistake is why Wolf believes that she needs to appeal to objective value in explaining meaningful lives. Subjective impressions of meaning are insufficient. Even though she admits that she has no theory of what objective value is, or of what has it and why, and even though she has no way to compare lives in terms of it—she says that there is no fact of the matter whether the life of a lonely philosopher or that of a beloved housewife is more meaningful or valuable—she believes that she needs this concept in her account. She writes, "There can be no sense to the idea of meaningfulness without a distinction between more and less worthwhile ways to spend one's time, where the test of worth is at least partly independent of a subject's ungrounded preferences or enjoyment, i.e., objective."[4] Commitment in itself does not create meaning in life, if what one is committed to is objectively worthless. A life of watching television soaps or sports events is not meaningful, no matter how committed to such activities a person is.

Steven Cahn questions not only Wolf's account of which activities and lives are meaningful and which are not; he dismisses the whole distinction as groundless and indeed pernicious.[5] Her judgments of lives with objective value and meaning reflect, he implies, simply her own subjective values: according to her, the lives of corporate lawyers and pig farmers are highly suspect, while presumably those of labor lawyers and epistemologists (whom others might accuse of playing glass beads games) are not. This amounts simply to disparaging the lives of others who find happiness in pursuits that seem worthless to her. Farmers and business executives would judge very differently even if they accepted her notions of objective value and meaningfulness. But they should not accept the latter concept, since appeal to it is a disguise for narrow-mindedness.

Cahn is right that some of Wolf's examples are bogus and that her appeal to objective worth as distinguishing her meaningful from meaningless lives does not do the work required of it. But, unlike him, I think there is something genuine in the intuition that a life of mindless repetition lacks something significant that is present in a life of deep personal relationships and self-fulfillment. Whether that something is properly termed meaning is another question, although I believe it is. Indeed, Cahn could just as legitimately have accused Wolf of changing the subject, since she provides no argument for the claim that engagement in objectively valuable projects has any connection with meaning in any ordinary sense. She might claim that this is a merely verbal matter, and that she is simply speaking of what others referred to when thinking about meaningful lives. Perhaps she has no interest in appealing to meaning in any more common usage. But I think it is worth inquiring why the notion of meaning does seem apt here. When we do inquire, we won't find any connection to the concept of objective value. That something is meaningful or imparts meaning does not imply that it has objective value. But at the same time Wolf appears to be right that being actively engaged and content in some mindlessly repetitive activity does not make one's life meaningful. In rescuing the notion of meaningfulness from Cahn's trenchant attack, we face the task of accepting this intuition without appealing to differences in objective values of different lives or activities in explaining it.

Not only won't the concept of objective value do the work that Wolf requires of it; it is a highly suspect concept in itself in the practical arena. Not that Wolf is alone in invoking it in this context. Stephen Darwall and John Cottingham, to name two, agree with her that meaning in life cannot derive from purely subjective values, but instead derives from engagement in objectively valuable pursuits.[6] Objective value plays the traditional role of God's plan in such contemporary philosophers' discussions of meaningful lives. Its pursuit is supposed to give our lives meaning or purpose without our having to create such meaning or purpose. It provides an external standard for our subjective values and pursuits to meet, validating the ways we value things (everyone thinks her own values objective) and providing reasons for the motivations we have. But just as God's plan would not create meaning in our lives unless we understood, accepted, and made this our plan or purpose for us, so objective value would remain irrelevant to our lives unless it connected to our concerns or motivations.

A dilemma then arises for proponents of this concept. On the one hand, objective value need have no connection with any of our current concerns or motivations. That is just what 'objective' means—independence from our subjective states. But if there were no such connection, there could be no practical relevance to the existence of such value. How could the world demand that all our concerns be other than they are? Could you accept a demand to not care for yourself or your loved ones and to pursue some conflicting values instead? And how could we recognize such value? We can judge what is valuable only from the perspective of what we value or find valuable.[7] Completely alien values would remain just that whether objective or not. It would be utterly mysterious how such an alien value could require or prompt motivation from us. Why would this value give us any reason to pursue it if it relates to none of our concerns? The only answer could be that we would be better off if we had such a concern. But how could we be better off if none of our informed concerns were better satisfied?

On the other hand, if objective values matched our own values or concerns, the appeal to them would be superfluous from a practical perspective. If we already care about what has objective value, then we are motivated to pursue it whether or not its value is objective. We do not care about things because we want our values to be objective; instead, things seem to have or lack value because we care about or value them, or, as Wolf views corporate law, we don't value them. Our focus on the objects of our concerns and not on our desires themselves makes the value of those objects seem objective. But, as in the case of colors and other secondary qualities, the phenomenology can be metaphysically misleading.

Wolf could reply again that being concerned, committed, or "actively engaged" in various pursuits is not sufficient for making them meaningful, and that their having objective worth must be the additional necessary condition that together with commitment is necessary for meaningfulness. Our question once more is whether we can account for meaningless commitment without appealing to this otherwise superfluous and mysterious notion of objective value. To answer it, let us return to the concept of meaning, which seems anyway to be independent of the concept of objective value.

Meaning is always a three term relation: something means something else to an interpreter. The paradigm, although probably not the origin of our concept of meaning, is linguistic meaning, based on conventional associations between terms and their referents. That this is the paradigm may be why the question of the meaning of lives seems inappropriate or even senseless to some philosophers. Lives do not literally refer to or symbolize anything, except perhaps for the lives of historical figures who are known for one action or effect. Patrick Henry symbolizes liberty to many, but you and I are not like that.

We can also say somewhat non-literally that certain people symbolize certain things to other people because of the way they affect their lives: decent parents mean security to their children. This comes a bit closer to what some see as the source of meaning in lives: their effects on others. It takes us, however, to a natural, as opposed to conventional, use of 'meaning': causes mean their effects and effects mean their causes. Clouds mean rain and smoke means fire. Similarly, we can say that person A means something to person B because of the effect that A has on B's life. But again this is not the primary sense we seek when we ask whether lives are meaningful, because usually we are interested in whether people's lives are meaningful to themselves, not to others. This allows, however, that an important source of meaningfulness in the life of a person can be its meaningfulness to others, the way it contributes to the meaning in their lives. Yet another related sense of meaning equates it with importance. "You mean a lot to me" means that you are very important to me. But when we ask whether a life is meaningful, we are not simply asking whether it is important, either to others or to oneself. Sisyphus might have thought it important that he stay alive even though he was leading a meaningless life.

There is a final most relevant sense of meaning that we invoke when we ask what people mean by various actions or remarks. "What did he mean by interrupting her speech, by running out on the field in the middle of the game, by saying that he would not run for office?" We raise such questions when we do not understand the point or purpose of the action or remark, the broader plan into which it fits. We want to know what broader concern of the agent makes her action intelligible to us or rational for her. When we ask for the meaning of a remark in this sense, it is not that we do not understand the language, but that we do not see the point or significance of the remark in the broader scheme of things, how it relates to an ongoing conversation or figures in the speaker's broader purposes.

Traditionally, the solution to the problem of the meaning of life appealed to just this notion of a broader plan or purpose into which each person's life fit. A life was considered meaningful by fitting into God's plan for it in his broader plan for all humanity or the universe as a whole. But while this answer involved a proper sense of meaning, it did not reveal the meaning of lives to those living them, since no one knows what such all encompassing plans are. And the idea that one's life is merely a miniscule tool in some super being's infinitely larger plan or purpose does not seem to afford that life an uplifting kind of meaning. All such grand narratives, whether supernatural or historical and political, simply swallow up the lives of the individuals who are unwitting pawns in them.

Nevertheless, the question of meaningful lives may not appear pressing until belief in such a plan is challenged or given up. At that point, just when the question becomes pressing, it may at the same time seem senseless, since there is no longer any super narrative scheme beyond a person into which his life can fit and in terms of which it can have a purpose. In the modern and postmodern ages we have lost faith in these religious and secular grand narratives that provide external purposes or plans for our lives. At least there is no such plan for the lives of ordinary people, but perhaps only for those fanatics who devote their entire time to a single cause. The causes to which we do commit ourselves are self-chosen, diverse, and not all consuming. So we have lost faith also in the idea that life itself, or all lives, have a single essence that could give to each the same sort of meaning. There is no single meaning of life. Thus, some philosophers will dismiss the issue entirely if they cannot accept the older responses to it.

But, as Kurt Baier points out, there can be meaning *in* lives even if there is no meaning *of* lives.[8] Changing the subject just this much allows us to rescue what does make sense in the original question far better than does equating the concepts of meaning and value. So, despite that error, Susan Wolf was correct to ask about meaningful lives and not the more traditional question of the meaning of life. Meaningful lives have meaning within them as they unfold. This meaning is internal to the lives as they are lived. But if internal to a life, the meaning must attach to aspects or episodes in it, since, as noted, meaning is a relation of an element to something outside it. 'Meaning in life' therefore refers to episodes or events in one's life that are meaningful and that thereby lend meaning to life as it is lived.

Events in a life acquire meaning by relating to each other as episodes in the pursuit of long term projects and personal relationships. Others have noted that such projects and relationships give life meaning, while merely repetition of particular actions or flitting randomly from one activity or brief pleasure to another do not. Indeed, life does seem to acquire new meaning when one embarks on a new project or relationship or deepens an old one, refocusing one's concerns and activities. But if left at that description of meaning generating projects, we are left wondering why meaning is what such projects but not particular actions in themselves provide, and the explanation may seem elusive. The answer emerges when we focus on events that point to other events as developments or precursors of them, giving them meaning in a quite ordinary sense, especially initiating and culminating events and those that change the course of an ongoing project or relationship.

This sense of meaning is quite ordinary in applying both to linguistic terms and to other sorts of nonlinguistic entities. Especially linguistic terms without concrete referents are said to derive their meanings from their places within sentences and inferential patterns. Like the life events we are discussing, they acquire meaning by relating to other terms in larger intelligible structures. The meanings of logical connectives, for example, are exhausted by the terms they relate and the inference patterns they allow.

An equal or perhaps better analogy is to elements within artworks. In musical pieces, for example, the musical phrases acquire meaning for competent listeners through their places in developing themes and harmonic progressions, pointing the listeners behind to what prepared for them and ahead in anticipation of developments and resolutions of dramatic tensions. A phrase or theme heard in a recapitulation has a meaning different from its first appearance in an exposition and from its transformation in a development section. A listener who hears and understands these differences grasps the unfolding meaning of the piece. This meaning derives from internal relations among the musical elements unfolding in an orderly way toward the ultimate goal or finale. Similarly, events in a fictional narrative are understood to foreshadow future developments or to fulfill earlier promises or resolve earlier tensions. When the reader grasps these relations, she interprets and understands the meanings of the fictional events in terms of their roles in the narrative structure. And it is the same in the messier domain of real life.

We get a better sense of a concept by comparing it to its negation, grasping the contrast drawn. From the negative point of view, to say that a life lacks meaning is to say that it lacks direction or intelligible progression. As usual, no one says it better than Shakespeare. When Macbeth complains that life is a tale told by an idiot, he is lamenting its lack of narrative intelligibility, the fact that its events fail to relate to each other in a progressive, intelligible pattern. But this very powerful lament suggests what meaning in life could or should be, and according to Macbeth, pompously purports or pretends to be (pretense in the person of a poor player strutting on the stage). A meaningful life, even according to Macbeth, who could find no such meaning, would be an intelligible succession of events giving meaning to each by relating it to others in an unfolding narrative that makes sense of each as a precursor of the next and culmination of the prior. Of course, Macbeth was wrong about his own narrative: more than in the life of any real person, the logic of events in his life simply led inexorably in the direction of a tragic end.

As the case of Macbeth makes clear, this account of meaningful lives does not reduce or equate the concept of meaning to that of value, but it does maintain a possible link between the two. Meaning can still derive from engagement in worthwhile or valuable projects or relationships, more easily sustainable than heinous projects and exploitative relationships, but value here is given an internal instead of external interpretation. Worthwhile aims do not maximize objective value, but consist in fulfilling our shared deepest values and achieving our comprehensive projects. Agents pursue projects that reflect their own values, and meaning derives from the way that pursuit of these concerns connects various activities and events into intelligible narratives. It is not the value of the goals that generates meaning, but the complex relations among the activities involved in their pursuit. That is why challenging goals that require sustained pursuit through a variety of means provide more meaning in the long run, and why satisfactions that come too easily seem shallow and relatively meaningless.

Of course success matters in several ways. Pursuits that fail may seem pointless in retrospect, especially if there was little or no chance of succeeding to begin with. My trying to be a great professional basketball player will not lead to a meaningful life for me no matter how long I persist in pursuing that impossible goal. In contrast, success brings a sense of fulfillment that heightens the meaning of the struggle to achieve it. And it relates the entire project to its external effects, giving it a meaning that failure lacks. If I am able to contribute significantly to the philosophical literature, then my philosophical pursuits have a meaning they would otherwise lack. They point beyond themselves to their results. But success is not a necessary condition for activities to contribute to meaning in life, since it is the ongoing pursuit of goals and relationships that ties these activities together in intelligible structures.

Just as meaning does not derive from the objective value of the goals pursued, so it does not derive from the nature of the activities in themselves. In itself shooting a ball through a hoop makes no more sense than throwing it as high as one can into the air; hitting a ball over a net is no different as an isolated action from hitting it into a net. These activities become meaningful when nested in a connected set of concerns validated by a social structure that orients them toward various goals. Throwing a ball through a hoop, as opposed to high in the air, can be at the center of such concerns as developing physical skills, competing, winning, earning respect of peers, creating school spirit, and having a lucrative career. That is why it can be a part not only of such long range goals, but even of a life plan for those with some chance of success at it. And these various goals into which the activity can fit relate it to many others and thereby render it a meaningful activity, while throwing the ball in the air is a strange waste of time.

Meaning here is tied not only to value, but to happiness. The continuous achievement of our central concerns that lends meaning to the activities involved connects with happiness as the global approval of the course of our lives over time. Just as success and the feeling of fulfillment that accompanies it reflects meaning in the activities that led up to it, so it leads itself to happiness, other things equal. But contentment with one's projects and relationships is again not sufficient for meaning. Wolf is right to reject Richard Taylor's claim that Sisyphus's accepting his lot and remaining content with his mindlessly repetitive task makes that activity meaningful. If Sisyphus thinks that the activity is meaningful, he is simply mistaken. It might symbolize something to him, such as the injustice of the world or the need to keep up the struggle, but it lacks relations to other activities and goals that would give it meaning in the full blown sense we invoke when we speak of meaningful lives.

Just as artworks and works of literature admit of different interpretations according to which the elements or episodes within them will have different meanings, so, as interpreters of our own lives, we can relate its events, and relate to them, in different ways. Trivially, events will take on different meanings for the optimist than for the pessimist, as they interpret them in different ways, as fulfillments or precursors of worse things to come. And different and incompatible ways of interpreting may be equally supported by the events themselves, which will have multiple and branching effects and causes. But not just any way of interpreting is justified. We may to an extent give meaning to the events we experience, but we are constrained by their actual sequences, just as interpreters of literary or musical works are constrained by the texts or scores as written.

Thus, as in the mythical world of Sisyphus rolling his stone, in the real world a life devoted to making sure one's clothes are in fashion by making trip after trip to the shopping mall, or one devoted to watching sports on television, seem meaningless even if the people leading those lives are perfectly content to do so. Such examples lead Wolf to conclude that a meaningful life must instead be devoted to objectively worthwhile projects. But we have seen that the contrast can be drawn without appealing to this suspect notion of objective value. It is revealing in the examples just cited to compare the life of a professional fashion designer or baseball player to that of the consumer or fan. Winning the

World Series can meaningfully be at the center of the player's concerns because it relates to and indeed organizes many other activities and concerns—desires for accomplishment, a successful career, and wealth, for example—and it culminates years of endeavor. For the fan there are no such organizing relations; the new season of passive watching simply begins shortly after the previous one ends. The actions and events in his life are simply repetitive instead of cumulative. This contrast between the meaningful and meaningless life can be drawn in terms of the internal relations among the activities that make it up, and not in terms of the objective value of the activities themselves. The challenge we posed to ourselves at the beginning to account for commitment to or contentment with meaningless projects without appealing to objective value that merely disguises our own values has been met.

Our debate on the question of meaningful lives is similar to a debate we might have on the topic of meaningful work, a more widely recognized social issue. Wolf, I am guessing, would say that work is meaningful if engaging to the worker and productive of objectively valuable products or results. Cahn might reply that any work is acceptable if the worker enjoys it, and that this is the only criterion, aside from the instrumental value of income, as far as the worker is concerned. I would say that work is meaningful if sufficiently varied and challenging, and if the worker welcomes the work as her own. The demand that the work be meaningful is separate from the demand that it be enjoyable or valuable.

Similarly, the meaningfulness of a life is only one aspect relevant to its evaluation, and a goal for the person leading the life that may have to be balanced against others. Meaning in life is not only distinct from happiness, as Wolf rightly claims, but might come into conflict with it. Unlike fictional characters, no real person's life is fully coherent, let alone coherent with those of all others. Seeking a perfectly coherent narrative for one's life would again be fanatic and narcissistic, not to be mention that meaningless activities and events can be fun.

In closing, I will return a final time to a modification of a previous example that divides Wolf's, Cahn's, and my positions. Wolf, I take it, would dismiss the life of the baseball watcher as meaningless, while Cahn would ask only whether the life was enjoyable to the person himself. I side with Wolf here on the question of meaningfulness. But now imagine that the person organizes a whole set of concerns and activities around watching baseball games. (We can also imagine that he does not neglect his family, that he has sufficient income to indulge his passion, and so on, so that moral questions do not interfere with our judgment.) He scrupulously plans trips to various stadiums in different cities, collects souvenirs from these trips, collects and trades baseball memorabilia, gradually building a collection that reveals the history of the sport, memorizes statistics from all the games he watches and from the sport's history, follows trades, potential trades, salaries, and so on. Furthermore, his expertise and involvement in the sport increases over time. I take it that Wolf would still brand such a life meaningless (assuming she knows and cares nothing about baseball) and would claim further that what makes it so is not the lack of internal relations among its activities, but once more its lack of objective value or objectively worthwhile projects.

Here I simply disagree, siding with Cahn's attack on her verdicts but not with his generalized conclusion regarding the category of meaningfulness. This life certainly does not fit my taste, although I am a sports fan, but the events in it do have meaning. As with any bearers of meaning, they point outside themselves and become intelligible in terms of their relations to these referents and to overall plans and goals. As events in a complex ongoing project, they refer back to earlier events whose promise they fulfill or forward to future events for which they prepare. Of course, this type of meaningfulness is a matter of degree, and it remains true in our modified example that each new baseball season simply begins a new cycle much like the previous one. But there is repetition in any life, perhaps necessary for stability and security, and in this one there is also progression as the memorabilia and experiences in different locales add to the earlier ones. Wolf may not approve of the meanings that accrue here, but then she does not approve of corporate law practice either, which does not prove to us that events in the life of a corporate lawyer are not as meaningful as those in the life of a philosopher. (As a philosopher with two corporate lawyer sons, I can testify that many interactions in their professional lives seem more exciting than my professional experiences—again not to be equated with meaning, but perhaps somewhat indicative of it.)

From a truly objective perspective, by contrast, the perspective of the world or the universe as a whole, one life matters as little as another. In the long run, as they say, we are all dead and gone, and there is little else to say. All effects we might have will disappear entirely, if they ever matter at all in the grand scheme of things.[9] Wolf dismisses such thoughts as "an irrational obsession with permanence."[10] But the universal perspective is the objective perspective, as opposed to the limited subjective temporal and spatial perspective that we normally occupy. The truly objective perspective that is supposed to reveal the true meaning and worth of our lives instead removes all meaning and value from view. That is another reason why we can only judge value from the perspective of our own values and standards.

In the end, from this alternative subjective viewpoint from which we always make our value judgments, meaning in life itself matters only to those who care about it. If all value for us derives ultimately from our concerns or from what we care about, this will be true also of the value for us of meaning in our lives. And this value will differ depending on how much we care about it. Some people prefer challenge, complexity, diversity, and long range projects in their lives that lend to them cumulative progression and narrative intelligibility. Others might prefer the more relaxed and comfortable routine of repetition. Eventually we all reach a point where the quest for new meanings itself seems pointless. But there is nothing wrong with looking forward to retirement on the golf course. So Cahn has the correct final word in his response to Wolf, "If a person can find delights that bring no harm, such discovery should not be denigrated, but appreciated."[11]

Notes

1. Susan Wolf, "Happiness and Meaning: Two Aspects of the Good Life," in E.F. Paul, F.D. Miller, and J. Paul, eds., *Self-Interest* (Cambridge: Cambridge University Press, 1997), 207-225, 209.
2. Ibid, 210.
3. The example is from Richard Taylor, following Albert Camus. Taylor claims that the agent's attitude toward his activity is all that counts. Richard Taylor, "The Meaning of Life," in *Good and Evil* (Amherst, NY: Prometheus, 2000), 319-334.
4. Wolf, p. 209.
5. Steven Cahn, "Meaningless Lives?" in *Puzzles and Perplexities* (Lanham, MD: Lexington Books, 2007), 89-91.
6. Stephen Darwall, *Impartial Reason* (Ithaca: Cornell University Press, 1983), 164; *Welfare and Rational Care* (Princeton: Princeton University Press, 2002), 89-90; John Cottingham, *The Meaning of Life* (London: Routledge, 2003), 66.
7. This point has been emphasized by Harry Frankfurt in many writings.
8. Kurt Baier, "The Meaning of Life," in E.D. Klemke, ed., *The Meaning of Life*, (Oxford: Oxford University Press, 2000), 101-132.
9. The point is emphasized by Thomas Nagel, "The Absurd," in *Mortal Questions* (Cambridge: Cambridge University Press, 1979).
10. Wolf, 215.
11. Cahn, 91.

4. The Relevance of Empirical Findings in Psychology to the Study of Philosophical Ethics

Tziporah Kasachkoff

Courses in ethics are usually taught without any reference to empirical data concerning how ethical judgments are actually made. This is not to say that ethical theorists have not defended their theories by reference to what they take to be empirical truths about human nature. Many ethical theorists—among them, Aristotle, the natural law theorists, utilitarians, and (even) Kant—claim that their theories not only take into account the way that, as a matter of empirical fact, human beings are constituted but, more fundamentally, that their theories are constructed in light of that account. (Whether the various accounts offered of the nature of human beings are truly empirical or only presented as such is a different matter.) There are also ethical theorists (non-cognitivists and moral relativists, for example) for whom an account of how human beings actually come to make their moral judgments determines the nature of those judgments and the criteria according to which they are to be assessed as true or false, cognitively meaningful or meaningless.

The claim that some empirical data about human beings must be taken into account in the construction of ethical theory is, therefore, not unfamiliar. Nor unreasonable: we all accept that moral claims rest on some empirical assumptions about the agents who are the objects of those claims and/or the circumstances in which they find themselves. (The famous dictum 'ought implies can' expresses this presumption. It is the announcement that the ascription of moral obligations rests on the acknowledgement of empirical capabilities—that certain moral claims have the weight they do only in light of certain empirical truths about us.)[1]

Recently, however, a growing number of professionals working in the field of moral psychology[2] have claimed that empirical facts—specifically, those of evolution—establish that contrary to what moral philosophers have generally assumed, the specific moral attitudes we have, the specific moral judgments we make, and the way we change our minds on ethical matters is not a matter of considering and then reflecting upon different reasons for and against our moral positions. Rather, the reasons we announce for our moral position or change in position are not true reasons at all for they do not serve as the premises from which we derive our moral attitudes and judgments. They are, rather, (at least for the most part and for most people) merely after-the-fact, made-up justifications of those judgments. Their conclusion is that since the reasons we give for our moral attitudes, judgments, and changes in position do not actually serve as their grounds, our moral judgments are not to be viewed as the outcome of reason at all. Moral reasoning is, generally speaking, a fiction. (It is worth pointing out that the raw empirical data presented as evidence for the view that moral reasoning is not a search for moral truth and that moral judgment is therefore not to be seen as the product of rational reflection are data with which philosophers *qua* philosophers are not generally acquainted. Most of the studies on which this view of moral reasoning relies are reported in journals of psychology and are cast in a rubric that is sufficiently technical to be somewhat opaque to those not working in the field. Consequently, philosophers who try to grapple with the conclusions of those psychologists who have done what are claimed to be the relevant psychological experiments are often restricted to those psychologists' own interpretations of, and inferences concerning, the results of these experiments.[3] Still, many philosophers have taken more than a cursory philosophical interest in these studies, and more than a few have found the 'evidence' presented—almost always portrayed as straightforwardly empirical and unequivocal—as findings that are open to a considerable range of interpretation and, as well, of contestation.[4])

In what follows, I want to examine the view that moral reasoning is, generally speaking, a chimera: when we are faced with making a moral decision regarding a person, act or policy, no true rational deliberation takes place. Instead, what occurs is a genetically determined emotional, intuitive, immediate response that we then present as a moral "judgment." On this view, moral judgment is driven not by reason but by evolution: we are hardwired by our genetic heritage to be disposed to react morally to certain events in particular kinds of ways.

In examining this view, I shall take the writings of Jonathan Haidt as representative. Haidt has published widely on this topic both alone and with many co-authors, in both the popular press and in academic journals.[5] Moreover, many of the moral psychologists writing on the topic refer (approvingly, for the most part) to his work.

Haidt and his co-authors' theory (which they dub the "social intuitionist model" of moral reasoning or 'SIM') is that empirical data concerning the evolutionary basis for our emotions in combination with empirical findings concerning the emotional basis for our sense of what is morally right and wrong support the view that human beings' moral responses (attitudes, judgments, likes and aversions) are but expressions of intuitive and automatic responses that are programmed in us by evolution for the purpose of allowing us to live in harmonious association with one another. To the extent that reason (logical analysis, the working out of logical inferences, and the weighing up of positive and negative considerations) is used in the making of moral assessments, it is only an epiphenomenon and plays no major role in the formation of those judgments. Any argument we present so as to ground our moral judgments in rational considerations has as its true purpose not the rational persuasion of others but the triggering of like intuitions in them.

However, Haidt and his colleagues do admit some exceptions to this account. On some occasions—which, on their view, occur only rarely—moral reasoning does indeed take place but when it does it is the outcome of social interaction—hence the name 'social intuitionist model' of moral reasoning—and so is to be regarded as a social phenomenon (though even in these cases, the moral reasoning engaged in by the individuals who are party to the interaction is held to be reasoning that is both "intuitive" and "post-hoc."[6])

Let us turn now turn to the evidence that is presented for the view that moral judgments are not, at least in the case of individuals, the outcome of any process of reasoning. It consists of the following:

1. In studies conducted by Haidt and a colleague, subjects hypnotized to feel disgust in the presence of certain cues invariably made moral judgments that were more severe in the presence of those cues than the judgments they made absent the cues that induced disgust. (The conclusion drawn is that feelings of disgust are either the cause of negative moral judgments or the cause of their being as stringent as they are.)
2. Haidt and his fellow researchers found that people who gave their reasons for a negative moral judgment concerning a particular act did not rescind their negative judgment on being given new information about the act that rendered the reasons they gave for their judgment irrelevant to it. (The conclusion Haidt draws from this is that since the subjects' moral judgments were not taken by them as having been undermined when the reasons they gave for those judgments were undermined, those judgments bore no relation to the reasons they gave for them but had, rather, a different and non-reasoned source, namely, a genetic disposition to form moral intuitions that were then expressed as moral "judgments.")

Before examining the above findings for their probative value with respect to the SIM thesis, I shall indicate those claims or implications of SIM that seem incontrovertible (and that, no doubt, have contributed to its popular appeal).

1. *We sometimes have 'intuitive' responses to situations, persons or acts, in that sometimes we have an immediate positive or negative feeling in response to a person, situation or act.*

Whether these feelings are, as SIM maintains, rightly characterized as having a moral dimension is a question that we shall return to below.

2. *Many people make moral judgments that they are hard put to justify.*

This hardly controversial point was noted by Plato over 2000 years ago. In Plato's *Euthyphro*, the main character is portrayed not as an idiosyncratic but rather as a typical example of the state of aporia, the state of perplexity at not being able to come up with a justification for one's position (though Plato does not restrict the state of aporia to perplexities that arise only in the context of moral judgments).

Whether the fact that people sometimes announce views for which they are unable to give good reasons shows that moral judgments are not properly the outcome of reasoning is another matter that I shall deal with below.

3. *Were humans devoid of feelings and sentiments, it is unlikely that they would have moral beliefs and moral motivations.*

Perhaps feeling of some sort is indispensable for having moral attitudes and making moral judgments. But even if this is so, the question that remains is whether moral judgments are mere expressions of those feelings or even the simple outcome of them.[7]

With these claims and the reservations concerning what follows from them in mind, let us now turn to the SIM thesis that moral judgments, though they are presented as conclusions of reasoned arguments, are typically and for the most part not conclusions at all for they are not arrived at through any process of reasoning but are, rather, direct reflections of 'moral intuitions.' Any reasons we give for our moral judgments are, on this view, merely window dressing—ad hoc maneuvers to make it look as if our judgments are formed on the basis of reasons when the truth is that any reasons we give for these judgments are merely "cooked up" in order to draw others into the orbit of our opinion. On this view, moral reasoning is retroactive: it rationalizes prior judgments rather than serves as a means by which we arrive at them.

The first thing to note is that even were it true that reasoning is not the basis on which any initial moral judgment is formed, it would not follow that we never engage in moral reasoning. For we might appeal to reason to assess whether our moral judgments, however initially formed, are morally right or wrong, morally well grounded or not. Experience suggests that moral reason is commonly employed in just this way: we form a moral judgment (perhaps in haste, or without reflection, or in some other way non-rationally) and then we might have occasion to ascertain whether that judgment stands up to the light of reason. We do this by trying to figure out what considerations are relevant to our judgment, what differential weights of importance and urgency ought to be assigned to these different considerations, and what follows from these calculations. In short, we often appeal to reason to evaluate the judgments we have made and in this way come to know whether, however initially formed, they can rationally be justified. (Consider, for example, how we might think through and revise our "spontaneous" moral views concerning sex, politics, or money.) So even if the authors of SIM are right—though there is no reason at this stage to believe that they are—that moral reasoning is not used to establish first order moral judgments, this would not show that moral reasoning is not used to assess what we may call second-order moral judgments, i.e., assessments of, and sometimes changes in, those judgments.

Three other considerations drawn from moral experience should make us skeptical of the claim that most people (even given the authors' qualification "for the most part") do not engage in moral reasoning. According to the authors of SIM, moral "reasoning" is a misnomer. What we have are 'automatic,' 'quick,' 'spontaneous,' and 'evaluative' feelings of like and dislike, feelings that are then articulated as assertions of praise or blame and designated as "moral judgments." But this identification of immediate evaluative intuitive responses as moral judgments fails to account for the moral judgments that we make in the absence of any intuition at all, as often happens when we are faced with the need to make a moral judgment about a situation whose moral contours are complicated or unclear to us. When we are called upon to make a judgment in the absence of any relevant intuition concerning which we must make that judgment, there can be no identification of moral judgment with intuition. (Are there clear intuitions that most of us could appeal to when it comes to making judgments concerning such vexing moral questions as whether to institute a school voucher system? Or open up an ecologically rich island to tourism so as to bring in useful revenues? Or use aborted fetal tissue for important medical research? Or clone pets?)

Second, it may be that with respect to a given situation we find not that we have no moral intuition regarding it but too many: there are some situations (generally but not always complicated ones) in which we have multiple intuitions, each of which pulls us in a different direction. In such cases, our moral judgment cannot reflect our spontaneous and immediate intuitions but will be called upon to adjudicate among them. To take a much appealed-to example: Most people surveyed report that they would find it morally loathsome to throw a person in the path of an out-of-control trolley in order to stop it from hurtling down the tracks and killing the five people working there even given that that is the only way to stop the trolley. But they also respond that it would be right to kill a certain number of innocent people if by doing so we can save a much greater number of innocents from dying, their intuition being that the more innocent lives saved, the better.[8] When we have such conflicting moral intuitions, discerning the morally best thing to do requires sorting out what is morally most salient in the particular situation that faces us—a 'sorting out' that we refer to as 'moral reasoning'. It cannot be true, therefore, that moral reasoning is always a rationalization of prior intuitions because in some situations it is precisely because our intuitions do not comport well with one another that we turn to moral reasoning to adjudicate between them.

A third reason for skepticism regarding the identification of moral judgment with immediate evaluative response is that many of our moral judgments have no plausible link to immediate evaluative intuitions or even to any emotion of like and dislike. In addition to moral judgments about particular actions and particular persons (where there may be some plausibility to the notion that our assessment takes place against the background of an immediate and intuitive attraction or aversion), we often make judgments about the general and relative moral importance of character traits or states of affairs, such as the judgment that being loyal is better (or less good) than being truthful, or that the duty to be kind is more (or less) stringent than the duty to keep one's promises. SIM's claim that "moral judgment is a product of quick and automatic intuitions"[9] loses plausibility when we look at these kinds of moral judgments for such judgments are not arrived at quickly and automatically but, typically, only after consideration of and reflection on a multitude of specific cases. Nor does our experience show that such judgments reflect the sort of "spontaneous evaluative feelings" that Haidt and his colleagues claim to be the hallmark of moral intuition. The point made above with respect to judgments about relative moral importance applies equally to judgments that express general moral principles (of the sort that are not merely inductive generalizations from individual cases) such as the principle that 'sons ought not to be punished for the sins of their fathers' or that 'ought implies can.' However one regards these assertions in terms of their truth or wisdom, these evaluative judgments can hardly be said to be the product of feelings and emotions that are 'unconscious,' 'automatic,' 'quick,' and 'spontaneous.'

From criticisms that have been made of the SIM thesis, its authors are not unaware that judgments such as those noted above present difficulties for their view. So later presentations of their thesis include exceptions to its core claim that moral judgment is not the product of moral reasoning: now that claim is emended as being true only "for the most part and for most people," philosophers (among some other few, though unspecified, groups) being one of the rare exceptions.

However, the incorporation of this last exception to the general thesis that moral reasoning is merely epiphenomenal to genetically determined intuitive, quick and automatic moral responses serves only to generate more quandaries. First, the sorts of judgments that require deliberation, deep reflection over time, and sometimes even discussion with others, are not judgments that are rare and not to be found among ordinary folk. Though non-philosophers may communicate their judgments and the process by which they arrive at them differently from the way in which professionally schooled philosophers articulate their judgments, there is no evidence that it takes philosophical training to be adept at the making of reasoned moral judgments (even if it takes philosophical training to conduct second-order analyses of those reasoned judgments). To be sure, non-philosophers sometimes make moral judgments that are determined by what they feel (rather than by what they think about what they feel). But sometimes so do philosophers. The question we must ask, then, is not whether affect ever determines moral judgment but whether—in the case of philosopher and non-philosopher alike—the direction may work in reverse and reasoned moral judgment may determine affect as much as affect may determine judgment. From what we know, not only are non-philosophers not the only people for whom moral intuitions sometimes serve as the sole basis for their judgments, but philosophers are not the only people whose moral judgments may be the outcome of appeal to moral reason.

Second, it is no advancement of our understanding of moral phenomena to be told by proponents of SIM that what we thought were instances of deliberate moral reasoning are really a matter of innate, spontaneous, and automatic responses that represent our evolutionary heritage but which are nonetheless not universally true for everyone. For while there may be legitimate exceptions to any scientific generalization, what is needed is an explanation of how, consistent with the evolutionary story that SIM tells, these exceptions come about.

Let us turn now from the question of the plausibility of the SIM thesis, to an examination of the evidence presented for it.

Evidence for the SIM Thesis

Haidt and a colleague report on a study that they conducted of subjects who, under hypnosis, were cued to respond with a feeling of disgust to certain words. After being brought out of their hypnotized state, most of these subjects' moral judgments of acts that were described with those "cue" words were more severe than their judgments of those same acts when those acts were described without the words to which the subjects had been programmed to respond with feelings of disgust. Here is how the authors of SIM describe their study and what they hoped to ascertain by means of it.

Under the heading Manipulating Intuitions, they write:

> [W]e ... directly manipulated the strength of moral intuitions without changing the facts being judged, *to test the prediction that... intuitive judgment... directly causes, or at least influences, moral judgments* [italics added]. [We] hypnotized one group of subjects to feel a flash of disgust whenever they read the word "take"; another group was hypnotized to feel disgust at the word "often." Subjects then read 6 moral judgment stories, each of which included either the word "take" or the word "often." Only highly hypnotizable subjects who were amnesic for the post-hypnotic suggestion were used. In two studies, the flash of disgust that subjects felt while reading 3 of their 6 stories made their moral judgments more severe. In study 2, a seventh story was included in which there was no violation whatsoever, to test the limits of the phenomenon: "Dan is a student council representative at his school. This semester he is in charge of scheduling discussions about academic issues. He [tries to take] <often picks> topics that appeal to both professors and students in order to stimulate discussion." We predicted that with no violation of any kind, subjects would be forced to override their feelings of disgust, and most did. But one third of all

subjects who encountered their disgust word in the story still rated Dan's actions as somewhat morally wrong, and several made up post-hoc confabulations.... One subject justified his condemnation of Dan by writing "it just seems like he's up to something." Another wrote that Dan seemed like a "popularity seeking snob." *These cases provide vivid examples of reason playing its role as slave to the passions* [italics added].[10]

The authors' conclusion that their subjects' behavior exemplifies Hume's claim that reason is 'a slave to the passions' is taken by them to follow from the fact that the subjects, having been hypnotized to feel disgust at certain cues, find themselves post-hypnotically responding to those cues by morally condemning behavior couched in terms of those cues. But when unable to justify their post-hypnotic condemnation by the actual facts as they know them, they end up making "post-hoc confabulations" to account for their otherwise inexplicable moral judgments.

But why is the subjects' behavior to be regarded as showing that their reason was doing the bidding of their passions? When people find themselves behaving in ways they can't account for, it is precisely as rational creatures that they search for something that might explain it. In the situation described, the reason for the subjects' behavior is hidden from them as they aren't told that they are acting under hypnotic suggestion and so (perhaps pathetically) they are driven to rely on invention. Is this reason in the service of the passions, or reasoning persons engaging in somewhat desperate attempts (as, not surprisingly, they must be in such circumstances) to find consistency between their judgments and the facts? The subjects' attempt to make sense of behavior that has no sense at all from their point of view is driven by the perfectly rational desire to foster consistency between their judgments and the facts as they perceive them, that desire being a requirement of rationality, not of passion.

According to the authors of SIM, if feelings of disgust incline us to form negative moral judgments when we would not otherwise have done so, or cause the negative moral judgments that we make to be more stringent than they otherwise would be, then feelings (of which disgust is but one example), not reason, are the driving force behind our (negative) moral judgments.[11]

It appears from the studies described by Haidt and his colleagues that, as a matter of fact, feelings of disgust do have an effect on moral judgments. But one should not take this as demonstrating that reasoning is irrelevant to moral judgment and that morality is but the linguistically articulated version of genetically determined intuitions. For one thing, while feelings of disgust may influence moral judgment, so too might fatigue, nagging hunger, indigestion, a spat with one's boss, and suffering from a bad case of poison ivy. Indeed, it may be the case that the content or stringency of one's moral judgments is affected by any strong affective state and not just those that evolution has determined us to feel for reasons of self-protection and survival.[12]

Proponents of SIM may be inclined to respond that if it is found that any number of negative affective states may influence the formation, content and stringency of our moral judgments, this would not undermine their thesis (that affective states, not reasoning, are the grounds on which moral judgments are formed) but rather provide confirmation of it. But this will not do because the thesis that moral judgment is not the outcome of reasoning but of genetically determined intuitions centers on the characterization of these intuitions as not merely spontaneous, automatic, quick, and immediate but—most important—as genetically determined evaluative responses. So if it turns out that any negative affective state—such as emotional stress, physical discomfort or hunger—generate, or produce a change in, moral judgment, the thesis that it is not reasoning that lies behind moral judgments but rather negatively valenced evaluative feelings for which moral judgments serve as proxy will have been undermined.

Furthermore, just as it might be the case that any strong negative affective state has an influence on the content and stringency of moral judgment, it might also be the case that strong negative feelings have an influence on any sort of judgment, moral or non-moral. If, for example, the presence of strong negative feelings have an influence on the nature of whatever scientific, economic, or political judgments are made under their influence, then the question of why feelings of disgust influence moral judgments will be part of the larger question of why, generally, affective states bring about changes in whatever assessments one is in the process of making. What we need, therefore, are not merely studies that show that disgust influences or alters moral judgments but that other, non-evaluative feelings do not have similar effects on judgments of other sorts.

Haidt and Bjorklund (Haidt's co-author and co-advocate of the SIM thesis) tie their view that moral judgment is a 'stand in' for moral intuitions to the view that disgust (as well as anger) are 'watchdogs of the moral world,' the implication being that disgust (and anger) are feelings that are intimately connected with moral beliefs and attitudes. But not only need there be no connection between feelings of disgust and moral evaluation, there need be no connection between feelings of disgust and any evaluative judgment—moral or non-moral. (We might feel disgust at, say, the sight of cockroaches or of someone eating his own vomit, without making any judgment—even a nonmoral one, regarding these things.) To be sure, sometimes disgust is felt towards that which we morally disdain, but just as commonly disgust is felt independent of any judgmental viewpoint (and is actually often a poor guide to judgment). So even if we agree that disgust is a genetically encoded feeling that guides behavior in terms of what we should avoid and what we should approach, this is not tantamount to an argument in favor of our viewing it as moral, or even evaluative, in nature.[13]

Second, the studies from which conclusions are drawn concerning a connection between feelings of disgust on the one hand and moral judgment on the other are, as we noted, studies that involve subjects who have been hypnotized to feel disgust. But since these conclusions are claimed to illuminate what is true of general moral psychology and of ordinary moral reasoning the question arises whether feelings that are hypnotically induced rather than those that arise in ordinary circumstances are the of sorts feelings that we should be looking at. An experiment that hypnotizes subjects so as to short-circuit their cognition and "synthetically" produce an affect that is devoid of meaning for them is one that we cannot be sure shows anything about a connection between negative affect on the one hand and general moral assessment on the other because we do not know how similar naturally occurring feelings are to feelings induced by hypnotic suggestion. What we need if we are to draw reliable conclusions about the connection between affect on the one hand and moral judgment on the other are studies that give us reason to believe that 1) hypnotically induced affect is comparable to non-hypnotically produced affect; 2) judgments made as a result of hypnotic influence are judgments that are sustained over a period of time (as non-hypnotically influenced judgments typically are, and 3) judgments made as a result of hypnotic influence are reasonably viewed as moral judgments.

I turn now to another argument advanced by Haidt and his co-authors in support of their thesis that moral reasoning is bogus (except, as noted above, for philosophers and for some others whose moral thinking takes place in social contexts). The argument is that the unlikelihood that our moral judgments are really the product of a search for moral truth is borne out by the fact that people have a tendency to search only for reasons that confirm their moral judgment and not for reasons that might undermine or disconfirm them.

It is true that sometimes—even perhaps often—people search for what confirms and not for what disconfirms their moral position. But this is difficult to understand only if we think that the goal of reaching correct moral conclusions is the only goal that people have rather than one that must vie with multiple other goals a person has, typically important among them being the goal of having oneself perceived—by oneself as well as by others—as being morally in the right. Which of a person's various goals is/are determinative of the sort of reasoning that that person pursues on a particular occasion may have to do with a variety of factors, such as that person's sense of confidence, her level of comfort with her audience, and the stakes of finding herself morally in the wrong. No doubt, when the goal of being perceived as morally in the right is dominant, the search for moral truth will most likely get sacrificed to a search for what confirms rather than for what disconfirms that person's moral position. But though this may show that the search for truth is not always a person's unique goal, it does not show either that it is not one of her goals or that it is not one of her important goals. The tendency people have to search for what confirms rather than for what undermines their position does not, therefore, necessarily reflect a lack of interest in moral truth or in moral reasoning; it may show only that that interest is not always paramount or always psychologically overriding.

It is worth noting that there is nothing unique about moral reasoning in this regard. People are no more likely to search out evidence against their political, social, psychological, religious, and even scientific positions than they are with respect to their moral positions. But no one would suggest that this fact shows that in these areas the goal of reasoning is something other than to reach correct conclusions.

Another and perhaps the chief argument offered by proponents of the view that moral judgments are (for the most part) not the outcome of reason is that people sometimes find themselves unable to state the basis for their moral judgments: after all, if a person has arrived at a moral conclusion on the basis of reasons, she should be able to state those reasons and if she cannot state the reasons for her moral judgment then it is fair to conclude that her judgment is not the conclusion of any process of reasoning.

There is no doubt that people sometimes announce moral views for which they are unable to give their reasons. Indeed, people sometimes make, and stick with, judgments that they are hard put to support in economics, science, psychology, and in the affairs of everyday life. But though SIM takes the fact that people are sometimes unable to justify their moral judgments as showing that, generally speaking, moral judgments are not the outcome of reasoning, they draw no such analogous conclusion regarding reasoning in these other areas. Perhaps SIM's differential treatment of moral judgments on the one hand, and other sorts of normative assessments on the other, is taken to be justified by findings concerning the phenomenon of "moral dumbfounding," a topic to which we shall now turn.

'Dumbfounded' Responses and What They Show

Haidt and his colleagues conducted experiments in which they found that people were unwilling to rescind or modify their moral judgments concerning certain taboo violations even after new facts supplied by the interviewers rendered the reasons the subjects gave for their judgments irrelevant to those judgments. The subjects were also unable to explain the reason for persisting with their judgment even after the reasons for it had been undermined—an inability that Haidt dubs 'the dumbfounded response.'[14] (Specifically, subjects were unwilling to change their judgment that consensual adult sibling incest was morally wrong even when the reason that they gave—that such incest produces physically damaged offspring—was later undermined by the interviewer telling them that there could be no offspring because the brother and sister used two forms of birth control.)

What moral dumbfounding shows, Haidt claims, is that moral judgments are not the outcome of moral reasoning but rather, the product of a genetically-determined 'anti-incest' module or 'modular intuition,' an intuition which, being genetic, is not revisable by other knowledge. (Significantly, subjects who revised their moral judgment in the light of new information supplied by the interviewer are not perceived by the authors of the study as casting doubt on the claim that it is intuition rather than reasoning that is at work in moral judgment but merely as those who "overruled" their intuition to come to an "uneasy" different moral judgment.)

The question before us, therefore, is: Does the refusal of subjects to give up their negative moral judgment despite the undermining of the reasons they presented on its behalf show that those reasons were not truly the grounds for their judgment and that the judgment was simply the causal product of unreasoned intuitive reactions 'dressed up' in the language of 'reasons'?

I suggest that it does not. First, in the context of the study, a 'dumbfounded' response on the part of the subjects may not have been an unreasonable one. Since in the real world moral judgments are responses to situations that occur within contexts in which decisions carry implications and actions have consequences, asking someone to make a judgment concerning a situation in which all these accompaniments have been nominally, and hence artificially, subtracted cannot but elicit a 'dumbfounded' response. To be sure, the subjects were not literally "dumbfounded"—it is not that they had nothing to say about the incest once the basis for their moral judgment concerning it was undermined by the experimenter. It was rather that, though they persisted with their judgment despite the invalidation of the reasons they gave for that judgment, they found themselves unable to explain this persistence.

But how seriously should we take a researcher's conclusions about general moral reasoning when these conclusions are based on experiments that require subjects not merely to make moral judgments about actions that the experimenter tells the subject are uncoupled from the consequences and implications usually—indeed perhaps always—associated with them, but also requires the subjects to render their judgment quickly, without the opportunity to mull over the issue, or discuss it with others, or spend time reflecting on the values inherent in their judgment? Under these conditions, the 'dumbfounded' response elicited by these studies reveals little about typical moral reasoning for this is not how, typically, we engage in moral reasoning. For Haidt and his colleagues to require that subjects make their moral judgments abstracted from the social and cognitive background that usually accompanies those judgments is to render the results of these studies irrelevant as an index of how human beings actually come to make their moral judgments. It therefore shows little about the nature of moral reasoning generally.

Of significance here are studies—to which the authors of SIM do not allude—that show that once a subject has committed him- or herself to a position, then whatever the subject matter on which the position has been taken, there is reluctance to rescind that position,[15] a finding for which various explanations have been offered, one of which is that people are disinclined to reverse their previously announced positions so as not to appear uncertain, lacking in confidence, unknowledgeable, illogical, or in some other way cognitively deficient. This suggests that the reluctance of the subjects in Haidt's studies to reverse their moral judgments in the face of the undermining of the reasons that they gave for those judgments may show less about the etiology of moral judgments than it shows about the psychology of self-perception, the perception of others' perception of one's cognitive abilities, and the connection between how one views the public reversal of one's position and the desire to 'save face.' To establish that perseverance with one's announced moral position in the face of the undermining of one's reasons for that position shows what the advocates of SIM claim it shows (namely that moral judgments, generally, are made independent of reasons), we would need to look at studies that compare how subjects respond to the undermining of the reasons they give for their moral judgments with how they respond to the undermining of the reasons they give for judgments about matters having nothing to do with morality. But SIM offers us nothing in this regard.

Other Aspects and Other Difficulties with SIM

The thesis we have been looking at claims that through evolutionary processes we have come to have genetic dispositions to respond morally to situations in ways that are felicitous to our survival in communal associations. These dispositions, we are told, take the form of moral modules in our brain, and serve as templates for moral response. Haidt identifies five such modules, each representing a different 'moral' concern (harm, reciprocity, purity, authority, and recognition of an ingroup/outgroup distinction). The modules are held to be genetically determined and so (presumably) are constant for all human beings although the form in which they find expression at a particular time and within a particular society is claimed to be environmentally determined. (For example, although according to SIM we all inherit a module for reciprocity, what counts as conduct that demonstrates reciprocity, as well as the determination of the sorts of behavior for which reciprocal conduct is required, may vary from culture to culture.) Thus is allowance made by SIM for cultural variance in the ways that the genetically encoded moral modules find expression despite their claim that the content of the modules is innate to, and so universal for, all human beings.

As for the differences in moral outlook that we find among members within a single cultural group—such as the differences we find between American political liberals and American political conservatives—these are explained by proponents of SIM as due to differences of emphasis that each places on the innate moral constants that, according to their view, are present in all. In turn, differences in emphasis are accounted for by the fact that "some people are simply born with brains that are prone to experience stronger intuitions from individual moral modules."[16]

Further variability—this time among individuals within the same subculture—is explained by the fact that:

> [l]earning, practice, and the assistance of adults, peers, and the media ... produce a 'tuning up' as each child develops the skill set that is her unique pattern of virtues. This tuning up process may lead to further strengthening or weakening of particular modules. Alternatively, individual development might be better described as a broadening or narrowing of the domain of application of a particular module.[17]

But these explanations will not do. With respect to the explanation offered for the differences in moral outlook to be found between American liberals and

American conservatives: It strains credulity to accept the implication that a liberal who becomes a conservative (or vice versa) can be taken to have undergone a transformation of his brain from being less (or more) prone to experiencing inherited material to now being more (or less) so. And although there may be some plausibility in accounting for human similarities in moral responses by positing a common innate heritage, accounting for our variability in these responses by recourse to the hypothesis that some of us have and some of us lack capacities to tap into this common heritage is another, clearly less plausible (and also clearly ad hoc), claim. It is also a claim that, though presented as an empirical hypothesis, comes unaccompanied by any empirical support.

With respect to the explanation offered for differences among individuals within the same cultural subset: The assertion that learning, practice, and the assistance of others help to 'tune up' one's moral modules and so to strengthen or weaken them amounts to an explanation without any explanatory power for we know no more about what 'tuning up' amounts to and how it is consistent with the evolutionary assumptions of SIM than we do about why, given the same genetic heritage, some human beings do and some do not elude its influence. The explanation offered here is as opaque as what it is introduced to explain.

Finally, as noted above, the authors of SIM present moral reasoning on the part of philosophers as an exception rather than as a counter-example to their thesis that moral judgments represent feelings rather than reasoning. But no explanation is offered as to how this exception comes about or is consistent with the evolutionary story that is told. Here too, as in the other cases, what we need and what is missing is an explanation of why—given the view that evolution has provided us with innate guides to moral behavior—we find that some people follow these innate guides and some act independently of them.

The Argumentative Strategy of SIM

Whether the authors of SIM are right or wrong about the empirical facts of moral decision making and what these facts show about whether moral reasoning actually takes place, the argumentative strategy they employ in the presentation of their thesis tends to discredit that thesis as scientifically sound. This is because every putative counter-example and every recalcitrant fact is dealt with in a way that merely pushes the concern raised by these examples and facts back one stage.

To the objection that, contrary to what SIM claims to be the case, we often change our minds about moral matters because of others' reasons and others often change their minds in response to reasons that we ourselves present, comes the response that moral judgments are the outcome of non-rational processes only "for the most part and for most people." Thus is a place provided for moral reasoning though it is claimed that such reasoning is rare and occurs only in the course of social interaction when reasoning 'runs through other people.'

To the objection that experience shows that there are individual and not merely social instances of moral reasoning, comes the response: "Yes, but only in rare cases, and only in some people (for example, philosophers)" though no account is given as to how these cases and these people escape the evolutionary net that, according to SIM, enmeshes us all.

To the objection that we find variation in moral attitude and behavior when we would expect to find likeness (given that we are genetically hard-wired to morally respond in the same way to the same cultural cues), comes the response: "Yes, but only because some have greater access than others to their genetically determined moral constants," though no explanation is offered as to how differences in access may come about.

The constant accommodation to counter-examples through successive additions to the SIM thesis creates the impression that its authors believe that the presentation of counter-evidence serves only to point out that their thesis has been incompletely stated and not that it is defective.

Admittedly, some pieces of counter-evidence to a thesis can be met with the rejoinder, legitimate in some cases, that there are exceptions to the generalizations that constitute that thesis. But such a reply must be accompanied by an explanation of why the suggested counter-cases should be regarded as exceptions. Otherwise, one is left to wonder what would count as disconfirmation of the thesis and whether consideration of it as an empirical thesis is warranted.

Concluding Remarks

Empirical findings may help us to understand the necessary conditions for our ability to make moral judgments and for our being inclined to morally respond to certain situations in one way rather than another. But we must bear in mind that what is billed as "empirical research" must be genuinely empirical. While it is extremely likely that, as SIM maintains, evolution has prepared humans for the task of ethical decision-making by predisposing us to respond in certain ways to certain situations, suggestions of likelihood fall far short of empirical proof. Proponents of SIM argue that the process by which evolution has prepared us to behave and think morally gives us reason to doubt that, apart from the exceptional case, reason is actually exercised in the making of moral judgments. I have argued that the arguments presented for this claim are deficient both in terms of empirical support and in terms of the inferences that are drawn from the 'findings' that are presented.

However, the view advanced by SIM is not merely unsupported; it is implausible. The claim that evolution has prepared humans for moral behavior through the implantation of moral modules that circumvent rather than make use of reasoning (which is itself evolutionarily developed) is less plausible than the view that, insofar as morality is genetically determined, it incorporates the exercise of reason rather than makes it redundant. Since the capacity for reason is itself an evolutionary product, the sentimental modules—if indeed, this is a constructive way to think about our innate preparedness to have certain moral responses and to make certain moral judgments—do not deliver morality to us; they simply constitute basic sentimental responses on which moral reason can exercise itself.[18]

We do not yet have an empirically sound account of how we come to make the moral judgments that we do. However, if and when we do, it is not likely (for the reasons given above) that we will find that the exercise of reason in the making of those judgments is gratuitous.

Notes

1. I am assuming that the 'can' referred to in the 'ought implies can' dictum refers to capabilities that are other than normatively determined. (If the drunk, because he is drunk, cannot do what he morally ought to, we may nevertheless rightly hold him morally responsible. For a discussion of some of the complexities, see Michael Stocker, "'Ought' and 'Can,'" *Australasian Journal of Philosophy*, 49. 1971.)

2. See, for example, J. Haidt, "The Emotional Dog and its Rational Tail: A Social Intuitionist Approach to Moral Judgment," *Psychological Review*, 108, (2001); Jonathan Haidt and Fredrik Bjorklund, "Social Intuitionists Answer Six Questions About Moral Psychology," in W. Sinnott-Armstrong, ed., *Moral Psychology*, Vol. 3 (2003); and J. Haidt, F. Bjorklund, and S. Murphy, "Moral Dumbfounding: When Intuition Finds No Reason" (Unpublished manuscript) (2004).

3. This is not to say that philosophers have remained uninterested in this issue. In 2006 Peter Singer devoted a seminar at Princeton University to the topic of the relevance of empirical data to our understanding of moral reasoning—an issue that he foreshadowed many years ago in a book that he wrote, in 1981, entitled *The Expanding Circle: Ethics and Sociobiology* (Clarendon Press). It was also the topic to which *Philosophical Explorations: An International Journal for the Philosophy of Mind and Action* devoted its entire March, 2006 issue, and on which Anthony Appiah has recently written *Experiments in Ethics* (Cambridge, MA: Harvard University Press, 2008).

4. See, for example, Cordelia Fine, "Is the Emotional Dog Wagging its Rational Tail or Chasing it? Reason in Moral Judgment" and Garrett Cullity, "As You Were? Moral philosophy and the Aetiology of Moral Experience" both in *Philosophical Explorations*, vol. 9, No. 1 (2006).

5. See, for example, Jonathan Haidt and Fredrik Bjorklund, "Social Intuitionists Answer Six Questions About Moral Psychology," op. cit.; J. Haidt, "The Emotional Dog and its Rational Tail: A Social Intuitionist Approach to Moral Judgment," op. cit.; J. Haidt, Frank Bjorklund, and S. Murphy, "Moral Dumbfounding: When Intuition Finds No Reason," (2004). Unpublished manuscript, University of Virginia; J. Haidt and M. A. Hersh, "Sexual Morality: The Cultures and Reasons of Liberals and Conservatives," *Journal of Applied Social Psychology*, 31, (2001); and J. Haidt and C. Joseph, "Intuitive Ethics: How Innately Prepared Intuitions Generate Culturally Variable Virtues," *Daedalus*, Fall, 2004.

6. Jonathan Haidt and Fredrik Bjorklund, "Social Intuitionists Answer Six Questions About Moral Psychology," op. cit., 11.

7. For a sensitive general discussion, see Joel Feinberg, "Sentiment and Sentimentality in Practical Ethics," *Proceedings and Addresses of the American Philosophical Association*, 56 (1) (1982): 19-46.

8. This latter response surfaces through their response to the question of whether an out-of-control trolley headed along tracks on which five people are working should be diverted to another set of tracks on which one person is working so as to avoid killing the five. Most people say 'yes' to diverting the trolley even though it means that an innocent person will be killed by the diversion. Reported by Steven Pinker, "The Moral Instinct: How evolutionary psychology and neurobiology are changing our understanding of what morality is, " *NY Times Magazine*, January 13, 2008/Section 6.

9. Social Intuitionists Answer Six Questions About Moral Psychology," op. cit., 2.

10. T. Wheatley and Jonathan Haidt, "Hypnotic Disgust Makes Moral Judgments More Severe," *Psychological Science*, 2005.

11. Although SIM claims that affect rather than reason is, at bottom, what morality is about, it focuses on feelings of disgust because it views disgust as one of the feelings that evolution has determined us to experience as a self-protective avoidance measure and therefore as one that may be presumed to be automatic and so not mediated by cognition or reasoning. For an interesting, if controversial, view of feelings of disgust and the role these feelings may play in our lives, see Martha Nussbaum, *Hiding from Humanity, Disgust, Shame and the Law* (Princeton University Press, 2004).

12. We might also raise the question of whether feelings of disgust have the evolutionary significance claimed for them by the authors of SIM. It seems more probable—in light of the fact that we are speaking not only of humans but of other animals as well—that it is not disgust but something more primitive that evolution has determined us to feel, a feeling which we humans later conceptualize as disgust and make use of as a self protective measure—and perhaps for other purposes as well.

13. For a nuanced account of disgust in relation to the issues raised here, see Nussbaum, op. cit.

14. "Social Intuitionists Answer Six Questions About Moral Psychology," op. cit., 14.

15. D. Peterson, H. D. Saltzstein, and C. Ebbe, "Sequential Effects in Social Influence," *Journal of Personality and Social Psychology*, 6, (1967); H. D. Saltzstein, and L. Sandberg, "Indirect Social Influence: Change in Judgmental Process or Anticipatory Conformity?" *Journal of Experimental Social Psychology*, 15, (1979).

16. Ibid.

17. "Social Intuitionists Answer Six Questions About Moral Psychology," op. cit., 25.

18. Some of the issues raised in this paper are the focus of an article that I have co-authored with Herb Saltzstein. Professor Saltzstein has added much to my understanding of developmental moral psychology and its literature.

5. The Teaching Profession

Peter Markie

In his essay, "A Sculptor in Snow," celebrating the career of Sidney Hook, Steve Cahn quoted Hook's description of one of the great benefits available to teachers, "although the teacher like the actor is a sculptor in snow and can leave no permanent monument of his genius behind, he can reach the minds of those who will survive him, and through them affect the future."[1]

Commenting on Hook's description, Steve wrote, "through the vision of excellence Professor Hook has projected to so many thousands of students, he has himself constructed a monument to the ideals of great teaching."[2]

Steve has done as much and as well. He has given his students and colleagues a model for every area of our professional lives and teaching perhaps most of all. I want to use this opportunity to articulate some of the insights that I ultimately owe to Steve with regard to college teaching.

The points that concern me unfold neatly from a single claim: College teaching is a profession. We sometimes think of a profession as any occupation that requires specialized knowledge. Lots of activities, from the practice of medicine to safecracking, are professions so conceived. My concept of a profession is richer in content and narrower in scope. Professions are identified by five closely related traits: expertise, commitment, authority, independence and a distinctive ethical role. Many activities we commonly count as professions (e.g., safecracking, plumbing) do not exemplify this combination of traits, but others do, at least when properly practiced. Medicine, the ministry and journalism come to mind, in particular. I shall develop this model of a profession and consider how well teaching fits it.

Professions

Professions involve the possession of some specialized knowledge, as well as skill in its application. Physicians are schooled in medical science and trained in its application to their patients. Ministers, priests, rabbis and the like are schooled in theology and trained in the spiritual counseling of their congregants. Journalists are trained in obtaining, analyzing and publicly sharing information.

Professions also involve a defining commitment to serve the welfare of others. Physicians are assumed to have a commitment to use their medical knowledge and skill to advance the physical and psychological welfare of their patients. Members of the ministry are presumably committed to using their theological knowledge and training to promote the spiritual welfare of their flock. Journalists are assumed to be committed to advancing the public's understanding of important events. This element of commitment underlies our sense of each profession as a noble calling and of professionals as dedicated individuals.

It is important to note that the relation between professionals and those they serve is not that between a service provider and a consumer. The parties in a mere service provider-consumer relationship are united by self-interest. Providers attempt to promote their own welfare by offering goods that may or may not be in the consumers' interest. Consumers select goods in an attempt to maximize their wellbeing. Neither party is dedicated to advancing the welfare of the other. In contrast, professionals and those they serve are united in a common effort to promote the interests of the latter. They are partners in a common cause aimed at advancing the wellbeing of one of them.

The professional's commitment to advancing the welfare of others is combined with a respect for their autonomy. Professionals don't offer their expertise as a replacement for the free, rational and informed choices of others; they offer it as a way of increasing the quality of those choices. Physicians present patients with information and options and help them, often though a process of education, to make their own informed treatment choices. Those in the ministry guide their congregants to a particular understanding of their lives but recognize the importance of their own free, informed acceptance of that understanding. The journalist's commitment to full and balanced reporting is based on the value of each reader or listener rationally arriving at his or her own informed view of the world.

Given their expertise and commitment, professionals speak and act with great authority within their practice. That they know better than the rest of us and are offering their views with concern for our welfare and respect for our autonomy gives us a good reason to trust their opinions. Professionals also act with a great deal of independence. We let them set the standards for training, certification and continuing competence in their area. They largely police themselves, and, insofar as society regulates a profession, the professionals play a major role in the design and implementation of the regulations. As is the case with their authority, professionals gain their independence on the basis of their expertise and commitment. Given their expertise, they know best how their practice is to be structured and regulated. Given their commitment to others, they can be trusted.

The last trait associated with professions is a distinctive ethical role. To join a profession is to change the ethical dimensions of one's life substantially, taking on new values, duties and rights. Some duties are common to all professions. Every professional has a duty to maintain the knowledge and skill that are the basis for his or her practice. Other ethical duties are profession specific, stemming from the particular nature of the profession's defining commitment. Suppose a physician discovers that her patient, an important public figure, has a serious medical condition. A journalist gains the same information from a different source. The public figure's neighbor gains it by happening to overhear a conversation between her and her spouse. Who has what obligations with regard to sharing this interesting information with others? The determining factors vary with the presence or absence of a professional role and from one profession to another. The physician has a duty of confidentiality, based on a commitment to promote the patient's welfare and autonomy, and need not worry about the public's right to know. The journalist has a duty to inform the public and no special duty of confidentiality to the public figure. The neighbor, having no professional relationship to the public figure, has neither a special duty of confidentiality nor a special duty to inform the public. Because each profession has an ethical dimension, being good *at* a profession involves being good ethically.

The ethical dimension of each profession is determined in part by a changeable compact between the profession and society. Our expectations for a profession help determine its members' responsibilities and, as our expectations change, so do the responsibilities. Consider how our expectations for physicians have changed dramatically over last century. The once accepted model of a paternalistic physician who treats but does not always inform has been replaced by the model of a physician who guides patients through their own choices regarding treatment options. The new model contains a revised understanding of a physician's responsibilities. It also supports changes in the training of physicians. Professional preparation includes a greater emphasis on the skills needed to communicate with and educate patients.

The successful maintenance of a profession's compact with society depends on the continuing professionalism of its members. In particular, professionals who would retain their authority and independence must maintain their expertise and commitment. If we decide that physicians lack the expertise they claim, we are much more inclined to mandate certification standards and procedures for them. If we decide that they are more interested in serving their bank accounts than their patients, we are more inclined to support hefty malpractice judgments to bring their unprofessional pursuit of self-interest in line with the promotion of their patients' welfare. When clergy are seen as potential pedophiles, their congregants demand a greater role in their selection, evaluation and assignments. Once we decide that journalists are shilling for politicians in return for the special access that will advance their careers, we are much less inclined to support shield laws. Each profession depends on its initial education programs and subsequent mentoring to ensure the professionalism of its members.

In all, professionals employ a special expertise for the benefit of others and act with substantial authority, independence and distinctive ethical responsibilities and rights. They operate within a changeable compact with society and their continuing to prosper within that compact depends on their continuing professionalism. Medicine, the ministry and journalism are professions so conceived.

What of college teaching? Is it a profession of the sort I've described? It is certainly thought to have all the necessary elements.

College Teaching

College teaching involves the possession of specialized knowledge and skill in its application. Each professor is expected to be a certified expert in his or her intellectual discipline and skilled at teaching it. Each is expected to maintain that expertise. Professors are assumed to be committed to advancing their students' knowledge and understanding in their discipline, as well as the students' general capacity for rational thought. Every university's recruitment materials speak confidently of its faculty's commitment to students. Sidney Hook's characterization of the liberal arts teacher neatly describes the central element of this commitment: "The primary function . . . of the liberal arts teacher is to help young men and women to achieve intellectual and emotional maturity by learning to handle certain ideas and intellectual tools."[3] Hook points out that this function is best served by the professor's development of an attitude of sympathy for students, where sympathy is "a positive attitude of imaginative concern with the personal needs of others."[4] A professor's commitment to the intellectual welfare of his or her students is also combined with a necessary respect for their autonomy. Teaching is not indoctrination. Professors guide students to understanding, and help them to develop the necessary skills to make their own determinations about what to believe.

Professors have extensive authority as teachers. We present the course material with little likelihood of being challenged in our pronouncements. We set the standards for student achievement and determine whether those standards have been met. The professor/student relationship is a power relationship, and almost all the power is ours. Students often get to evaluate our performance after the fact in course evaluations that play some role in salary, tenure and promotion decisions, but their role is relatively minor. Even when faced with student complaints, most administrators hesitate to overrule a professor's pedagogical decisions for fear of the charge of violating the professor's academic freedom.

Our independence is almost complete. We generally have significant control over what courses we teach and even more control in what we teach in them. The details of the course design, from requirements to grading standards, are, almost without exception, simply up to us. We help create the standards for our own evaluation and, within the practice of peer review, we are responsible for applying them to our colleagues.

Being a professor includes a distinctive ethical role. Our professional relationship with students involves duties to present the material accurately, protect confidences, maintain fairness in evaluation and avoid misusing our authority. Since we teach as part of a cooperative venture with other faculty, we also have duties relative to our colleagues. Our duties can change with society's expectations for higher education. Insofar as the burden of teaching basic skills is shifted up the educational ladder, it becomes part of our responsibility. As universities are expected to prepare students to succeed in a global economy, our obligations in designing courses and requirements change accordingly.

College teaching thus displays all the defining traits of a profession. It is a profession in the same way that medicine, the ministry and journalism are, when practiced at their best: a noble activity in which dedicated persons employ their hard won knowledge and expertise in the service of others. This way of understanding college teaching is not new. As my references to Hook suggest, I think it is very close to the view he presented in *Education for Modern Man* almost fifty years ago. Nonetheless, this understanding has yet to be widely and seriously accepted by those of us engaged in the activity. It has yet to fully inform either our sense of ourselves as teachers or our actual practice. Consider just one example of how we have not honored the fundamental expectations that accompany the conception of college teaching as a profession.

The following proposition is both true and generally accepted: Potential professionals require training in both their subject matter and its application in order to achieve professional competence; members of a profession should neither recommend nor employ beginning practitioners unless they are competent. We expect the training of physicians to include both a mastery of medical science and a mastery of clinical skills. We expect that that training will be closely supervised, and we expect that it will include the deliberate inculcation of those basic values that help define the successful practice of medicine, such as a commitment to the welfare of patients and a respect for their autonomy. We expect that medical students will be evaluated on their skills in the practice of medicine and on their demonstration of the values that define its proper performance. We expect that members of the medical profession will not certify or recommend students for professional practice unless they are competent in these areas. We have similar standards for training in the ministry and journalism. Divinity students need to learn to be effective spiritual counselors. Journalists need to become skilled at interview techniques and to have such values as the need for fairness and balance in their reporting inculcated in them through professional training.

If we actually understood college teaching to be a profession in the same way as medicine, journalism and the ministry, we would have this expectation for it. Yet, the situation has not changed since Hook noted "the absence of any training in college teaching, despite the fact that there are certain common psychological and philosophical principles which hold for all varieties of instruction."[5] Graduate students continue to serve a tepid apprenticeship as teaching assistants. They are given courses to teach but receive scant supervision, assistance or instruction in effective teaching techniques. Little to no effort is made to inculcate in them the values that define good teaching or to acquaint them with the ethical dimension of their profession. Seldom is it even suggested to them that they are entering a profession.

Our failure to display a strong professionalism in college teaching has cost us. It has encouraged critics who would restrict our authority and independence under our compact with society and limited our ability to respond to them successfully. Calls for us to cater to students as customers cannot be effectively met by the claim that we already treat them as much more, if we have shown little interest in their welfare. Calls for us to prove the value of our teaching relative to various assessment tests cannot be met by the claim that we are focused on the broader goal of developing thoughtful human beings, if we have shown no such concern. If we would secure the position of college teaching in our society and, in particular, the authority and independence that are so vital to its success, we must take its status as a profession seriously. A new professionalism must inform both our conception and practice and, perhaps most of all, our preparation of the next generation of the professorate.

Of course, many individuals have already taken this step in their own careers. They practice college teaching as a profession and, in doing so, fit Hook's description of the successful college teacher as "a *dedicated* person, strong in his faith in what he is doing, worthy not only of honor in a democracy but of a place in its councils" (his emphasis).[6] I was fortunate to meet one of them early in my career. In addition to being a teacher, mentor and friend, Steve Cahn has given me, like so many others, an excellent example of what it is to be a professor. Let us follow his lead.

Notes

1. Sidney Hook, *Education for Modern Man* (New York: Knopf, 1963), 235.
2. Steven Cahn, "A Sculptor in Snow," in Paul Kurtz, ed., *Sidney Hook: Philosopher of Democracy and Humanism*, (Buffalo, New York: Prometheus Books, 1983), 153.
3. Hook, 219.
4. Hook, 229.
5. Hook, 218.
6. Hook, 234.

6. Philosophy and Its Teaching

David M. Rosenthal

1. The Humanities and the Sciences

A striking difference between those fields we classify as humanities and those we regard as sciences is the attitude within each field toward its history. Learning about literature, music, or the visual arts requires becoming knowledgeable about a significant amount of the history of those areas. And education in these fields, at whatever level, invariably involves some study of great accomplishments in the past.

By contrast, scientific work and standard scientific textbooks make little reference to the history of the science in question, and such reference is typically relegated to the appreciative mention in passing of important empirical discoveries or theoretical innovations. And professional training in the sciences, both graduate and undergraduate, involves no serious examination of the achievements or methodology of past scientific work, no matter how impressive and influential those achievements may have been.

Progress dominates thinking in the sciences, and that emphasis may seem to explain such casual and occasionally condescending reference to the history of the sciences. But progress occurs in the humanities as well; even if some of the greatest artistic accomplishments are well in the past, there is remarkable innovation in style, technique, and methodology in the various arts. Some of the most monumental accomplishments in the sciences, moreover, are historical; nobody is likely to surpass the quality and importance of Newton's achievements, and few will ever equal those of Einstein. So it is unlikely that attitudes towards progress or past accomplishments can explain the divergent attitudes that fields in the sciences and humanities exhibit towards their own history.

We can better understand this contrast by appeal to a characteristic feature of the arts. Nobody today writes in the manner of Milton, Racine, or Shakespeare, or composes in the manner of Bach or Beethoven, or paints in the style of Vermeer, Renoir, or Da Vinci. Even Picasso's early, somewhat ostentatious paintings in the styles of various past masters were more to show his prodigious abilities than they were original artistic endeavors. Still, past artistic achievements often influence current work in ways that critics and professors delight in tracing. And the past even influences new styles that purport to break with the past, since those breakaway styles are developed in reaction to influential work of predecessors. A full appreciation of work in the arts often, if not invariably, requires understanding previous work.

Nothing like this is true in the sciences. Current work in the sciences always builds on past theoretical and experimental accomplishments. Contemporary scientific work would be unthinkable without the theoretical breakthroughs and empirical findings of Newton, Faraday, Poincaré, Lavoisier, and Einstein. Still, such work is typically presented as part of our current body of scientific knowledge; the way in which that knowledge builds on past accomplishments is at best relegated to footnotes.

There are exceptions; scientists do sometimes appeal directly to the thinking of Darwin and of Freud. But that is arguably because there is still considerable scientific controversy in the relevant scientific fields, which are not yet operating on a firm, widely accepted scientific foundation. The theoretical innovations of Darwin and Freud therefore remain relevant to contemporary scientific debate.

This explanation of the contrast between the sciences and humanities as regards the study of their histories reflects a recognized difference between those two groups of disciplines. Progress in the sciences makes significant consideration of past work relatively unnecessary. From the point of view of ongoing scientific investigation, any achievement worth studying is simply incorporated into the current statement of our scientific knowledge. So far as scientific knowledge is concerned, the current state of things is enough.

The kind of progress that occurs in the arts, however, does not result in any similar irrelevance of past accomplishments. Whatever innovations occur in style, technique, or methodology, or in our thinking about the humanistic disciplines themselves, the great achievements of the past continue to demand study on their own right. Past work is not simply assimilated into the current state of knowledge, as in the sciences. We learn from past works in ways that we could not learn from any contemporary accomplishments.

This contrast is largely due to differences of goal. In the sciences, we aim to get at the truth about reality, and to explain those truths by constructing theories that cover a wide range of phenomena and enable the prediction of new phenomena. Any empirical discoveries and theoretical innovation worth studying are accordingly incorporated into the current state of scientific knowledge.

The goal in the arts is different. The aim there is to produce works of beauty and sublimity, works that capture our thoughts about and outlooks on the human condition and that we find moving, inspiring, and affecting. Such works may well express truths we find difficult to capture in scientific terms, but those are not the truths we seek in the sciences. These truths are typically either those of common sense or generalizations from common sense; they are not subjected to empirical test and we do not seek to subsume them in theoretical structures. Moreover, artists and critics typically find different truths expressed in particular works of art, and we may well not follow a particular artist's word about the significance of that artist's works. So there is no way to incorporate the truths we find expressed in works of art within an articulable body of current knowledge. The need of artists and critics to study past works is inescapable.

Teaching in the sciences and humanities, at both the undergraduate and graduate levels, follows suit. To get a grounding in the humanities, students must be acquainted in some serious way with a good sample of the great works of the past. But students in the sciences have no corresponding need to know anything about the history of their field, and seldom know more than standard passing references to great breakthroughs. The history of science figures in scientific teaching only as the respectful tipping of our collective hat to great past achievements, not as anything essential to an understanding of the relevant field.

2. Philosophy and Its History

It is instructive to compare practices in philosophy and its teaching with those in the sciences and arts. Philosophy is today typically classified among the humanities, though in the 16th, 17th, and 18th centuries it was seen as continuous not with the arts, but with the sciences. And both work and training in philosophy today plainly follow the pattern described above for the arts and other humanities. A substantial part of any undergraduate philosophy curriculum consists of the study of historical figures, sometimes without any explicit mention of relevant contemporary work. Even anthologies that stress current work often also include historical work, as though to build a bridge from past to present. And work on contemporary issues often alludes to historical work, sometimes even when the issues under consideration were not pursued or even recognized before the current day.

This emphasis on the history of philosophy seldom occasions notice or comment, since serious attention to historical work is characteristic of the humanities, and philosophy is typically seen as among the humanities. But the early modern view of philosophy as continuous with the sciences prompts the question whether its classification with the humanities reflects anything essential about philosophy, as against simply being a convenience for librarians and university administrations.

There is a familiar picture of philosophy on which it fits comfortably within the humanities, and on which we would expect the emphasis on history. Philosophical work is sometimes seen not as an investigation of the truth about things, but as the development and elaboration of various perspectives on reality. Philosophy presents us with ways of seeing how things fit together and the place that individuals and humanity in general occupy in the overall scheme of things.

What we gain from philosophy, on this picture, is not much like what the sciences have to give us. Rather, the understanding philosophy offers is something like that which we get from plays, novels, and poetry. On this way of seeing philosophy, Aeschylus, Shakespeare, and Dostoyevsky are philosophers along with Hegel, Nietzsche, Heidegger, or Dewey, and we learn from them all much the same kind of thing. It is largely a matter of literary taste which of these authors we prefer and with which we connect most naturally, both intellectually and otherwise. This view of philosophy underwrites its classification among the humanities. This picture also underlies and may seem to warrant the persistent and pervasive sense, in popular culture as well as much literary work, that philosophy in the Anglo-American tradition is dry, uninteresting, and sterile.

The emphasis on the history of philosophy is also understandable on this picture. The history of philosophy provides an impressive range of perspectives on reality and the place of humanity. These perspectives sometimes complement and reinforce each other, though they often clash, presenting mutually incompatible views. We learn much from examining and comparing these perspectives, both when they fit together and when they are mutually incompatible. On this picture, whatever progress occurs in philosophy would never outweigh the benefits of studying the great philosophical systems of the past. We learn from those works in something like the way we learn from the great past creations in music, art, and literature.

But this picture of philosophy, though it justifies its classification as a humanity and explains its emphasis on its own history, leaves out a lot that has been considered central to philosophy throughout that history. The attitude of the great philosophers that constructed these alternative, often incompatible systems has seldom if ever been that of great literary figures whose work offers alternative perspectives. Rather, their attitude is that of scientific theorists who develop alternative theories. They assume that at most one of the philosophical systems gets things right, and they advance arguments in favor of their own. They see themselves as trying to set philosophy onto the "secure path of a science," as Kant famously put it (B Preface to the *Critique of Pure Reason*, Bvii).

Indeed, the language of perspectives is typically foreign to the writing of philosophers. Hobbes and Descartes did not see themselves in the third set of Objections and Replies to the *Meditations* as differing about perspectives on reality, but about the truth on various issues. Nor is some quasi-literary perspective in question when Aristotle takes his predecessors to task for concentrating on only one of the four causes, or when Kant talks about the failures of rationalism and empiricism. Similarly throughout the history of philosophy; the great figures we study saw themselves as trying to get at the truth about things, much as scientists see themselves as doing.

Philosophical work often purports to employ different methods from those used in the sciences to arrive at the truth. And the issues and questions about which they seek the truth typically differ as well. But subject matter and method aside, the goals are much the same. Whether the issues pertain to metaphysics, ethics, aesthetics, or other branches of philosophy, philosophical writing seeks correct answers to particular questions.

Contemporary work in philosophy is no different in this respect. The questions and issues have changed somewhat in various ways, and there are new ways of dividing philosophy into subspecialties. But now as in the past, philosophical work aims at establishing the truth about particular matters.

This poses a problem for understanding the nature of philosophy, and a consequent problem about how best to teach it. If the goal of philosophy is to establish truths about specific issues, what matters is the truths it manages to establish. And then it should simply catalog and organize those truths, revising them as needed, but presenting at every stage the body of knowledge that philosophy has so far come up with. It should, in short, operate present as the sciences do. But in this case, it will be no more obvious in philosophy than in the sciences what benefit is to be derived from studying the history of the field.

This problem plainly carries over to the teaching of philosophy. As noted at the outset, a large portion of both undergraduate and graduate curriculums is typically devoted to the history of philosophy. But it's unclear why that should be if philosophical work aims primarily at the establishment of truths about particular issues. It might be useful for undergraduates who don't intend to pursue further work in philosophy to know something of its history. But that cannot by itself explain the prominence within the philosophy curriculum of courses on its history.

3. Why Study the History of Philosophy?

There is a variety of explanations put forth for this prominence. But it is arguable that none of the standard explanations is satisfactory.

One explanation often offered cites the way in which contemporary work in philosophy is sometimes inspired by the work of a particular historical figure. The early work of Stuart Hampshire owes much to his study of Spinoza, and J. L. Austin's extensive knowledge of Aristotle plainly figures throughout his writing. But such cases are relatively unusual; the most telling influences in contemporary philosophical work are typically late nineteenth- and twentieth-century writers. Contemporary work does, as mentioned earlier, sometimes refer to historical figures, but such reference is typically made largely in passing, and contributes little if anything to the argument or position being developed.

Another explanation sometimes advanced is that students cannot come to grasp contemporary philosophical issues without knowing the historical antecedents that led to those issues. This is highly implausible. Many students today display an impressive command of issues at the center of all areas of contemporary work in philosophy, and yet have no significant knowledge of the history of philosophy.

This is not surprising, given that relatively few contemporary issues occur in historical discussions in the same way. Contemporary issues are almost always transposed somewhat relative to their historical cognates, and occur now in theoretical contexts that would have been unrecognizable in earlier periods. So appeal to history antecedents in learning about contemporary issues may fail to help students grasp the exact nature of those issues as they figure in the contemporary literature, and may even invite some confusion about them. The appeal to historical antecedents of contemporary discussions frequently necessitates compensatory theoretical adjustments, so that historical context does not skew students' understandings of contemporary work.

Another explanation sometimes offered for the emphasis on the history of philosophy applies mainly to the undergraduate curriculum. It is said that it's easier to read and understand the great historical figures than to delve straight into contemporary journal articles, which are often technical and less accessible than classical philosophical writing. The great works of the past accordingly are said to provide a convenient ramp up which the student can progress, eventually getting to contemporary work.

Many great philosophers were also gifted literary figures, and reading them may in that way be far more inviting than reading any contemporary work. And many of the great philosophical works are landmarks in our cultural heritage; it is arguable that every college curriculum should include Plato's *Republic*, John Stuart Mill's *On Liberty*, parts of Descartes's *Meditations* or *Discourse of Method*, and perhaps of one of Hume's *Inquiries*.

But the argument for having these and similar philosophical works in any undergraduate curriculum is not because they facilitate an understanding of the contemporary literature in philosophy, but because of their cultural importance generally. And putting literary and cultural value to one side, the strictly philosophical content of contemporary work is seldom as difficult to understand as even the most widely used classical texts. The texts just mentioned continue to occasion extensive debate about their meaning and their major claims and arguments. There is little in the contemporary literature that would sustain such debate, and little that requires it. In studying the great classical works, students often end up with little more than a cartoon picture of arguments that are pivotal to those works; consider standard treatments of Descartes's *Third Meditation*, or Plato's theory of forms. The current literature in philosophy may be dry, technical, and uninviting in a literary way, but it is seldom nearly so hard to understand.

Indeed, so far as the distinctively philosophical issues are concerned, there is much contemporary work that addresses these issues in relatively self-contained and accessible ways. These are often successfully used to stimulate undergraduates' interest in these issues, and to prepare them for more demanding contemporary work. Focusing solely on effectiveness in getting undergraduates to understand contemporary work in philosophy, and bracketing the acknowledged cultural importance of the great classical figures, it may well be less fruitful to have students read them than to read select contemporary work.

There are other standard explanations for the emphasis on the great classical works in the philosophy curriculum. But it is arguable that they are unconvincing in explaining the substantial place of historical teaching in the philosophy curriculum. Indeed, the failures of the explanations just surveyed suggest considerations that undermine other standard explanations.[1]

4. The Historicist Explanation

There is, however, a particular response to this problem that has recently come to be widely discussed and is worth independent consideration. On this view, the standard attitude philosophers, both classical and contemporary, have held toward their own work is simply misguided. Despite their pronouncements, the goal of philosophy is not to establish truths about various issues, but rather to develop and articulate a perspective on the nature of reality and the place of individuals and humanity generally in the overall order of things. The popular picture of philosophy described in the preceding section is, on this account, correct, despite the somewhat scientific pretensions of philosophy itself.

On this view, then, the goal of studying the history of philosophy and training students in it is not to better understand philosophical progress. We should not think of that history as the development of arguments for and against positions about perennial problems articulated by earlier thinkers. Rather, we should see the history of philosophy as offering a virtual conversation that the great figures have among themselves, a conversation whose twists and turns can have a general edifying effect. To study the history of philosophy is to eavesdrop on and perhaps add our own commentary to that conversation. This, in broad strokes, is the view of philosophy and its history championed by Richard Rorty,[2] as well as in much post-modern hermeneutics.[3]

Such a picture has become influential in the view of philosophy held in many academic literature departments. But it has not taken hold in most philosophical work, largely because it fails to do justice to actual philosophical practice, historical or contemporary. Still, it sometimes happens that intellectual work can misrepresent its own significance, and that may be the case with philosophy. Perhaps practitioners of philosophy are, as Rorty argues, in the grip of an inaccurate picture of their own discipline, a picture inherited from an earlier, more naive age. So we need carefully to assess the merits of this revisionist view of philosophical work.

A useful way to evaluate Rorty's historicist attitude toward philosophy is to examine the implications it has for a particular philosophical issue. And it's convenient to do this by considering Rorty's own example of such implications in the case of the mind-body problem. Mind-body materialists such as J. J. C. Smart and D. M. Armstrong had argued in the 1950s and 1960s that we can accommodate qualitative mental states within a materialist framework only if descriptions of such states are topic neutral as regards being physical or mental.[4] Only then, they held, will such qualitative states be physicalistically respectable.

Rorty concurred, arguing that the very concept of the mental precludes anything that is mental from being physical. So mind-body materialism is defensible only in an eliminativist version; we can sustain mind-body materialism only by arguing that there is nothing that is properly classified as mental. And such eliminativism is itself defensible, he argued, because we can describe, explain, and predict everything we now describe, explain, and predict without any using any mental vocabulary at all.[5]

But this eliminativist resolution of the mind-body problem points, Rorty urged, toward a historicist understanding of philosophical problems themselves, and hence of philosophy. If we no longer describe anything whatever as mental, and indeed dispense with the very category of the mental, we eliminate not only mental descriptions, but the mind-body problem itself. And that, Rorty maintained, is all to the good. Debate for several centuries now about the mind-body problem has arguably produced no useful breakthroughs or progress; dualists and materialists both still thrive in the philosophical literature, and remain as unaffected as ever by the arguments of the other side. This suggests, Rorty argues, that the very issue itself is a false problem, admitting of no convincing solution. And it thereby helps sustain an eliminativist resolution to that apparent problem. The sense that the mind-body problem involves some serious issue is illusory, the result of the needless use of a mentalistic vocabulary loaded with anti-materialist implications. Teaching students that there is a substantive issue here misleads them and distorts their understanding of the relevant literature.

In *Philosophy and the Mirror of Nature* and subsequent writings, Rorty forcefully and eloquently argued that this is true of most of the issues that have dominated philosophical discussion in the Western tradition. We should, he urges, adopt a historicist picture of the questions that have defined philosophical discussion, questions that have continued for centuries to resist straightforward, substantive answers. But though philosophical discussion and debate seldom if ever yield decisive answers, they can often on the historicist picture be edifying. We should study and teach such discussion and debate as a virtual conversation about some of the perspectives available for seeing how our knowledge, practices, and preferences fit together. We should see the so-called problems of philosophy as conundra that arise in developing these perspectives, not as problems that demand and can yield to decisive solutions. They are creatures of particular cultural developments, and have no standing independent of those cultural occurrences.

But the argument for this historicist picture is flawed. Consider again Rorty's case study of the mind-body problem. A naturalist materialism requires jettisoning mental vocabulary, according to Rorty, because that very vocabulary harbors anti-materialist implications. This view of our mental vocabulary is itself controversial, and without it there is no reason to adopt an eliminativist view. But even if Rorty is right about our mental vocabulary, a mind-body materialism would not require jettisoning that vocabulary; we could instead just strip that vocabulary of its anti-materialist implications. As Rorty has forcefully argued, there is no firm line between the meaning of our terms and the theories we take to govern the application of those terms.[6] So we can construe any anti-materialist implications not as part of the meaning of mental descriptions, but rather as an added theory about the nature of the mental. We can then retain our mental vocabulary and consider the claims of materialist and dualist theories on their merits and adjudicate between them.

Rorty would urge that we can understand what made issues about mind-body materialism seem problematic to generations of philosophers only if we see anti-materialist implications as literally built into the meaning of our mental vocabulary. And it is only in those terms that we can construe mind-body materialism as involving genuine intellectual problems. But this argument is unconvincing. For one thing, if anti-materialist implications were built into our mental vocabulary, dualism would automatically win. And if dualism's winning were a conceptual matter, mind-body materialism would be conceptually inconsistent, and it would be hard to see how the debate between dualism and materialism could ever have seemed to be problematic. People do sometimes get entangled in conceptual contradictions. But on Rorty's view the conceptual inconsistency is relatively straightforward, and it's implausible that this would have lasted for centuries. Rorty's picture cannot after all do justice to the apparent problematic character of that debate.

Rorty's idea is that an issue will seem problematic in a distinctively philosophical way only if it is stubbornly persistent and seems to resist straightforward resolution. But whether something seems problematic is relative to whether we think we have a resolution. Once a widely accepted resolution is at hand, the problematic air that had earlier surrounded an issue recedes, and may well disappear altogether. Its problematic character comes to have only historical significance, and reconstruction of its having appeared to be a genuine problem will inevitably seem strained. As Nelson Goodman had noted, because the goal "in philosophy [is] to make the obscure obvious . . . the reward of success is banality. An answer, once found, is obvious."[7] To argue that we must construe philosophical issues in terms of what has made them seem problematic is to deny any possibility of resolution.

5. Scaffolds and Connections

Rorty's historicism offers both an explanation and a justification for the prominent place that the history of philosophy occupies within the standard curriculum. If philosophy is best seen as a virtual conversation among the great figures, possibly along with a contemporary commentary on that conversation, the history of philosophy must be as central to the teaching of philosophy as it is in any of the humanities, and in much the same way.

But this historicist picture fails to do justice not only to the way philosophers operate and see their own work, but also to the substantive disputes that drive that work. Historicism about philosophical problems generally, like historicism about particular issues such as the mind-body problem, sees those problems as not being genuine questions that admit of serious answers. But that way of construing these quandaries itself rests on a substantive, controversial position about the nature of these problems. On that position, philosophical quandaries arise not from clashes among competing theories, but from the adoption of optional vocabularies that embody problematic assumptions. But without an argument that these assumptions are essential to the relevant vocabulary, rather than being added by the choice of theory, such historicism begs the question against the standard view of philosophical issues, on which these issues pose genuine questions that have definite answers. So we cannot rely on the historicist picture to explain the emphasis by philosophy on its history.

The problem, to recapitulate, is that philosophy, like the sciences, aims at getting the truth about various issues. So the history of philosophy should represent progress towards that goal, and we should be able then simply to dispense with the history of that progress. We should be able to study and teach the things that philosophy has so far gotten right, along with the catalog of pressing outstanding problems. If the history of philosophy is useful at all, it cannot be in the way it characteristically is in the arts and other humanities, in which the dominant goal is not simply to get at the truth about things.

We can, however, understand how the history of philosophy is useful in philosophical education without thereby treating philosophy like one of the arts. And this way of understanding the usefulness of the history of philosophy actually underwrites an particular analogy between philosophy and the other humanities.

In discussing methodology in philosophical work early in *Experience and Nature*, John Dewey writes of "those astounding differences of philosophic belief that startle the beginner and that become the plaything of the expert."[8] Every student of philosophy is familiar with the striking phenomenon Dewey is referring to, though it is equally striking that this phenomenon is seldom explicitly mentioned. The history of philosophy is a great collection of systematically developed views, which seem not only incompatible each with the others, but often incommensurate as well.

The arguments that drive each of the great systems also suggest apparent refutations of the others. So it seems one can simply pick and choose among them to suit one's own theoretical disposition and proclivities. Historical development accordingly seems altogether irrelevant in comparing and evaluating these theories. One could, for example, present the synthetic *a priori* of Kant's critical philosophy as undermining Hume's claim that relations of ideas and matters of fact exhaust the kinds of judgments there can be. But one could equally go in the opposite direction, arguing that Hume's dichotomy refutes Kant's notion of synthetic *a priori* judgments. No wonder progress is rare in philosophy, and seldom if ever occurs in connection with system building. And no wonder Dewey saw the resulting "differences of philosophic belief [as] the plaything of the expert."

It is these same apparently incommensurable differences among philosophical systems that Hume evidently had in mind in writing of

> the justest and most plausible objection against a considerable part of metaphysics, that they are not properly a science; but arise either from the fruitless efforts of human vanity, which would penetrate into subjects utterly inaccessible to the understanding, or from the craft of popular superstitions, which, be-

ing unable to defend themselves on fair ground, raise these entangling brambles to cover and protect their weakness.[9]

It is hard not to have some sympathy with Hume's complaint. In no other respectable area of intellectual inquiry is there so much theoretical divergence about substantive questions over so long a period of time.

Dewey understood the "astounding" differences in systematic philosophical conviction in characteristically pragmatic terms, urging that such differences result from some theoretical "[c]hoice that is disguised or denied." And he argued that the proper resolution to these striking conflicts in philosophical conviction was to be explicit about every pivotal theoretical choice, treating each choice as a theoretical "experiment to be tried on its merits and tested by its results" (30/35). If we think of Dewey's recommendation in terms of our testing each philosophical system by its theoretical payoff in explaining and describing things, that is doubtless a sensible strategy. We should isolate and expose hidden assumptions and intellectual procedures, and evaluate the resulting theories in terms of their doing justice to and explaining the relevant phenomena. Such pragmatism about theories and theoretical reasoning is unexceptionable, in philosophical contexts as elsewhere.

Hume, by contrast, argued that the many apparently irresolvable conflicts among philosophical systems are due simply to the occurrence in those systems of terms that literally have no meaning. We can accordingly get rid of such fruitless clashes by testing the relevant vocabulary for meaningfulness. The proper use of this method, he urged, "might render every dispute equally intelligible, and banish all that jargon, which has so long taken possession of metaphysical reasonings, and drawn disgrace upon them" (21). But whatever one's diagnosis of and prescription for the plethora of incompatible systems, success in philosophical work plainly requires that we largely operate independently of them. Dewey is doubtless right that their incommensurability results from the way each system incorporates and builds on assumptions not shared by others. And as Plato argued, it is self-defeating and fruitless to reason from hypotheses taken simply as given;[10] we must subject all hypotheses and assumptions to scrutiny, taking none as privileged or immune to revision.[11]

The merits of Dewey's pragmatist methodology and Hume's quasi-verificationism aside, the character of the mutually incompatible philosophical systems that concerned them point towards an explanation of the role in philosophy of its history. The careful study of any of the great systems reveals a plethora of connections among various issues of interest in philosophical work, issues that, considered on their own, typically seem largely independent of one another. Because the ties these systems articulate among such issues tend to hold across a variety of systems, we can understand those connections without being committed to any particular system. So a system that is arguably mistaken and wrongheaded in every other way may nonetheless be especially revealing about the connections that hold among seemingly disparate issues. One need not be at all tempted by the specific claims in Kant's critical philosophy or Hegel's

Phenomenology of Mind to learn much about the connections among various issues that these systematic works articulate.

Unlike the work of great philosophical system builders, contemporary work tends to focus on individual issues or small clusters of them. This tight focus has proved exceptionally salutary. Although many major theoretical disagreements remain, such careful work has charted out areas of broad agreement, and has crystallized in fruitful ways the major theoretical divides that require further work. But a corresponding disadvantage in studying such contemporary work is that it seldom provides an opportunity to explore the many important connections among the various issues that individually receive such careful attention.

The study of major works in the history of philosophy, by contrast, offers rich opportunities to explore these connections. Any of the great works in the standard canon of Western philosophy reveal a multitude of ties among philosophical questions that afford students an appreciation of the scope and nature of philosophical work. And this advantage of studying such works is wholly independent of "those astounding differences of philosophic belief that startle the beginner and that become the plaything of the expert." And because the connections among issues are largely independent of particular positions taken on the issues themselves, we need not evaluate the beliefs that particular philosophical systems embody to learn much about those connections. The great systems provide intellectual scaffolds for issues, through which we learn about the connections among them, independent of whatever positions we may come to take on those issues.

6. Interpretation and the History of Philosophy

The variety of competing systems that occur in the history of philosophy suggests a second way in which studying in which history can be useful, once again independently of the merits of specific claims and arguments found in any system. The problematic feature of these systems to which Dewey dramatically drew attention is that they are not only incompatible, but incompatible in ways that seem to resist resolution. This apparent recalcitrance to resolution results in the scandalous aspect of philosophical work that Hume complains of. How can the best thinkers in any respectable intellectual discipline hold such incompatible views? And how can a respectable field of inquiry harbor such incompatible views that for so long resist any serious resolution, and with no promise of resolution in sight?

But that very feature of philosophical systems, however frustrating, encourages an intellectual activity essential to philosophical thinking. Understanding what others say invariably calls for some measure of interpretation. This interpretive activity must answer to three constraints, which can occasionally pull in different directions. Most basic is our construal of individual words homophonically, as meaning what we would mean by them, where such construal is largely independent of context. But we also seek to interpret others' remarks so as to make them come out true as often as possible, at least true by our lights. In interpreting others' remarks, we understand them as much as possible both as using words as we do and as making claims that we can endorse.

These two interpretive goals can collide; sometimes our projecting our way of using words onto others results in seeing them as saying something untrue. We then have a choice between construing the relevant remarks as false and seeing them as involving what we regard as a nonstandard use of words. Typically we adjudicate automatically between these competing possibilities, but it may sometimes be that nothing tips the balance.

There is, in addition, a third factor that sometimes comes into play. Statements often fall into patterns of inference, and when they do we try to interpret those remarks so as to see those inferences as valid. And even when another's remarks do not fall into explicit inferences, we try to construe their remarks as jointly compatible, which involves the kind of connection that figures in inference. Two remarks are jointly compatible only if each fails to imply the denial of the other. As with the constraints of homophonic interpretation and construing remarks as true by our lights, this third desideratum again may conflict with the other two. We may be able to preserve our use of words and truth as we see it only by construing another's remarks as jointly inconsistent or as constituting an invalid inference.

Interpretation accordingly involves the charitable maximizing of three factors: seeing others as using words as we do, as making true statements, and as advancing valid arguments and mutually compatible claims. When these constraints conflict, as they often do when others differ with us, we must somehow strike a balance among them.

Applying charity of interpretation in these three ways to the things others say typically is wholly effortless and occurs without our noticing it, but it is also unavoidable.[12] And the way we balance constraints pertaining to words, statements, and inferences is also typically automatic and effortless. But when it seems that we cannot satisfy all three constraints, we are likely to think consciously about how to construe the remarks in question, and therefore how to balance the three desiderata. As the things others say increasingly diverge from anything we ourselves are inclined to say, the likelihood increases correspondingly that the need to construe and so to balance the three constraints will explicitly command our attention.

The things people say very likely never conflict more dramatically than what we find when we examine the great philosophical systems. The "astounding differences of philosophic belief that startle the beginner" to which Dewey called attention doubtless present as great a challenge to charitable interpretation as we can find anywhere. How can we charitably construe the conflicting claims and arguments of such systems? Even if one is partial to the views embodied in one particular family of systems, how can we charitably interpret those systems that are starkly incompatible with our favored view?

Sharp disagreements occur also in the contemporary philosophical literature, but nothing like those that characterize the great classical systems. For one thing, it is typically pretty clear how to understand the words used in the contemporary literature. Though advocates of different positions do sometimes use words in divergent ways, the general convergence of idiom that occurs in the contemporary literature often obscures such divergence. Nor is there serious difficulty in understanding the disputes; in the ordinary case an author argues against specific claims or arguments couched explicitly in the other person's words.

Conflicts among the classical systems are typically more difficult to calibrate. In part this is because in developing a system, other authors are seldom mentioned. But the more important factor is that the systems tend to differ from one another in holistic ways that often cannot be captured in any unique way. We may seek to encapsulate the difference between Plato and Aristotle about form and between Hume and Kant about whether relations of ideas and matters of fact exhaust the possibilities. But even there the two parties to each dispute would differ about how to characterize their dispute.

Moreover, such disagreements typically affect every aspect of the philosophers' systematic thinking, leaving little that we can construe in a neutral, independent way. This raises challenges for the charitable interpretation of both parties to such a dispute. There is little one can say about what such systematic thinkers mean that does not require extensive interpretive work.

The study of the history of philosophy accordingly affords an especially rich opportunity to practice in the interpreting of challenging texts and to sharpen one's interpretive skills. Indeed, this is the major activity in such study. The great systems are seldom presented as a model for how to engage in philosophical inquiry or what to think about particular issues. Rather, our work on the challenging problems of interpretation that those systems present us with results in our being able to construe all philosophical writing, including the contemporary literature, in subtler and more systematic ways. The most productive readings of classical philosophical texts are typically those that most successfully maximize and balance these three interpretive constraints. So our reading systematic work in the history of philosophy forces us to make our interpretive activity explicit, and so to consider how to balance the homophonic translation of words against the charitable construal of assertions and arguments. Practice with charitable interpretation of difficult texts is therefore a second way in which the study of the history of philosophy can be important.[13]

As with the first explanation for the emphasis of philosophy on its history, which appealed to connections among seemingly disparate issues, this second explanation is again independent of how we evaluate claims and arguments that occur in the works we study. Indeed, as noted earlier, it is because most classical texts are questionable in respect of their claims and arguments that the need for extensive interpretive work in studying the history of philosophy is not only necessary, but also obvious.

7. Transcending the Systems

There is a yet another benefit that can come from studying the great philosophical systems. Though it is seldom that any of those systems strikes anybody today as having gotten things right, the way these systems clash about specific issues sometimes provides an opportunity to transcend theoretical conflicts between those systems.

As noted in section 5, the fruitless disagreements among the great systems typically result from the adoption by each system of specific hypotheses or assumptions rejected by other systems. The interpretation of these systems can help crystallize the undefended assumptions that operate in this way. So in addition to giving us practice in charitable interpretation, studying the great systems can also stimulate us to think about how to go beyond the question-begging assumptions those systems embody, and thereby reach a stable, defensible position on the relevant issues.

There are several ways this can happen. We may come up with a salutary reformulation of questions or a change of subject, which resolves an issue while sidestepping or disposing of the conflict that dominated earlier thinking. Or by isolating the undefended assumptions that led to such controversy, one may be able simply to approach the issue in a way that steers clear of those assumptions. So the study of fruitless disputes among the great systems can suggest novel ways to come to terms with the issues those systems failed to resolve. This is sometimes a third benefit of studying the history of philosophy.

The foregoing explanations of the importance of the history of philosophy point to a striking parallel philosophy has with the other so-called humanities. We expose ourselves and our students to the great works of music, literature, and the visual arts in part because these are examples of the best that has been done, and sometimes, we may think, the best that can be done. Similarly with the great works of philosophy. But the problem was that, unlike music, literature, and the arts, philosophy aims at getting the truth about things. And if the great works of past philosophers don't do that, why study them?

An acceptable explanation for the central role in philosophy of its history must therefore be independent of whether any of the great historical systems do get at the truth about things. And the explanations offered here satisfy that demand. Independent of getting at such truths, these works display a multitude of important connections that various issues have with one another. And independent of getting at such truths, studying those works sharpens our interpretive skills in ways that the study of contemporary work in a largely familiar idiom tends not to do. Finally, such study can suggest new approaches to issues that transcend the conflicts the great systems embody. It is these benefits that warrant the central place in philosophy of its history. As with the other humanities, we study the history of philosophy for reasons independent of the search for truth.

There is an important pedagogical moral that we can draw from these reasons for studying the history of philosophy. The history of philosophy is sometimes presented to students in bite-sized selections, as though to put on offer a kind of zoology of odd philosophical positions and arguments. Such brief selections may well serve to make students familiar with the major touchstones of the field, putting them in the picture as regards the divergent views which have dominated past discussion and debate. But such brief selections are unlikely to exhibit many connections among superficially disparate issues, offer much of an opportunity to sharpen one's interpretive skills, or suggest ways of transcending past systematic discussions. If the foregoing argument is correct, we should expose students to selections of historical works sufficiently large to give them a sense of rich systematic connections and daunting interpretive challenges.

Notes

1. For further examples, see David M. Rosenthal, "Philosophy and its History," in *The Institution of Philosophy*, ed. Avner Cohen and Marcelo Dascal (Peru, Illinois: Open Court, 1989), 141-176, § 3.

2. *Philosophy and the Mirror of Nature* (Princeton: Princeton University Press, 1979), e.g., 378, and chs. VII and VIII; and *Objectivity, Relativism, and Truth*, vol. 1 of *Philosophical Papers* (Cambridge: Cambridge University Press, 1991).

3. See, e.g., Shaun Gallagher, "Conversations in Postmodern Hermeneutics," in *Lyotard: Philosophy, Politics and the Sublime*, ed. Hugh J. Silverman (London: Routledge. 2002), 49-60.

4. J. J. C. Smart, "Sensations and Brain Processes," in *The Philosophy of Mind*, ed. V. C. Chappell (Englewood Cliffs: Prentice-Hall, Inc., 1962; New York: Dover, 1981), 160-172; D. M. Armstrong, "The Causal Theory of Mind," *Neue Hefte für Philosophie*, Heft 11, 1977, 82-95; reprinted in slightly revised version in his *The Nature of Mind* (St. Lucia, Queensland: University of Queensland Press, 1980), 16-31.

5. "Incorrigibility as the Mark of the Mental," *The Journal of Philosophy* LXVII, 12 (June 25, 1970): 399-424, and *Philosophy and the Mirror of Nature*, ch. 2. For more on these issues, see Rosenthal, "Mentality and Neutrality," *The Journal of Philosophy*, LXXIII, 13 (July 15, 1976): 386-415, and "Keeping Matter in Mind," *Midwest Studies in Philosophy*, V (1980): 295-322.

6. See, e.g., "Criteria and Necessity," *Noûs* VII, 4 (November 1973): 313-329, and *Philosophy and the Mirror of Nature*, Part II.

7. *The Structure of Appearance*, second edition (Indianapolis: Bobbs-Merrill, 1966), xix.

8. John Dewey, *Experience and Nature* (Chicago & London: Open Court, 1925; revised edition, New York: Norton and London: Allen & Unwin, 1929), 30; reprinted in *John Dewey: The Later Works, 1925-1953*, vol. I, edited by Jo Ann Boydston, associate textual editors, Patricia Baysinger and Barbara Levine (Carbondale and Edwardsville: Southern Illinois University Press, 1981), 35.

9. Hume, David, *An Enquiry concerning Human Understanding*, in *Enquiries concerning Human Understanding and concerning the Principles of Morals*, ed. L. A. Selby-Bigge, 3rd edn. revised by P. H. Nidditch (Oxford: Clarendon Press, 1975), 11.

10. *Republic*, 511a2-8.

11. Cf. W. V. Quine, "Two Dogmas of Empiricism," in *From A Logical Point of View*, second edition, revised (Cambridge, Massachusetts: Harvard University Press, 1980), 20-46, esp. § 6.

12. On the need for charitable interpretation, see Quine, *Word and Object* (Cambridge: MIT Press, 1960), § 13; "Carnap and Logical Truth," in *The Ways of Paradox and Other Essays*, revised and enlarged edition (Cambridge: Harvard University Press, 1975), 107-33; and Donald Davidson, *Inquiries into Truth and Interpretation* (Oxford: Clarendon Press, 1984) 2nd edition, 2001, essays 9-11. On an interesting way in which we must balance constraints on charitable interpretation, see Quine, *Philosophy of Logic* (Englewood Cliffs: Prentice-Hall, Inc., 1970), ch. 6.

13. For more on this second explanation, see Rosenthal, "Philosophy and Its History," §4.

7. Philosophical Humor, Lewis Carroll, and Introductory Philosophy

John O'Connor

The philosopher Ludwig Wittgenstein once remarked that it would be possible to write a serious philosophical work that consisted of nothing but jokes. Whether or not this is true, humor can help to involve students in the study of philosophy, not only by making the subject more interesting to them, but also, if the humor is philosophically sophisticated, by showing students that philosophy oftentimes involves taking seriously questions that in ordinary life might be considered silly or even absurd. I find that students who can laugh at a philosophical joke already demonstrate a potential for philosophical understanding.

During four previous semesters, I included Lewis Carroll's *Alice's Adventures in Wonderland* and *Through the Looking Glass* among the required reading for my twelve sections of Introduction for Philosophy.[1]

Lewis Carroll was the pen name of Charles Dodgson, who was a Professor of Mathematics at Oxford University in the nineteenth century. He published a number of scholarly writings in logic and mathematics, along with the two "Alice" books and an extensive variety of humorous prose and poetry, word games and puzzles. According to one source Lewis Carroll is the third most frequently quoted author in the English language. While the Alice books are his most famous works, he did write two articles for *Mind,* the leading English philosophy journal at that time.

The choice of the two Alice books was easy. They are easy to read, contain a large number of memorable characters (the Cheshire Cat, the Hatter and the March Hare, the Queen of Hearts, Humpty Dumpty, Tweedledum and Tweedledee, and the Red Queen, among others), and include a number of observations and conversations that are almost stunning in the way that they mirror important philosophical arguments and insights. They continually call attention to the fact that language can be a source of misinformation and miscommunication (as well as information and communication)—a point made explicitly by such philosophers as Berkeley, Nietzsche and Wittgenstein. They require the reader to enter into a series of adventures that challenge commonsense ideas of space and time, cause and effect, sense and nonsense, and dreaming and wakefulness, which is just what good philosophy often does.

It is possible to allot the Alice books a separate section of the syllabus, as one does with a Plato dialogue or Descartes' *Meditations*. I decided, however, that it would be better to assign two chapters of *Wonderland* and then *Looking Glass* each week throughout the term. Informal polls in my classes indicated that students much preferred to read Alice as we went along, rather than all at once. Some said they read Alice first before trying to read the regular assignment, which could be on occasion fiendishly difficult. Others said that they read Alice after the other assignment, as a sort of reward.

Before each class I would reread the assigned chapters, and make a list of between 15 and 20 brief items. I would note where Alice went, whom she met and the gist of their conversations. I would also note any relevant philosophical happenings: paradoxical statements, word play and puns, and similar items.

In addition I would prepare brief quiz questions on the Alice books (and on the other readings assigned for that class). The questions were not difficult, because I wanted to encourage the students to do the reading and reward them for their efforts. Many of the correct answers were only one or two words long. Some sample questions: Alice finds herself swimming in a pool of what? (Her tears.) Who was the lizard Alice kicked up the chimney? (Bill). Each quiz would consist of two to four questions on Alice and two to four questions on the other reading. The quizzes, in which I gave in almost every class, counted for 10% of the final grade.

I would give the quiz at the beginning of the class by reading the questions aloud and allowing the students between one and two minutes to complete the quiz. The quizzes were collected immediately, and graded and returned at the next class. There were no make-up quizzes, although I did drop the three lowest quiz grades at the end of the semester and did not penalize these students for authorized medical absences. Once students learned that the quiz for, e.g., an 11:00a.m. class would be given at exactly 11 o'clock, the number of students who came on time increased dramatically.

After the quizzes were collected, I would ask students if they had noted anything funny, interesting, or perplexing in the Alice reading, or if they had any questions. About half the time one or more students responded and we had brief discussions on the points they raised. Then I would go quickly through my list of items, making sure that students were following the story and, more importantly, stressing the philosophical points and plays on words. Often I would ask the students questions such as "Why weren't the dishes washed at the tea party?" Usually one or more students (and occasionally the whole class) would explain that Time was angry at the Hatter and just stopped at six o'clock teatime. Since it was always tea-time, there was never time to wash the dishes.

One class favorite was the passage in which the King of Hearts tried to remove Alice from the trial of the Knave of Hearts. He cited "Rule Forty-two: *All persons more than a mile high to leave the court.*" When Alice protested that the King had just invented the rule, the King replied that it's "the oldest rule in the book," to which Alice appropriately responded that if it is, it should be rule number one.

I found that when discussing such items the students would often end up explaining the jokes to one another.

On occasion I would take a more substantial amount of time to explain a particular fallacy or paradoxical claim or larger philosophical point, and, where appropriate, link it to topics considered in the non-Alice part of the course. Some specific examples are presented below.

At the end of the first semester during which I assigned the Alice books, I asked students to submit anonymous written statements on whether or not they would encourage me to continue the assignment. Of the 85 who responded, 83 said yes.

In his recent review in *The New York Times* of Martin Gardner's *The Annotated Alice*, Adam Gopnic makes the following observation about *Alice's Adventures in Wonderland* and *Through the Looking Glass*:

> We return, therefore, to the original puzzle: why does this book work so well, better, even than the other books Gardner has annotated? Perhaps it is because *Alice* is what literary theorists call—or if they don't yet, they ought to—a "hub" book for modern thought, in the same way that Memphis is the hub airport for modern packages. Everything flies into it, and mostly everything flies out of it. Carroll deliberately packed it with everything he thought about, and everything in it has the life of an idea: Victorian piety in parody form, mathematical and logical speculation, bits of philosophy—even the sentiments are intellectualized, made strange. Ideas fly out, because ideas flew in. (Very few books—perhaps only *Gulliver's Travels* in the 18th century and *Ulysses* and *Finnegans Wake* in the 20th—are hub books of quite this kind, and in Joyce once can still feel that the flights out have all been cancelled because of fog.)[2]

What Gopnic refers to as "bits of philosophy" have stimulated lots of philosophers to mention Alice in their writings. Peter Heath, in *The Philosopher's Alice*, published in 1974, lists the names of close to fifty philosophers who quote or allude to Alice, and notes that, at that time, the list was "only the beginning."[3] Presumably, twenty-seven years later, the list would have hundreds of names.

In what follows I hope to demonstrate how teachers of philosophy can put those "bits of philosophy" to service in introducing their students to significant philosophical arguments, distinctions, and ways of thinking. I will also attempt to show that using the Alice books to supplement traditional introductory course materials not only provides students with an accessible, entertaining, and at times delightful way to become acquainted with philosophy, but also, on a more subtle level, introduces them to philosophical humor.

Teaching an introductory philosophy course provides the instructor an opportunity to acquaint students with important philosophical distinctions and topics "along the way," as well as to provide them with a more comprehensive understanding of some significant philosophical views. To indicate how valuable the Alice books can be in carrying out these activities, I will give threw instances drawn from my courses.

First Example

Consider the distinction, stressed by pragmatists and positivists among others, between a "disagreement" concerning a matter of fact and one that is "merely verbal." A famous instance of this distinction is presented by William James: A man wanted to catch a glimpse of a squirrel that was clinging to a tree. The squirrel was on the opposite side of the tree from the man. The man moved around the tree, but the squirrel, by moving at the same rate, kept the tree between itself and the man. When the man had traveled completely around the tree, he still hadn't seen the squirrel. The question under consideration is: Did the man go around the squirrel or not? As James points out, the question is not one of fact, but of the meaning of the phrase "going around."[4] If "going around" means "being to the north, east, south, and west" of the squirrel, the answer is yes. But if "going around" means "being in front, on one side, in back of, and on the other side of" the squirrel, the answer is no.

Consider now the following exchange from *Alice's Adventures in Wonderland*:

"Take off your hat," the King said to the Hatter.
"It isn't mine," said the Hatter.

When I asked one class where the source of confusion lay, a student suggested that the King (mistakenly) thought the Hatter owned the hat he was wearing, and the Hatter's response was designed to enlighten the King. Clearly the student took the issue to be one of fact: Did the hatter own the hat he was wearing? But after further consideration the class reached the conclusion that the King was using the phrase "your hat" to mean "the hat you are wearing," perhaps the normal sense of the words in such a context, while the Hatter was using it to mean "the hat that I own (as a personal possession, not as a part of my business)." This interpretation treats the confusion as "merely verbal." I was able, I hope, to make clear the distinction in a way that was entertaining, at least to some students, without having to devote a significant amount of time to the matter, and without having to explain to the students why I was bothering to discuss the distinction. It just developed naturally in our reading of Alice.

Second Example

Depending upon what materials the instructor uses in the course and the order in which those materials are presented, it may be possible to use passages from Alice to expand a point made earlier in the course. For example, in my opening lecture I spend some time discussing paradoxes, using the Liar Paradox and two examples from Lewis Carroll's non-Alice writings, one involving a crocodile and one involving training to become a lawyer.

The sentence "This sentence is false" always evokes some laughter when I present it after trying to convince students that "This sentence is English" is true, and "This sentence is very long" is false. In my discussion I indicate that some philosophers have proposed the view that what is wrong with the paradoxical sentence (and indeed the other two) is that each refers to itself, but given time constraints I don't go into any real discussion of metalanguages, the use-mention distinction, etc.

Consider the following passage, which we read near the end of the semester, from *Through the Looking Glass*:

> "...The name of the song is called '*Haddock's Eyes*'."
> "Oh, that's the name of the song, is it?" Alice said, trying to feel interested.
> "No, you don't understand," the Knight said, looking a little vexed. "That's what the name is called. The name really is "*The Aged Man*."
> "Then I ought to have said 'That's what the song is called'?" Alice corrected herself.
> "No, you oughtn't: that's quite another thing! The *song* is called "*Ways and Means*," but that's only what it's called, you know!"
> "Well, what *is* the song, then?" said Alice, who was by this time completely bewildered.
> "I was coming to that," the Knight said. "The song really is '*A-sitting On A Gate*': and the tune's my own invention."

Once the students have read this, I use the occasion to point out that the idea of "levels" of language that the White Knight, in a sort of Marx Brothers semi-incoherent way, embodies in his discussion, offers a way to understand the proposed solution to the Liar Paradox that I had mentioned in my opening lecture. Now I take the time to discuss metalanguages and related topics. (I think this works better than attempting to lay out the details in the first class, before students have had a chance to get familiar with how philosophers think.)

I explain that by distinguishing among what the name of the song is called, the name of the song and the song itself, the White Knight is in effect drawing attention to the difference between talking about a thing (the song) and talking about its name. As mentioned above, one form of the Liar Paradox is generated by the sentence "This sentence is false," which upon reflection is seen to be false if it's true and true if it's false, creating a paradox because no sentence can be both true and false at the same time.

Some philosophers have concluded that in talking about a thing (e.g., a song) we use what is called the object language, while in talking about words in the object language (e.g., the name of the song) we must ascend to a metalanguage. If we wish to speak about words in the metalanguage, we must use a metaphysics-metalanguage, and so on. The key point is that no meaningful sentence can be in two levels of language simultaneously. These philosophers argue that since the paradoxical sentence refers to itself it violates the principle of language and thus is really nonsensical. As a result it cannot be either true or false, thereby eliminating the contradiction. What is especially helpful is that the topic is raised in the context of reading Alice, and thus doesn't require that the instructor interrupt the regular assignments to pick up a loose end from the opening class.

To be honest, I have no way of knowing that if this way of presenting the materials is more effective than doing it differently. All I can say is that it is more fun for the instructor, and presumably for some (or many) students.

Third Example

The Alice books also provide an opportunity to the instructor to clarify the students' understanding of classic philosophic texts and arguments. In my introductory classes I have the students read Descartes' *Meditations*. Later the semester in *Through the Looking Glass* we encounter Tweedledee and Tweedledum, who tell Alice that she is only a character in the Red King's dream. Alice naturally objects, leading to the following exchange:

> "I am real," said Alice and began to cry.
> "You won't make yourself a bit realler by crying," Tweedledee remarked: "there's nothing to cry about."
> "If I wasn't real," Alice said—half laughing through her tears, it all seemed so ridiculous—"I shouldn't be able to cry."
> "I hope you don't suppose those are real tears?" Tweedledum interrupted in a tone of great contempt.

A number of students realize that Alice is in effect saying "I cry; therefore I am." Although the *Meditations* doesn't contain the sentence "I think, therefore I am"—it's in the *Discourse*—it naturally came up in our earlier discussion of Descartes.

When I asked the students whether they thought Descartes would agree with Alice or Tweedledum and Tweedledee, I found (somewhat to my disappointment) about half voted for Descartes and half for the two brothers. This result provided me with an opportunity to clarify Descartes' view and stress the sweeping nature of his doubt. It is true that Descartes thought he had established his own existence, and thus might be believed to sympathize with others trying to establish their own existence, at least following the sixth meditation. Nevertheless, some of the better students realized that, given the situation, Alice had no basis to claim to know that her tears were real, echoing in a way Descartes' doubts about the existence of material objects. This provided me not only with an opportunity to clarify Descartes' view, but also to stress the importance of realizing that a conclusion may be true but that unjustified premises do nothing to establish its truth.

Since the Alice books are so rich, it is likely that instructors who wish to introduce philosophical distinctions or clarify points raised earlier in the class will find several opportunities to do so, and to do so in a manner that is more vivid and memorable than might otherwise be possible. For example, there is a discussion involving the White King's use of "Nobody" as a name, providing a good example of the point that surface grammar is not a reliable guide to referential structure. Humpty Dumpty's claim that "When *I* use a word...it means just what I choose it to mean—neither more nor less" raises in a vivid way the issue of conventionality of language. The White Queen's account of a world in which punishment precedes trial and trial precedes crime, provides a link to a discussion of utilitarianism and fairness, and her claim that "I've believed as many as six impossible things before breakfast" raises William James' query as to whether or not what we believe is up to us. These are, of course, only examples. The Gardner and Heath volumes supply many more.

The Gardner and Heath volumes both contain the full texts of the two Alice books with extensive annotations. Heath focuses more on philosophical matters, while Gardner includes reference to physics, mathematics, literature, Victorian society, and Lewis Carroll's life, among other things. Both are valuable as references for instructors, especially the latest edition of the Gardner work.

Some instructors might want to put the Heath and Gardner books on reserve for the course. Since the Heath book is currently out of print and the Gardner work is reasonably expensive, it is probably best not to try and use them as texts for the course. Fortunately several inexpensive paperback editions of the two Alice books are available.

Having emphasized the virtues of using the Alice books in an introductory philosophy course, I should point out two possibly negative consequences of such use, one minor and one more significant.

1. As mentioned previously I would give frequent in-class quizzes on assigned readings, including Alice. On those occasions where there were two assignments for a single class session: Alice and, e.g., Mill or Kant or Berkeley, I would find some students had read Alice and skipped the harder assignment. This way they could get at least a grade of 50 out of 100 with a minimum of work. (One way to deal with this would be to count the Alice questions as only one-third of the grade.)

2. Even though the time devoted to the Alice books each class meeting was quite small—typically five to seven minutes (these classes met twice a week)—it did, during the first semesters I used Alice, have an impact on how thoroughly I could cover some of the other assigned readings. Some of the more subtle points concerning, e.g., utilitarian and deontological theories, were compressed or omitted, and student understanding was slightly diminished. My solution was to omit one reading from my usual syllabus. But occasionally

the discussion stimulated by the Alice books threatened to impinge on the time needed to cover other material. I believe this is the sort of problem that many instructors would find to be an invigorating challenge.

On balance it is clear to me that the use of Alice books made the course more interesting to teach, and based upon the comments of several students, more interesting to take. But beyond that, I believe that introducing students to philosophy through humor gives them an opportunity to develop a deeper appreciation of the subject and perhaps also an appreciation of why some very bright and slightly odd people dedicate their lives to it. I think that would be a nice gift to give our students.[5]

Notes

1. *The Annotated Alice: The Definitive Edition*, Introduction and Notes by Martin Gardner (New York: W.W. Norton, 2000).
2. Gopnic, Adam, "Go Ask Alice Again," *The New York Times Book Review*, (December 5, 1999), 60.
3. *The Philosopher's Alice*, Peter Heath, ed., (New York: St. Martin's Press, 1974) 247.
4. James, William, "What Pragmatism Means," (from Chapter II of *Pragmatism*), in Max Fisch, ed., *Classic American Philosophers*, (New York: Fordham University Press, 1996), 128-136.
5. The author would like to thank William Paterson University for sabbatical year support that made possible the completion of this paper.

8. Shake 'Em Up: On Teaching Weird or Irrelevant Philosophical Views

David Shatz

> [T]he aim of teaching is to make apparent the connections between seemingly esoteric material and the students' own sphere of experience.
> —Steven M. Cahn[1]

Among Bertrand Russell's many *bon mots* is this gem: "The point of philosophy is to start with something so simple as not to seem worth stating, and to end with something so paradoxical that no one will believe it."[2]

Teachers of philosophy, especially in introductory classes, feel the force of Russell's remark with sometimes unnerving regularity. Many students would rather stick with what is "so simple as not to seem worth stating," and they often find the problems their professors raise and/or the solutions that philosophers proffer irrelevant and weird. We all know that dealing with this reaction is one of the profession's great challenges. In this essay I offer some thoughts about meeting that challenge.

My suggestions are reflections of my own experience, and I do not seek to foist them on others whose students and intellectual setting, as well as personal inclinations, differ from mine. Most likely the profession's members will report a wide variety of experiences and concomitantly a plurality of strategies for dealing with less-than-welcoming student reactions to course material. It happens that the students I teach by and large have philosophical proclivities, since most have been brought up in religious homes and were educated in elementary and high schools in which theological problems and conundra crop up on a daily basis. But this general rule admits of many exceptions even in my own school, particularly because having thought about, say, why God allows evil, does not entail that one will be excited by Cartesian skepticism or Berkeleian idealism.[3] And I would think that, for professors who teach a different population, the problem of motivating weird or irrelevant seeming views will be that much more arduous.

1. Philosophy as Naiveté

To some extent, the difficulties in engaging college students to learn and do philosophy are surprising. In his fascinating book *Philosophy and the Young Child*,[4] Gareth Matthews demonstrates through anecdotes and interviews that philosophy is a natural activity, evident in early childhood. Young children frequently ask questions like "Papa, how can we be sure that everything is not a dream?" "where does my bellyache go when it goes away?," "what part of me is really me?" "how does the person who makes the dictionary know what the word means?" When told that he can't be in two places at once, Matthews's son points out that sure he can—he can be in the bedroom and the house at the same time. My own son, then in fourth grade writing a book report on the late baseball star Roberto Clemente, became perplexed over the teacher's question, "If you were this person would you have done anything different?" After all, he wondered, if I were truly him, I would have done exactly the same thing; and had I done anything different, I wouldn't be him. (Spoken like a true Leibnizian.) Whereas psychologists like Jean Piaget dismiss children's questions, claiming they display simple errors in reasoning, Matthews argues that it is Piaget who is erring—his supposed replies are not convincing, and the child's question remains in force.[5] The people who do understand the child's perplexities, their depth and tenacity, are writers of children's books—Lewis Carroll, for example, or L. Frank Baum, or James Thurber. When Humpty Dumpty declares to Alice that he can choose to make the world "glory" mean "there's a nice knockdown argument for you," or indeed whatever he wants it to mean, he is raising the important question of whether a word's meaning is determined by the idea or mental picture that the speaker or writer has in mind when using the word.

But if philosophy is a natural activity, why do many college students find it hard to relate to? Why must they *cultivate* naiveté, as opposed to having it naturally? What happens, Matthews suggests, is that our young Socrateses are socialized into thinking that their questions are silly or irrelevant. Parents patronize the children and direct them to other pursuits. Adults "aren't themselves interested in philosophical questions. They may be threatened by some of them."[6] (I presume because they have no answer, and/or the questions challenge their world view.). Perhaps not recalling that they once had similar questions, they let the matter drop or perhaps even *make* it drop. Also (this is my own point) as a rule philosophy is not taught pre-college. Eventually the questions disappear from the consciousness of teenagers, and for that matter, adults. The sentiment emerges that "[p]hilosophers seem to ask questions that no one wants to answer and to tell us what no one wants to know. Who needs them?"[7]

Matthews endorses Robert Spaemann's description of philosophy as "institutionalized naiveté." Philosophy "provide[s] an institutional setting in which people will be encouraged to ask questions so basic that grappling with them seems to all of us some of the time, and to some of us all of the time, quite naïve." Now, "in children, naivete comes naturally, without institutional encouragement." The challenge of teaching philosophy, then, is to reawaken the students' naiveté within an institutional setting.[8] For this purpose, it is important that the philosopher not become so preoccupied with technique or with consulting and understanding the views of other philosophers that he "lose[s] sight of the questions and perplexities that first called the techniques forth."[9]

If Matthews is right—and he has had many, many dialogues with children that provide evidence for his view—then taking philosophy seriously involves, I would say, not growing up but growing down. It involves getting at a core naïve question or perplexity and restoring a student's lost interest. Unfortunately, there is no obvious or straightforward way of restoring childhood innocence, so to motivate philosophy we need new ways to engage and excite. Tips from other philosophers are a dime a dozen, many requiring props like cartoons, Monty Python episodes, movies like the "Matrix" trilogy and "Crimes and Misdemeanors," or even, as Woody Allen suggested, field trips to meet the Creator. Such devices are certainly pedagogically useful, and I am all for them (except Woody's). Nevertheless, I want to suggest ways to make seemingly irrelevant or weird views and problems somewhat more friendly, understandable, relevant and plausible *without* props and gimmicks (except humor; see anon). My proposals reflect arguments that are actually used by the philosophers being studied or by other philosophers.[10] I will also critique some alternative pedagogic responses to perceived irrelevance or weirdness.

As for a definition of "weird view"—my colleague Margarita Levin wryly suggests this blatantly circular one: "A weird view is a view that initially seems weird, and after it is explained and the arguments for it made clear, *still* seems weird."

2. Teaching about Skepticism

"Why should I worry about being a brain in a vat or the victim of an evil deceiver? We all know the water's in the pot and the car is in the driveway. It's crazy to think we don't know those things. While I understand that a Cartesian or modern day skeptic is not saying that there *is* a powerful deceiver or a vat containing brains, but only asserts that we can't rule out this possibility, it's crazy to think even that these scenarios *may* be real. Why are we bothering to question what everyone knows to be true?"

Philosophy will sound even crazier for the student when she is asked to contemplate the scenarios that power skepticism about other minds and memory, or is asked to entertain the possibility that the next time she releases a ball from the twentieth floor of the Empire State building, it will go up into the heavens instead of straight down. Add now the fact that most of us think that skepticism has not been refuted, and many that it cannot be refuted, and we seem to be wracking students' brains over a question that, apart from lacking an existential grip, admits of no answer anyway.

I have found that bright students ask "why bother with this" no less frequently than weaker ones. Bright students want to find good reasons for studying what they study; they have reasoned-out ideas of what is important and what is not. They think in terms of the value of different intellectual endeavors, and need convincing that a particular intellectual exercise is worthwhile. Many find philosophy worthwhile, but others find that some of its questions serve no useful purpose. Weak students, by contrast, often see college as a game where you just play by rules and get your diploma. You have to take humanities courses to graduate? So take them. It's not interesting or relevant? So what. It's weird? Just do as asked. College is dull anyway. Weak students may drop the course, but more likely due to its difficulty than to principled, sophisticated doubts about its value. I heard of one class where the professor did such a poor job motivating a discussion of skepticism that the bright students dropped while the weak ones remained—which magnified his frustration many times over.

Let me present now several strategies I've heard for dealing with student complaints about skepticism, followed by my comments on each and then my own favored suggestions.

1) *"Shake 'em up"*: Here the professor asks the student to recall *why* Descartes raised skeptical questions. Descartes had discovered that long-held beliefs of his were false, and this made him wonder whether any belief is secure. The point of raising skeptical challenges is to put us ever on guard for the pernicious effects of prejudice, upbringing, and unquestioning acquiescence. It is to make us self-critical, to wake ourselves from (in Kant's great phrase) our dogmatic slumber. No, we should not abandon everyday common sense beliefs, this strategy says. But it is the posture, the attitude, that counts. We should be critical of our views on such matters as politics, religion, and ethics. And that is the point of questioning everyday beliefs about external objects or (moving beyond Descartes) the existence of other minds and the reliability of memory and induction. What the student must focus on, in this approach, is the overall moral of the story: epistemic humility. Skepticism about external objects, other minds, memory and induction merely illustrate how unwarranted and ungrounded even universally held beliefs can be, and hence a fortiori, beliefs that are actually controversial. The student is not expected to draw a skeptical conclusion about everyday beliefs, but is expected to appreciate the importance of questioning.[11]

Comment: The weakness in this approach is that it speaks out of both sides of its mouth.[12] Question, question, question; but don't give up everyday beliefs just because you can't answer questions about their warrant. Once the student realizes, as he or she must, that self-criticism leads us to be skeptical about the reliability of our senses, memory and inductive practices, along with belief in other minds, the student might very well consider that his or her other beliefs (politics, religion, ethics) should be held to weaker standards than the professor wants. After all, truly rigorous standards push us to a weird position, namely skepticism about commonsense beliefs. To present the point another way, the student will construct a parity or "same boat" argument. That is: I should not be troubled by my inability to logically prove my political, moral, religious, scientific, and historical views, because common sense beliefs, which my professor admits I should not give up, likewise can't be proven. The result of parity arguments is epistemological anarchy and the Balkanization of belief. Anything goes. The desired result—rigorous self-criticism—is not attained but rather undermined.[13]

Thinking about it further, the student will want to know whether life is even livable if we maintain a constant state of self-criticism. Constant examination of prior beliefs will lead to instability as well as to agnosticism about myriad questions big and small. Methodological conservatism (roughly, the view that the mere fact that a belief is already held gives it at least some added epistemic merit, at least when it is otherwise "tied" with its competitors) has strong attractions.[14] Maybe it's even an adequate solution to skepticism: leave me alone, Skeptic, for even though my beliefs are underdetermined by the data, I'm home free since I antecedently accept a non-skeptical position and have not been given reason to *deny* what I held previously. Hence, the strategy of saying that skeptical arguments should make us critical of our other beliefs may backfire and lead to an epistemology in which criticism of one's existing belief system on the grounds of insufficient warrant may be easily parried.

2) *"Look, this is what philosophy is. Take it or leave it. If you don't care about Descartes' questions, take a different class."* The professor could give this advice in a snooty, angry tone, or in a perfectly patient, sympathetic, and sensible one. The sensible point is: Don't take courses you don't like. If you don't care to know about the early explorers, don't take a course about them. If you don't like differential calculus, drop the course. And so too with Philo 101.

Comment: While this reply is straightforward and honest, it isn't going to win students over to philosophy. It is not an answer to the challenge of motivation so much as a capitulation—a confession by the professor that he or she has no answer.

3) *"Solve it or die."* One philosopher I know tried the following strategy. He asked the student, "Don't you consider yourself a rational person?" The student said yes. The professor asked: "How can you consider yourself rational if you don't have an answer to this most basic of questions!!! You will be intellectually dead."

Comment: The student will have a family, hold down a gratifying job, live a luxurious happy life—and have no clue how to ultimately justify her belief in her child's existence. Nonetheless she will be rational. In fact, if not having an adequate answer to Cartesian skepticism makes one irrational—then 100% of the world's population may be irrational.

4) *"Think about it or die."* This is a weaker form of strategy #3—thinking, not solving, is crucial to being rational. The professor asks: "How can you consider yourself rational if you don't *think about* this most basic of questions!!!"

Comment: Rational people don't have to think about everything, let alone beliefs whose acceptance will make life unlivable. And 98% of the world doesn't ask the question. Should we really say they are all irrational?

5) *"Laugh it up."* When I run into weirdness in texts I am teaching, I sometimes decide—selectively—to induce myself and my students to lighten up. I laugh at how weird the view is, and let students laugh with me. I forget who it was who said that for every crazy view imaginable, some philosopher or other has held it. That's worth quoting at such junctures. Also there is Wittgenstein's wonderful saying: "To solve the problems of philosophers, you have to think even more crazily than they do."[15] So a bemused "only philosophers would think of that" establishes a certain empathy with students that facilitates teaching. Sometimes it is good for students to see that we don't take ourselves too seriously and that we can be self-deprecating in a humorous way (as we often are in conversation with one another). This is the diametric opposite of the preceding four approaches because those others all take philosophy with ponderous and perhaps overbearing seriousness. Needless to say, turning weirdness into humor must be used selectively, or we project a total lack of seriousness and impart the thought that philosophy is a joke. But humor has its place in our pedagogy.

Comment: All that said, one issue we do not want simply to laugh off is skepticism. It is too central to epistemology to be dismissed that way. We can show students that we know how weird or crazy skepticism seems, but after that we will have to come up with an account of why, despite its weirdness and laughability, it is worth studying.[16]

6) *"Hume is right."* My own favored strategy with skepticism is to put forward a Humean perspective. The Humean strategy gives full-throated acknowledgment to the thesis that skepticism cannot be refuted. It *celebrates* that failure. For it shows that the failure is highly instructive: it teaches us something about ourselves. We are not the rational beings we thought we were. We are beings of habit, instinct, and hard-wiring (to use an anachronism). Children and horses make inductive inferences as we do; and as Hume remarks, even if some abstruse argument can justify induction, beings who use induction don't use any such argument.[17] Thank goodness we don't think with full, deductive rationality, or we could not live. (Hume does view resistance to induction as madness, and distinguishes rational and irrational, hence my slippery phrase "full, deductive rationality.")

A true skeptic, of course, will not allow anyone to draw conclusions about what human beings are like and why they do the things they do. Such empirical claims are liable to skeptical doubt just like anything else is. But what Hume was proposing was essentially this: you can't solve such problems, so move on. Be true to human nature. Do some philosophy, but on the whole take common sense for granted.

> Abstruse thought and profound researches [says nature] I prohibit, and will severely punish, by the pervasive melancholy which they introduce, by the endless uncertainty in which they involve you, and by the cold reception which your pretended discoveries will meet with, when communicated. Be a philosopher, but, amidst all your philosophy, be still a man.[18]

To be sure, we don't want students to take quotations like these so far as to delegitimize philosophical exploration. If we do, our courses should be evacuated or cancelled. A result like that would make the appeal to Hume self-defeating, to say the least. But the Humean perspective can actually *nurture* philosophical discussions of knowledge by stimulating a fruitful exploration of different senses of rationality and different accounts of epistemic norms. Professors who are naturalists, as Hume and Quine were, may be content to turn epistemology into psychology and reduce epistemic norms to a specification of the reliability of different cognitive processes. But this is still and all a philosophical position, and it is open to philosophical examination. The challenge for the non-naturalist professor is to salvage a notion of norms of rationality while teaching students that they must accept that our strongest beliefs are not fully rational. The discussion will prove interesting and relevant.

Introducing Hume while doing Descartes has worked for me. Students are struck by the disconnect in themselves: they see that they reason in certain ways and hold certain beliefs while knowing full well that they have no real warrant for doing so. The name of the game is not "justify your beliefs," but rather, "what can we learn about ourselves from the fact we can't justify them and yet (contrary to the *ancient* Skeptics) we can't shake ourselves loose of them?" Discovering and contemplating the disconnect between what we believe and what we think is justified is interesting, challenging to explain, and deeply instructive about the nature of human beings. Students learn as well that the overexamined life, a life in which absolutely everything is questioned, is not worth living. While they should appreciate that by trying to give a description of human psychology, Hume, as my professor put it to me, "contradicts himself on every page"—that is, his strategy is problematic—that is exactly the point: an appreciation that they "suffer" from this dissonance too gives students something to learn from the failure of rebuttals of skeptical arguments.

As a practical matter, this strategy works best when Descartes and Hume can be positioned in adjacent parts of the syllabus. In topics-centered introductory courses or epistemology courses this can be done easily enough. In historically structured introductory courses, introducing Hume when doing Descartes will be awkward—but not impossible. And the instructor will also not want Hume to end all discussion of skepticism, since skepticism is prominent in post-Humean thought. These problems demand further thought but are not in my opinion all that intimidating.

7) *Use the ancient Skeptics:* Before leaving the topic of skepticism, I make an iconoclastic recommendation: that skepticism not be introduced via Descartes's scenario of the evil deceiver.[19] A better choice is the ancient Skeptics' Trilemma Argument. Suppose you believe that *p*. What justifies your belief that *p*? Say it's your belief that *q*. But what justifies your belief that *q*? Say it's your belief that *r*. But what justifies your belief that *r*? The regress goes on. The attempt to justify belief that *p* will come to grief, because it either generates an infinite regress, generates a circle, or introduces a self-justified belief. None of those alternatives are acceptable, skeptics argue. I find that this argument works

better to motivate skepticism than Descartes' because it lacks the element of a weird scenario. It's a purely abstract argument. Likewise, students are absorbed by the question of how the use of reason can be justified. If is justified by rational argument, we have a vicious circle. This interests them.[20] In short, introducing the *Meditations*' arguments only after the arguments that do not depend on a wild skeptical scenario will help with the problem of motivation. When discussing the ancients, no one will bother to say, "but I *know* I'm not a brain in the vat," because the discussion has nothing to do with brains in vats or evil deceivers. Instead they will reflect on the *structure* of their reasoning.

In sum, while I can attest only to my own experience, I propose strategies 6) and 7) to deal with the weirdness of skepticism.

3. Ethics vs. Epistemology

In his celebrated and controversial *The Closing of the American Mind*, Allen Bloom begins as follows: "There is one thing a professor can be absolutely certain of: almost every student entering the university believes, or says he believes, that truth is relative."[21] I think that there is an intriguing difference, though, between classes in epistemology and classes in ethics. In epistemology, students enter with common sense intuitions and find skepticism strange. They need goading and persuading to regard the skeptical stance as something to be grappled with. In ethics, we find the opposite pattern. Students *enter* with philosophical views—relativism, skepticism.

Relativist views often come out ferociously in early classes. Under bombardment, the professor, no matter what his or her ultimate view of relativism, basically has to convince the students that they have strong moral convictions—be it about Hitler, people who torture babies, or racists and sexists. Whatever the ultimate fate of relativism and skepticism in later discussion, students have to somehow be made to feel the force of ethical intuition, because surely moral philosophy cannot be *so* simple as to render the relativist or skeptical position a no-brainer before classes have even started. Beyond the examples I have given of strongly held beliefs, atheists in the class could be asked how they can raise the problem of evil without endorsing a standard of ethics that differentiates good from evil;[22] theists could be asked how the inference "we must be grateful to God, for He has done good things for us" holds up if all ethics is relative. (The principle that one must be grateful to a benefactor is an ethical principle.) Or, the professor may ask whether abolishing slavery constituted moral progress and whether reformers like Martin Luther King redressed objectively wrong practices. Confronted with the fact they may really and truly have strong ethical convictions, the students may say, "yes, I have those beliefs, but they are just relative [to me, to my society, to my family]." But the professor will press them further: do you really believe that? Why, if relativism is right, does it matter to you which beliefs you or anyone else has? And don't you think you have good reasons for your beliefs? In addition, the professor may seek to demonstrate the incoherence or self-refuting character of relativism.

The point, I repeat, is that whereas in epistemology, college students must learn to suspend their commonsense beliefs and get comfortable with skepticism, in ethics, it is the reverse—they start with a skeptical or relativist position and must work their way back to own their ethical intuitions. You have to show them that, judging from their judgments, they don't really believe the philosophical positions they espouse. Later, after they finally come to see the strength of their own ethical convictions and to appreciate that an invocation of relativism sounds disingenuous—at that point, we can introduce relativism and skepticism in a rigorous way (as opposed to the loose, word-on-the-street version they started with) and subject them to careful examination. The positions take on significance only when it is established that students do have ethical convictions and that therefore the truth of relativism and skepticism would be surprising.[23]

Since I have a platform, I offer a few more words about the disconnect between students' convictions and their relativistic or skeptical views. When I start an ethics course by giving out a case study, such as variants of the trolley problem, and ask students for their views, they write answers that reflect often strong moral intuitions about the active/passive distinction. But when I use intuitions as litmus tests for evaluating utilitarian and deontological theories, inevitably someone asks how we can trust our intuitions, even the one that it is wrong to prosecute an innocent person for the sake of greater utility, and even the very ones about the active/passive distinction that they revealed when I give the trolley cases.

There is a story about a professor—it may have been my late mentor Sidney Morgenbesser—who got fed up with the relativism wielded by his students in early classes. In the fifth class or so, he gave a quiz, collected the papers, and then, with a perfectly straight face, declared that he didn't have time to grade the exams so he would give all people of one gender As and people of the opposite gender Cs. Immediately there erupted a loud student protest. "It's not fair!! It's not fair!! This is unjust!!" To which the professor replied, "I don't get it. For four days now I've been hearing how there are no well grounded ethical judgments. They're all relative. Now all of a sudden you have strong convictions?"

Interestingly, few of Matthews's examples have to do with ethics.[24] Children, in my experience, do not question the supposition that if one ethical view is correct, opposing ones are incorrect. As they mature, they see that different cultures have different standards—the view of descriptive relativism—and move from there to normative relativism, the view that no moral judgment is better than any other. It is only by means of the greater knowledge of the world that is acquired in teenage years that they become relativists. Even though some may already know about diversity, they often think "I'm right, they're wrong." By contrast, and I depart here from Bloom's sweeping generalization, they seem to take areas like science as monolithic and absolute, possibly because textbooks convey the message that there are absolute truths in science (alternative views are often not represented).[25] Be that as it may, what I am suggesting is that in ethics our aim should be precisely to *display* the weirdness of relativism and skepticism by showing students who hold these views that they have strong moral beliefs. After that weirdness is demonstrated, relativists and non-relativists in the professoriate may go their separate ways, the one group making the students comfortable with the weirdness, the other leaving them in discomfort. I am now verging on another issue, and that is whether professors should advocate particular views. If they ought not, then at least students by this point in the course should be able to sense the disconnect between relativism and their intuitions and be presented with options for dealing with it.

4. Dealing with Other Weird Views

Returning now to epistemology and metaphysics, in this section I sketch some strategies for dealing with weird views other than skepticism. In formulating these strategies, I cite as illustrations a small sample of additional weird views held by classical philosophers.

A) *Show that, although the view is weird, the philosopher in question found the alternatives problematic, and convey just how serious and recalcitrant those problems are.*

    Consider Berkeley's Idealism, which, on a weirdness scale of 1-10, rates an 11. There are no objects outside our minds except other minds; and our perceptual states are caused by God, save for some states that we generate on our own. This position is weirder than skepticism. Skeptics *doubt* whether there is an extramental material world. Berkeley flatout denies there is such a world. Some of Berkeley's objections to Locke's Representative Theory of Perception don't work well, but he does have a good point when he says we have no way of checking whether our ideas match the outside world. Provided that students see this skepticism as an embarrassing result for the Representative Theory, they will see how Berkeley ended up where he did and why he proudly proclaimed himself as free from skeptical worries. (Since there is no extramental world, there is no problem of proving there is.) Similarly, Nicholas Malebranche's occasionalism, the view that God is the only cause of events, including the rising of our arms upon the occasions of our intending to lift them, and the shattering of windows on the occasion of rocks hitting them, is fed in part by the obscurity of Cartesian interactionism.[26] You might call this a "negative campaigning" strategy on the part of the philosopher being studied. The professor can put it to good use.

B) *Point out the most interesting and long-lasting parts of the philosopher's arguments.*

    In a key argument, Malebranche stressed that there is no logically necessary connection between what we ordinarily call causes and what we ordinarily call the effects of those causes. This view is important and accessible, and it influenced Hume, who developed it in, to say the least, a rather different direction.

C) *Show the students what they would need to understand to solve the problem.*
Zeno's argument for the unreality of motion (I assume that was the point of his paradoxes[27]) stimulates an account of motion and the infinite. Zeno could also be used to illustrate the disconnect problem, since he denigrates the senses and embraces the supremacy of reason. The latter point holds also for his mentor Parmenides's view that there is no change.

D) *Show how religious sensibilities play a role in the development of philosophical positions.*
Malebranche thought that believing that things other than God have causal powers is the essence of paganism. Berkeley held this as well. Again, according to Leibniz, each monad has its own internal principles of development, and, furthermore, "has no windows," i.e., it does not interact with the outside world (= other monads). Yet, though each monad just goes about its business, in isolation from others, we experience the world as operating under ordered and stable laws. There is a "pre-established harmony." Leibniz found this universe of monads breathtaking testimony to the greatness of their creator. It is as if thirty people in separate rooms, and independently of one another, were playing notes on instruments as they saw fit—and the result were a gorgeous symphony. Louis Loeb has argued that religious considerations played a key role in early modern philosophy, and in particular accounted for philosophers' embracing certain problematic theories as well as arguments that were bad and/or tendentious.[28] The professor could use the discussion of religious sensibilities to discuss alternative theistic world views and in particular to get at the different sensibilities of occasionalists on the one hand and, on the other, philosophers who see God as operating according to teleological natural laws. (I like to ask students how an occasionalist would do play-by-play at a baseball game. "And God swings...")

Such contemporary views as David Lewis' position that nonactual possible worlds actually exist here and now together with the actual world, or its cousin, a view of cosmologists that there are multiple universes, a view often put forth to repel fine tuning arguments for the existence of God, will have to wait for another occasion.

5. Envoi

My colleague once saw the following on a student's evaluation of her introductory philosophy course: "This is the only course I have taken in which I knew less when I finished than when I started." Well spoken. We want students to probe, to question, to broaden the horizon of possibilities they consider worthy of their attention. But to make such a wide array of possibilities relevant to their thinking, we need to impart how consideration of these possibilities reveals truths about themselves, exposes the difficulties in world views we take for granted, and extracts the appealing features of even weird alternatives.

If I am right, that view is not weird.[29]

Notes

1. Steven M. Cahn, *Problems and Perplexities* (Lanham, MD: Lexington Books, 2007), 138.

2. Russell, "The Philosophy of Logical Atomism," in ed. Robert C. Marsh, *Logic and Knowledge: Essays 1901-1950*, 2nd ed., (New York: MacMillan/Capricorn Books, 1971), 193.

3. I say this while fully acknowledging that not only were Descartes and Berkeley theists, but God did heavy work in their epistemological and metaphysical systems.

4. Matthews, *Philosophy and the Young Child* (Cambridge, MA: Harvard University Press, 1980). See also his *Dialogues with Children* (Cambridge, MA: Harvard University Press, 1984).

5. The Piaget agenda that Matthews considers (pp. 37-55) includes the questions "What is thinking?," "What is the relationship between a word and its meaning?," "What are dreams and where are they located?," and "What things are alive and what things are conscious?"

6. *Dialogues with Children*, 73.

7. Ibid., 94.

8. Ibid., 94-95.

9. Ibid., 83-84.

10. As I noted earlier, students who are brought up in religious environments raise, while still young, numerous questions that their secular counterparts do not need to grapple with. They ask: "Why does God let people do bad things?," "How did He create the world?," "Where is God?," "I don't understand what happens to people after they die. And where can I find them?" These youngsters, I think, hold on to philosophical questions much longer, and remain keenly interested in high school. Often the questioning deepens their commitment. But again as noted earlier, interest in theological conundra does not entail interest in philosophical problems more generally.

11. This is the approach called "mitigated skepticism" that Hume describes in sect. 12, pt. 3 of his *Enquiry Concerning Human Understanding*. (His stress is on humility and tolerance vis-à-vis metaphysical views.) Though I will question the effectiveness of this Humean concept in our immediate context, we will see later that Hume's philosophy provides the basis for another, more successful strategy. I am struck by a contrast between Descartes' skepticism and Hume's mitigated skepticism. Descartes says: don't trust the beliefs you got from others, see what you can justify to yourself. Hume says: don't too much trust beliefs you get from yourself, be tolerant of others' views.

12. This objection to Hume's "mitigated skepticism" is put forward also by Terence Penelhum, *God and Skepticism* (Dordrecht: Reidel, 1983), 127: "How can he recommend that we confine ourselves to the reflections of common life, when their presuppositions are as incapable of rational justification as the pretensions of metaphysics? Surely Hume should either indulge both or reject both? How can skepticism consistently be mitigated?" Ira M. Schnall replies to Penelhum's charge of inconsistency in "Hume on 'Popular' and 'Philosophical' Skeptical Arguments," *Hume Studies* (forthcoming as of

this writing). I learned of Schnall's paper too late to adequately incorporate it into the present discussion. Nevertheless, Penelhum's question is one that students will naturally pose, and it is not clear that a good reply to Penelhum translates into a successful distinction that students will buy. If it does so translate, then, in the spirit of mitigated skepticism, I will humbly count strategy #1 as an additional good strategy.

13. These remarks are highly relevant to the use of parity arguments in philosophy of religion today. The danger of epistemological anarchy is well known to philosophers involved in that discussion. See, for example, Penelhum, *God and Skepticism*, ch. 6

14. See my *Peer Review: A Critical Inquiry* (Lanham, MD: Rowman & Littlefield, 2004), chap. 3, and the literature cited there.

15. Wittgenstein, *Culture and Values*, trans. Peter Winch (Oxford: Basil Blackwell, 1980), 75.

16. For more on humor as a pedagogic strategy, see John O'Connor, "Philosophical Humor, Lewis Carroll, and Introductory Philosophy," *APA Newsletter on Teaching Philosophy* 1,1 (fall 2001): 182-85.

17. See the last paragraph of *Enquiry Concerning Human Understanding*, 4.

18. *Ibid.*, section 1.

19. But I hasten to note that the ancient Skeptics proffered as well (inter alia) arguments based on the possibility of dreams and hallucinations.

20. Ira Schnall correctly suggested to me that Lewis Carroll's "What Achilles Said to The Tortoise" would be a good reading to introduce to point out difficulties in the structure of deductive reasoning.

21. Bloom, *The Closing of the American Mind* (New York: Touchstone Books, 1987), 25.

22. As Ira Schnall pointed out, though, the atheist student could counter that he is offering a reductio ad absurdum of theism, which does embrace an objective ethic.

23. On responding to relativism, see also Nancy Daukas, "Classroom Relativism as a Pedagogical Opportunity," *APA Newsletter on Teaching Philosophy* 3,2 (spring 2004): 2-6.

24. But there is a good example on p. 28 of Matthews's *Philosophy and the Young Child* (Cambridge, MA: Harvard University Press, 1980): IAN (six years) found to his chagrin that the three children of his parents' friends monopolized the television; they kept him from watching his favorite program. "Mother," he asked in frustration, "why is it better for three people to be selfish than for one?"

25. See Thomas Kuhn, "The Function of Dogma in Scientific Research," in A. C. Crombie, ed., *Scientific Change* (London: Heineman, 1963).

26. Malebranche is not taught in introductory courses, and is not normally taught in History of Philosophy classes. But he ought to be taught in the latter, since he provides an alternative to Cartesian interaction and influenced Hume. See Louis Loeb, *From Descartes to Hume: Continental Metaphysics and the Development of Modern Philosophy* (Ithaca, NY: Cornell University Press, 1981), 191, 355-56.

27. For a different view of his aims, see Wallace I. Matson, "Zeno Moves!," in Anthony Preus, ed., *Before Plato* (State University of New York Press, 1999).

28. Loeb, *From Descartes to Hume*. See especially the quotation on p. 113: "We must distinguish between the articulated grounds for the conclusion and the motive which led the philosopher to assert it," as well as the quotation from Maurice Mandelbaum on p. 228. On the religious motivations of individual philosophers, see: on Descartes, 68, 113-14; on Malebranche, 222-28; on Berkeley, 267-68; on Leibniz, 312-16.

29. Knowing Steven Cahn and collaborating with him has been one of the genuine

pleasures and privileges of my career. No professor who has been exposed to Steve and his writings can remain unaffected by his thoughtful, insightful, and important reflections on teaching. Quite apart from the valuable specifics of his suggestions and analyses, his making us conscious and reflective about our pedagogy and other challenging aspects of academic life has enriched and deepened our self-understanding of the life path we have chosen. I thank Margarita Levin, Ira Schnall, Atara Segal, and my wife Chani, who thinks all my views are weird, for their comments.

9. Global Norming: An Inconvenient Truth

George Sher

Mr. Adam Pendicks has asked me to write in support of his application to your institution, and I am obliged to do so. Adam is a sixth-year graduate student in philosophy here at Ragland University, where he has compiled a satisfactory though undistinguished record. Overall, I would place him in the third quartile of the students in our program.

Adam is currently writing a dissertation under my supervision on a variation of a possible objection to a potential difficulty with a defense of the killing/letting-die distinction that two philosophers, Arve Suissinnen and Benson Hedges once deployed, the former in the late 1960s and the latter in the early 1980s. Although the Suissinnen-Hedges line has not achieved wide currency—no one, to my knowledge, has actually said anything about it—a careful refutation of the variant of the possible objection to the potential difficulty that Adam discusses would nevertheless be an incremental addition to our understanding of the topic. Although Adam has now completed drafts of five of his seven chapters, the dissertation won't be in any shape to defend by this coming September, and I'm not sure about the following September either. There is, however, a probability greater than zero that some of it will eventually be published.

Adam is sometimes helpful in discussions. I rarely have to explain things to him more than twice, and when he manages to avoid irrelevancy, his points can be helpful targets for others. I think of him more as a student than a colleague.

Adam's social skills, like those of many in our profession, leave something to be desired. He is, however, a well-meaning person whose inappropriate laughter and other gaffes are rarely held against him. For the most part, he fulfills his duties adequately. Any department that hires him will gain a faculty member who will meet with his classes. I recommend him with all the enthusiasm his candidacy deserves.

The department in which I teach has just been conducting a job search, so I have just finished reading about 150 sets of letters of recommendation, not one of which is anything like this letter for Adam Pendicks. Over the years, I have read many other letters, and have written many myself, and not one of them was anything like this letter either. Yet many graduate students do of course rank in the third quartile—a full quarter do—and not a few are socially maladroit, derivative in their thinking, and/or at best indifferently dependable. Since most faculty members are at least decent people, and since a good number are admirable human beings, their routine willingness to omit some facts and to stretch others beyond the breaking point can hardly be attributed to a simple lack of veracity. Its source, rather, is a tension, often severe, between two different and equally legitimate moral demands, one the duty to tell the truth, the other the obligation to do one's best to get jobs for one's students. The basic difficulty is that it is logically impossible both to tell the full truth and to write a letter that will get a student a job that he would not get if the full truth were told.

Although this is hardly a tragic choice, I do think it is a genuine moral dilemma. I think, that is, that those who must write on behalf of their students are sometimes in a position in which anything they do will be at least somewhat wrong. When a faculty member's being in this position is not due to any prior wrongdoing or negligence on his part, it is a case of bad moral luck.

There are of course some who believe neither in moral dilemmas nor in moral luck. To these optimistic souls, keeping your nose clean means never having to say you're sorry. Applied to the case at hand, what their position comes to is either that (1) anyone who now must either violate his duty of veracity or fail to fulfill his obligation to a student must previously have created the problem by doing something he shouldn't, or that (2) our obligations to our students never require that we distort the truth or omit important facts, or that (3) we owe our students plenty of distorting and omitting, but doing these things in letters of recommendation is not wrong. To bring out the full scope of the letter-writer's plight, and also to score some general points against the optimistic dilemma-denier, I now want to argue against each claim.

Consider first the proposal that whenever everything a recommender can do would be wrong, he must have put himself in this position through some previous moral lapse. This proposal concedes that letters of recommendations may confront us with genuine dilemmas, but denies that these are ever unavoidable. In the jargon, it downgrades what appear to be dilemmas *simpliciter* to dilemmas *secundum quid*. But where, exactly, has Adam's advisor gone wrong?

There are a number of possible places, some farther in the past than others. Early on, the advisor may have fallen short by entering a profession that generates obligations that regularly conflict with the duty of veracity. More recently, he may have erred by accepting employment at an institution whose students are not strong enough to win every competition on their merits. Still more recently, he may have gone wrong by agreeing to supervise a weak student or by subsequently agreeing to write on that student's behalf. But none of this is at all plausible. Locating the wrong act at the point where the advisor entered academic life is silly because the academy is at least no more morally tainted than any other institution and is probably less tainted than most. Criticizing him for joining an institution that enrolls students whose prospects will be harmed by truthful letters is unreasonable both because every graduate program has such students and because jobs at the places with the fewest such students are beyond the reach of most job-seekers. Identifying his moral lapse with his agreement to take on a weak student is objectionable both because we often cannot tell how our advisees will pan out and because anyone who avoids weak students to keep his hands clean merely shifts the moral burden to his colleagues. And, finally, to say that the advisor should not have agreed to write on behalf of his weak student is merely to relocate the dilemma; for anyone who takes on an advisee has already undertaken a de facto commitment to write on that student's behalf.

Given all this, those who claim that letters of recommendation never confront us with moral dilemmas may retreat to their second option. They may argue not that any apparent dilemmas can be traced to earlier moral lapses, but rather that we are never obligated to distort or omit important truths to further our students' prospects for employment. But how, exactly, is this last claim to be defended in its turn? The argument can hardly be that we can't be obligated to distort the truth because distorting the truth is wrong, since whether distorting the truth in this context *is* wrong is just what is at issue. Moreover, although it sounds good to say that Adam's advisor did the right thing by telling the full truth, it doesn't sound quite as good to say that he did the right thing by writing a letter that he knew full well would doom Adam's chances for employment. This last claim would certainly be hard for Adam to swallow ("with supporters like that . . . "), and given that none of us actually write such letters despite the near-universality of student waivers, the rest of us evidently find it hard to swallow too. There is, to be sure, the occasional maverick who prefaces his recommendations with the disclaimer that unlike his weak and compromised colleagues, he intends to write only the plain and unvarnished truth and hopes his students will not be harmed by his stubborn integrity. However, remarkably, the students on behalf of whom such letters are written turn out to be just as uniformly superior as all the others.

Given all this, those who deny that letters of recommendation confront us with dilemmas may find it advisable to retreat once more. Instead of maintaining either that anyone who has only wrong options has only himself to blame or that our obligations to our students never require that we distort or omit important truths, he may take the position that we often *are* required to distort or omit but that doing so in letters of recommendation is not wrong. Of all the strategies for denying that recommendations confront us with genuine dilemmas, this is the one that seems the most promising. One obvious thing that can be said for it is that even when the currency is very inflated, some letters remain clearly stronger than others, and so real distinctions can still be made. A different but related point is that the need to convey real information has led to the development of a kind of code which any veteran letter-reader can decipher. Taken together, these facts suggest that instead of distorting or omitting important truths, hyperbolic letters may convey accurate information non-literally. Because there's nothing wrong with expressing oneself non-literally as long as the message is clear, we may after all seem capable of fulfilling all our obligations without violating our duty to be honest.

But I don't think we can get off the hook quite this easily; for precisely because we know that our inflated letters will automatically be downgraded, we also know that keeping our students competitive means inflating our letters further to withstand the inevitable downgrading. If "he is among the finest minds of his generation" will be translated as "he is competitive with some of the better students at very good institutions," then we cannot set him apart from the competition without touting his virtues in even more fulsome terms ("the very finest mind," "many a generation"). Instead of having to abuse the truth in plain language, we now have to abuse it in recommendationese, but nothing else has changed. As I have said, the basic problem is that it is logically impossible both to tell the full truth and to write a letter that will get a student a job that he would not get if the full truth were told.

So what's a philosopher to do? In a word, what we all do: compromise. To serve both masters, we must make concessions to each. To do what we can for our weaker students, we can try to write letters that will not disqualify them outright and that may be overlooked if their other letters come in stronger, while to preserve at least a tenuous connection to the truth, we can avoid saying things that are flatly false while playing up every scrap of positive information that is even marginally relevant. Like democracy, it's the worst way of doing things except for all the others.

Over the years, I have witnessed many impressive efforts to airbrush students whose prospects would be damaged by a candid assessment, and in the spirit of professional solidarity, I want to share some of what I've learned. To keep a weak student in the game, a letter-writer can do any or all of the following. First, he can discuss at great length the interest and importance of the problem to which his student is proposing an uninteresting and unimportant answer. Second, he can magnify the student's accomplishments by defining his specialty narrowly enough to guarantee that he will be one of the best at it. Third, he can finesse the all-important question of how this student stacks up against others by comparing him to weaker past students of whom few readers will have heard. Fourth, he can make the student sound good by saying positive things that somehow sound like they're job-related but really aren't. Finally, he can bring his letter to a satisfying conclusion by ending with a resounding but meaningless expression of support. When these techniques are used together, and when they're backed by strategic omissions as required, they are virtually certain to locate any letter squarely in the no-man's land between truth and falsity.

Let me end with an example. I began with a letter that gave Adam Pendicks no chance of being hired. Here, by contrast is one that gives him a fighting chance.

Mr. Adam Pendicks has asked me to write in support of his application to your institution, and I am delighted to do so. Adam is a sixth-year graduate student in philosophy here at Ragland University, where he is working on the later stages of a dissertation on the moral importance of the act/omission distinction. This distinction occupies a strategic position in both theoretical and applied ethics. Within the theoretical realm, the distinction raises fascinating questions about the scope and nature of moral responsibility, and disagreements about its importance can be seen to underlie many of the disputes between consequentialists and their opponents. On a more applied level, some version of the distinction informs many common beliefs about end-of-life decisions, famine relief, and other topics of pressing practical importance. Given all this, it is obviously crucial to gain a clearer understanding of the distinction, and that is precisely what Mr. Pendicks's project is intended to yield. He is already one of the world's two leading experts on the line of inquiry that he is pursuing [author's note: Arve Suissinnen passed away in 1992], and he will in due time be recognized as the single leading expert.

To convey a sense of the regard in which Adam is held here, it may be helpful to compare him to some of our other recent graduates. As far as I can judge, the consensus in our department is that Adam is somewhat better than Waxie Links, formerly of the Friendship Institute and now at Fulham A&M, that he's probably also better than Bibi Freund, who recently received a tenure-track appointment at Land O' Lakes University, but that he ranks just a touch below Lance Puller of Snake State. Adam is an enthusiastic contributor to the life of our close-knit community whose infectious laugh will be greatly missed when he leaves. I am pleased to recommend him warmly.

Isn't that better?

10. Intercollegiate Athletics and Educational Values: A Case for Compatibility

Robert Simon

College sports, particularly as played by teams from athletically elite Division I institutions of the NCAA, have come under increasing critical scrutiny. Various scandals, involving recruiting violations, misbehavior by athletes including alleged criminal activities, and significant academic fraud, have attracted much public attention but as critics have noted, the problems of intercollegiate athletics go deeper. Of particular concern are lack of academic involvement by some, perhaps many, elite athletes, the recruiting of athletic stars many of whom may have little if any interest in or aptitude for higher education, and consequent low graduation rates in some highly visible sports, primarily men's basketball and football, at some athletically elite institutions. Critics maintain that the problems go well beyond highly publicized scandals; rather the extensive amount of time intercollegiate athletics teams devote to travel, competition, and practice, which in many elite sports involves commitments for virtually the entire year, in effect assigns priority to athletics over academics. On this view, intercollegiate athletics are in conflict with and often undermine the academic mission of the university.

However, criticism has not been restricted to institutions with major athletic programs. For example, the Ivy League in Division I and the nation's most selective liberal arts colleges, such as those that play in the New England Small College Athletic Association (NESCAC), have long been thought to be shining examples of the value of intercollegiate athletics at their best. Such schools do not award athletic scholarships, have high standards for admitting recruited athletes, and aim at integrating athletics and academics within their institutions. However, recent studies, such as the widely cited *The Game of Life*, have argued that intercollegiate athletics even at these kinds of institutions is harmful to the academic enterprise.[1] This is because, according to the book, athletes make up a significant proportion of the student body of such schools, between 30 and 40 percent of the student body, yet do not perform nearly as well as other students in the classroom, thus dragging down the academic atmosphere at the entire institution.

Such critical views have attracted considerable support from many college and university faculty. These men and women quite naturally see the academic purposes of their institutions as of the highest priority and are alarmed by the manner in which intercollegiate athletics seems to undermine those purposes and even threaten the academic integrity of their programs.

In this paper, I explore the extent to which their views are warranted and offer an assessment of the claim that intercollegiate athletics as currently constituted is inconsistent with the academic mission of the university. In particular, I argue that many of the values that Steven M. Cahn has defended in connection with higher education, including its role in promoting critical inquiry and civic values, can also apply to some forms of intercollegiate athletics.

Of course, the label of intercollegiate athletics covers a diverse set of practices and institutions, ranging from athletically elite large state universities through different layers of Division I, which, with the exception of the Ivy League, normally involves award of athletic scholarships, to the more regional but nevertheless often intense competition at Division III, where no athletic scholarships are awarded and significant attempts are made to integrate academic and athletic goals. Any attempt to draw general conclusions about intercollegiate athletics must be sensitive to such differences, since conclusions about one sphere of competition may be inapplicable to others that differ significantly from it.

Three Theses: Irrelevancy, Incompatibility, Mutual Support

To sharpen our discussion, let us consider three claims that might be made about the relation of athletics to academics within institutions of higher learning. According to the first thesis, athletics simply are irrelevant to the main mission of the university that is conceived of as intellectual, not physical. On this view, athletics are at best a tolerable but sometimes distracting extracurricular activity but with no real connection to the function of colleges and universities. While the implications of such a view sometimes are unclear, it might be thought to lead to the following argument. Since athletics are not vital to the educational mission of the university, which always should take priority over other activities, athletics should not be assigned the importance they presently have, particularly at athletically elite Division I institutions. Rather, they should be assigned a recreational role, perhaps best pursued at the level of intramurals or loosely organized student clubs.

According to a second view, expressed by the more robust Incompatibility Thesis, intercollegiate athletics undermines or is incompatible with the academic mission of colleges and universities. Although some may assert this thesis as a conceptual truth, it is best understood as making an at least partially empirical claim: namely that in the context of actual higher education in America, intercollegiate athletics operates so as to undermine or conflict with major academic goals that colleges and universities should be pursuing. For example, the practice of recruiting athletes may be held to interfere with the educational goal of recruiting the most academically qualified student body.

A third thesis, that I will call the Mutual Support or Reinforcement Thesis, often is defended by representatives of athletic departments but also by some educators and philosophers of sport. It states that rather than undermining academics, intercollegiate athletics *properly conducted* actually can reinforce the academic mission of colleges and universities and even contribute more directly than the critics acknowledge to the support of academic values.[2]

The third thesis may be understood in a variety of ways. For example, it might be understood as claiming that important values presupposed by or expressed in athletic competition are identical to or sufficiently similar to those presupposed by or expressed in academic inquiry, so key values in each sphere of activity are the same or similar. It also might be understood as at least partially causal in asserting that when properly conducted, appreciation of the values central to athletic success can encourage adherence to those values in academic pursuits. It might also have an epistemic version; that illustration of certain values in athletic contests can reveal them or make them known and appreciated by wider audiences. Finally, it might function critically, as when violation of key athletic or parallel academic values are grounds for criticism; for example, when students or student-athletes are not sufficiently dedicated to achievement or honest with themselves about their weakness. So although this position can be developed in a variety of ways, and might apply differently at different levels of intercollegiate competition, it expresses an important alternative to the irrelevancy and incompatibility hypotheses.

In what follows, I will make a start toward evaluating these three approaches by considering three specific responses to the Incompatibility Thesis. Evaluation of these responses will give us some idea how to evaluate the dispute between adherents of the Incompatibility Thesis and supporters of Mutual Support or Reinforcement.

Three Responses to the Incompatibility Thesis

Provision of Entertainment as a Public Service

Many critics of intercollegiate athletics start with the surely acceptable premise that a primary mission of the university is academic and intellectual and then jump to the conclusions that the *only* major or fundamental missions of the university are academic and intellectual. This inferential jump is questionable, however. Surely, the academic and intellectual mission of the university might sometimes be compromised in the interests of student safety, for example, as when a controversial speech is postponed to prevent widespread violence, or when budget allocations are assigned to preserve the beauty of the campus rather than to strengthen an academic department, or when schools devoted to purely professional training receive support from the institution that might have gone to the humanities, arts, or sciences. These examples, while debatable, suggest that the nature of the fundamental mission(s) or function(s) of the university is ethically controversial.

If the mission of the university is conceived more broadly than purely academic and intellectual, why wouldn't it plausibly be extended to cover the provision of public service, including the provision of entertainment to the student body and wider community that intercollegiate athletics can provide? According to proponents of this view, it is clear that the university provides entertainment for the community in a variety of areas including theatre, music and other performing arts such as dance, as well as through programming on college sponsored radio and television stations. Intercollegiate athletics is simply another way in which academic institutions provide this good to their students and staff and to the population at large.

Indeed, proponents of this view argue, the university may have a duty to do so. Thus, Peter French, who as we will see is critical of other sorts of defenses of intercollegiate athletics, points out that the mission statements of many universities, especially large state institutions, include explicit mention of service to the community, often including reference to serving the economic and cultural needs of the population. Similarly, some mission statements of athletic departments, sanctioned by their universities, specifically include entertainment among the functions of their programs. Developing this line of thought, French maintains that:

> The honest and potentially successful defense of intercollegiate athletics, especially including the elite sports, is that they are the way, or at least one way and probably the most visible and successful way the university responds to its public service obligations in the area of public entertainment. In fact, they likely touch the lives of more members of the public in a positive and effective way than any other service the university may extend in that direction.[3]

Accordingly, once we abandon the assumption that the only fundamental mission of the university should be purely academic, encompassing teaching and scholarship in recognized academic disciplines, the sponsorship of intercollegiate athletics can be defended as fulfilling other legitimate functions of the university. As French puts it, "the tension in the university, particularly within the faculty, that sets the academic and athletic side of the campus at odds is caused by the general failure to appreciate the multiple missions of a contemporary university and on the part of the academic faculty typically to think that only their function is the 'real' mission of the university."[4]

How should such a position be evaluated? First, even if correct, this position applies with the most force to highly visible sports, such as men's football and basketball and perhaps women's basketball, at large athletically elite universities, particularly state institutions. It has less force at a small liberal arts college that emphasizes the excellence of its undergraduate education. I believe intercollegiate athletics does have an important function at small liberal arts colleges, but the case for such a conclusion may have less to do with provision of entertainment to the wider community than with other factors. So even if French's argument does have force, that force is greatest when applied to high profile sports at athletically elite levels of the NCAA and loses strength (although probably not to the vanishing point) when applied to different sorts of institutions or to lower profile sports.

A second criticism is that even if the university does have an obligation to provide entertainment, the kind of entertainment provided by athletics differs in kind from other kinds the university legitimately provides, such as concerts and art exhibits, Programs in the arts, as French recognizes, arguably have a much more direct link to the academic programs of colleges and universities than intercollegiate athletics. These can be defended as extensions of academics while, at least according to the critics, athletics cannot.

Is this second criticism decisive? I think not, for two reasons. First, as we have seen, the issue of what activities of the university are fundamental is itself an ethically contested issue. To assume that only entertainment closely linked to academic programs is legitimate is to beg the question about what functions universities should fulfill. More important, however, the objection begs the question in a more basic way. If the presumed divide between athletics and academics is nowhere near as deep as the critics assume and if there is or can be a significant degree of coherence and mutual support between the two, then intercollegiate athletics does not differ from university sponsored entertainment in other areas, such as the arts, to the degree critics assume. I will explore this point more fully in later sections of this paper.

That leads to the third criticism of the entertainment defense; namely, that athletics involves abuses of academic ethics that other activities of the university, including artistic performances, normally do not. If this means that some scandals have plagued high profile athletic programs at elite Division I schools, including cases of academic fraud, it clearly is true. Low graduation rates, particularly of minority athletes, at some institutions clearly are unacceptable. Moreover, if admissions standards for athletes differ so drastically from those of other students that a significant number of athletes are unprepared for college level work and as a result their academic course load is so diluted as to be educationally vacuous, then the charge of abuse is warranted.

However, such abuses occur mainly in high profile sports at some institutions and are not a reason for regarding all forms of intercollegiate athletics, even at the Division I level, as involving abuses of academic values. Moreover, the NCAA has taken some significant steps to raise graduation rates and insure that athletes are taking a core of serious academic courses. For example, Division I athletic programs with poor graduation rates will have the number of athletic scholarships they can offer reduced, providing a significant incentive to make sure athletes graduate. Even if incentives exist to circumvent such rules, perhaps by diluting the academic content of courses to which athletes may be steered, stricter rules do set a standard and significant penalties can deter violations.

A broader concern, however, applies even to elite athletic programs that provide opportunities for and encourage athletes to pursue their education and graduate. The intensity of competition, the travel and missed class time involved in playing a national schedule, the extended length of seasons, and off season training schedules may involve so great a commitment of time that the pursuit of educational goals is severely compromised. Thus, revenue is generated when high profile teams earn national ranking but that requires playing a national schedule, with the scheduling of games influenced more by attractive time slots on television and the need to travel extensively to play other national powers than requirements of class attendance.[5] These factors do raise issues of concern for those who would defend elite high profile intercollegiate sport as presently constituted.

French's defense of elite high profile intercollegiate sports as forms of entertainment legitimately provided by the university does have some force however. It is at least arguable, as he suggests, that provision of entertainment is one of the legitimate functions of colleges and universities, particularly large public institutions. However, such activity is legitimate only if it does not undermine the chances for the athletes in such programs to receive an education, does not subvert academic norms (as would be the case with academic fraud), and, more broadly, only if it does not involve a kind of disdain for the academic mission of the university which comes to be regarded as an obstacle to athletic participation rather than a significant aspect of the student athlete's intellectual and personal development.

There is another issue raised by the entertainment argument and its critics, however, that suggests both sides rely on a perhaps dubious common assumption. That assumption is that athletics and academics are two sharply distinct kinds of activities. However, as we will see in the next two sections, that assumption itself is open to serious challenge.

The University and the Teaching of Skills

French's discussion has called our attention to the point that attempts to characterize the mission or function of the university are normative in character and often contested. In a recent paper, former professor of philosophy and then university president Myles Brand, now President of the NCAA, has pointed out that much of what goes on in contemporary academic institutions involves the teaching, development, and exhibition of skills.[6]

Many such skills can be critical and highly analytic, such as learning how to formulate and criticize arguments, or how to design a double blind clinical trial. Others, however, such as those exhibited in dance and musical recitals, involve performance and exhibition of skills. Brand raises the issue of why the exhibition of some skills, say in dance, is considered within the boundaries of the academic enterprise and often receive academic credit towards graduation, but exhibition of other skills, such as those exhibited by athletes, is considered non-academic and extra curricular at best. Does this boundary line distinguishing the academic, understood to include dance and musical recitals, and the non-academic, understood to include intercollegiate athletics, have an acceptable justification or is it arbitrary and unjustified?

Brand's target in his paper is what he calls the Standard View that he claims is held by many academic faculty. According to the Standard View, intercollegiate athletics is an extra-curricular activity, outside the boundaries of the academic enterprise. According to Brand, however, the Standard View expresses a prejudice against the body.[7] Like French, Brand believes the academic critics of athletics have too narrow a view of what colleges and universities should be about. But where French argues for a pluralistic view of the mission of the university, including purposes beyond the purely academic, Brand argues for a broader notion of what counts as academic than he believes many faculty critics of intercollegiate athletics accept.

Brand starts from what he calls a "seemingly small point," namely that "When the educational experience of student-athletes is compared with those studying the performing arts such as music, dance, and theater, as well as the studio arts, it is difficult to find substantive differences."[8] Thus, like student athletes, student musicians practice a large number of hours, often more than is required, perform with various musical groups, some college sponsored, and often admission is charged to such events. Performance and practices often are intense. In addition, there is competition for places in the performing groups, and for students with the talent necessary for participation. Some preference may be given in admission to talented students in the arts and some may have aspirations for professional careers, although, as is the case with student athletes in the NCAA, almost all go on to careers in other areas of endeavor. According to Brand, "These similarities point to a convergence of educational experiences between student-athletes and others . . . but the activities of the student-athletes alone are not considered to be academic, or to be in conflict with academics."[9] Is there any plausible justification for this distinction?

Defenders of the Standard View would most likely reply that it is the intellectual content of academic courses that distinguish them from intercollegiate athletics. However, Brand maintains that in many performance courses in the arts, what is being taught are skills; "knowing how" rather than "knowing that." Moreover, athletics also involves content, such as knowledge of various strategies and the proper responses to them, as well as (this is my own addition) the ability to distinguish between morally acceptable and unacceptable conduct within the sport. In any case, in actual artistic performance, such as a concert or dance recital, it is not the "knowing that" which is most crucial but rather the exercise of skills at an appropriate level of excellence.

Although Brand's position does raise significant issues about the sharpness of the line between the academic and the non-academic, which is perhaps yet another dualism that might be called into philosophical question, it itself faces serious questions. Critics might maintain, for example, that the goal of elite intercollegiate athletics seems to be to win and to generate the revenue produced by winning, not to express artistic or intellectual values, as is the case with performances in music, dance, and theater.

However, while this criticism does not lack all force, it does seem overdrawn. First of all, the overwhelming majority of intercollegiate athletic contests do not involve high profile sports and are not intended to be revenue producing. Second, while artists normally may not aim at "winning," they do aim at excellence in performance. Similarly, although the cult of winning may have gotten out of hand in many area of sports, intercollegiate athletes often can be seen as aiming at excellence as well, with winning the natural by-product of top performance just as acclaim or the earning of an award can be the by-product of outstanding achievement by an artist. So there might be a difference, as the critics argue, between performance in athletics and the arts but perhaps not as sharp a one as the criticism might initially suggest.

Brand's critics also might argue that music and dance are embedded in a long tradition of intellectual development. Performance in these areas takes place in a context of artistic thought and often expresses or illustrates important themes of human existence or basic human values. However, athletics also can be studied as taking place within a tradition and a history. Moreover, athletic competition can express or illustrate important values such as dedication, excellence, and perseverance in the face of adversity. Brand's case would be stronger, however, if intercollegiate athletes not only participated in sports but also studied their history, social significance, and the ethical dilemmas that arise within them, just as artists may not only perform but also be students of art as well. In other words, Brand's argument would apply most fully when intercollegiate athletes not only participate in sports but also study them within an academic framework just as artists often take courses in, say, the history of music, art, or theater.

In addition, Brand's argument raises the issue of just which skills should be regarded as within the proper domain of a university or college education. If we include not only dance recitals and musical performances but also playing basketball and soccer, what about skillful performance in activities ranging from poker to cooking, to gardening, to playing Monopoly? Must we become so inclusive that no exercise of skill can be left out of the umbrella of the academic? Moreover, should we view those exercises of skill that do seem to be closely related to the academic enterprise, possibly including athletics, to be offered for academic credit or should they be viewed as adjuncts that reinforce a more traditional academic education but which, as Elaine of "Seinfeld" might express it, are not "credit worthy."

In fact, we might distinguish between a strong and weak version of Brand's thesis. According to the strong version, participation in intercollegiate athletics is credit worthy, at least if performances in the arts also are credit worthy. According to the weaker thesis, participation in intercollegiate athletics, while not credit worthy, is not merely extracurricular either. Rather, it ought to be seen as more closely related to performances that are recognized as academic, and thus as an important adjunct to the academic program.

Brand's argument does suggest that doubt is warranted about where the line should be drawn between the academic and the extra-curricular. The case for the weak version in particular is worth considering and may be reinforced by considerations I advance in the next section of this paper. While those who believe athletics falls on the non-academic side of the line would probably still maintain that it lacks the intellectual content and association with traditions of high art that are the hallmarks of the truly academic, it may be quite difficult, as we have seen, to articulate these notions in a way that clearly and effectively undermines Brand's approach.

Rather than pursue these points here, I want to explore the question of whether intercollegiate athletics might have educational value from another angle, by focusing not on the skills exercised in performance but on what might be called the cognitive virtues presupposed by the pursuit of excellence in athletics.

Athletics and Cognitive and Moral Virtues—An Assessment

To begin this section, I want to describe a theory or model of competitive sport, one I and others have defended elsewhere, that I believe will prove highly relevant to our inquiry into the relation of academics and athletics.[10] This theory, which might be called sport as a mutual quest for excellence through competition, not only helps to explain why so many in fact find competitive sport so fascinating but also provides an ethically defensible account of it as well.

According to an important analysis of the nature of sports by the philosopher Bernard Suits, sports are a sub-class of games.[11] Games, in turn, are defined by rules but the rules have an unusual feature. The constitutive rules of games create obstacles to achieving the primary task of the game that to an outsider may seem unnecessary. In one of Suits's examples, a bystander can't understand, if a person to whom he is talking wants to get from point A to point B as quickly as possible, why he doesn't drive there. However, the person in question is a runner in a marathon and must conform to the rules of the race, including starting at a certain time and running the course rather than taking short cuts or using alternate forms of transportation. Similarly, the rules of checkers create obvious obstacles to removing the opponent's pieces from the board; for example, they prohibit simply knocking them to the floor. Games, Suits suggests, are activities that involve overcoming unnecessary obstacles created by the constitutive rules. His suggests that games, including all or most sports, are fascinating and interesting because they involve the participants testing themselves against these artificial but challenging barriers to success. More specifically, in competitive sport, the participants challenge themselves to meet the test created by the rules, overcoming the special obstacles that are sport-specific, including the moves and strategies of the opponents.

Of course, it is debatable whether Suits's analysis, as he more fully develops it, provides necessary and sufficient conditions for an activity being a game.[12] Rather than pursue that issue, let me turn to how this account, which only has been sketched here, might apply to our inquiry.

First, but not most important for our purposes, this account explains a good deal of what makes competitive sport so fascinating for participants and spectators alike. It is interesting to try to meet challenges that are well designed to bring out the best in us, and also interesting to see others attempt to do so. Over the course of a full season, or athletic career, a narrative is generated with high and low spots, chances for improvement, failures, and successes. Tiger Woods' lifetime quest to surpass Jack Nicklaus's record for the most number of major championships in golf is one such story. So is the story of the basketball team that starts its season with a string of losses but is able to turn things around to win the rest of its games, as is the story of the talented team picked as the best before the season but which loses many of its games, even to inferior opponents, due to the inability of its members to overcome differences and work together. Failures, and what can be learned from them, are just as much part of such narratives as are successes. Even if the participants on the team that loses because of lack of cooperation do not learn from their experience, observers may draw accurate conclusions about the need to overcome differences in pursuing common goals. Clearly, these conclusions can be important outside as well as inside the world of competitive athletics.

Second, as the last example suggests, athletic contests also have a normative structure. This structure has several levels. One is the level of identification and cultivation of personal virtues that lead to success in meeting the challenges of one's sport. These can include the familiar ones of dedication and commitment but also might involve honesty about one's abilities and those of opponents, willingness to accept criticism and to strive to overcome weaknesses, and respect for the challenges set by the constitutive rules of the contest. What is not always noted, however, is that in the good athletic performance, such values are also expressed and revealed to a wider audience; for example, the audience may appreciate the virtues exhibited by skilled athletes and even hope to emulate them in their own lives. Finally, such norms may provide grounds for criticism, as when athletes do not show respect for the deepest values of their sport or when they avoid playing worthy opponents simply to rack up win after win against deliberately chosen inferior opponents.

Athletes often are called upon to make moral choices concerning fairness, sportsmanship, and respect for the values implicit in the traditions and structure of their sport. Indeed, the model of the athletic contest as a mutual quest for excellence suggests that opponents not be regarded as mere things, obstacles standing in the way of one's own victory, but as facilitators who make the good contest possible. Thus, David Duval, once ranked the number one golfer in the world, expressed this attitude, and showed respect for his sport, when he remarked about competing with Tiger Woods that "If I come head-to-head against him at, say, the U. S. Open, I want him to be playing as good as he can play because I want to beat him when he's playing his best. It would be a heck of a lot better, if you know he gave you all he's got, and you beat him."[13]

Indeed, such a view of the athletic contest shows why winning is a significant but nevertheless imperfect indicator of athletic success. A winning record is a sign of excellence at meeting the challenge of a sport only if attained (at least for the most part) against worthy opponents. Right now, I happen to be the best basketball player on my block, which considering my age and declining skills might be thought surprising. Of course, the next best player is four years old and cannot shoot the ball high enough to reach the basket. My string of victories against her, unfortunately lacks all significance, since the element of challenge is missing.

In fact, as several commentators have argued, athletic competition has many parallels with dialogue in critical inquiry.[14] In sports, each opponent reacts to the choices and skills of the other, tries to anticipate and respond to strategies, and over time to overcome weaknesses so as to mount a better challenge in the future. Similarly, in critical inquiry, we respond to the challenges of intellectual critics, try to anticipate their strategies, and consider how best to overcome weaknesses in our own position. In each case, we can learn a great deal about ourselves and others through subjecting ourselves to intellectual and to sporting challenges, so both can contribute to the process of self-examination and intellectual and moral growth. And just as Duval wants to beat Woods when Tiger is playing at his best, participants in critical dialogue should want to address the strongest version of alternate positions rather than formulations made of straw.

Of course, we need to be careful about reducing competitive sport to an alternate form of inquiry or assigning it a monolithic function or goal. Competitive sports can be played or observed purely as a form of amusement or entertainment, or pursued for reasons of health, friendship, or engaged in to achieve external rewards like fame and fortune with little regard for the internal values of the practice. However, it also is important to note that these other functions or goals often are parasitic on the idea of pursuing excellence through challenge. Thus, if we were only interested in health, we could simply exercise and not play sports competitively or even watch them. Moreover, much of what sports audiences find entertaining about sport is precisely the pursuit of excellence in the face of challenge.

What all this suggests is that competitive athletics can and often does have a relationship of mutual reinforcement of academics in intercollegiate contexts. This is most likely to actually occur and probably can best be fostered in the atmosphere of Division III of the NCAA, and in Division I conferences such as the Ivy League which at least make attempts to integrate athletics and academics (although even they may improve their effort in these areas), but perhaps with some modifications can apply to other areas of intercollegiate athletics as well.

In particular, if many of the values involved in intercollegiate athletics, conceived of along the lines of the mutual quest for excellence, have parallels in intellectual inquiry, emphasis on commonality of virtues necessary for success in one area can help promote development in the other. Of course, the nature of any causal link surely is complex and highly dependent on contextual factors. For example, it is likely to be stronger the more attempts are made to integrate athletics and academics and weaker the greater the emphasis on generation of revenue for the institution and competitive success at the most elite levels of intercollegiate sport. Now, some skepticism about causal links between development of athletic and academic virtues may be warranted in some contexts. However, general skepticism about whether development of cognitive and moral virtues in sports sometimes reinforce parallel virtues in academic endeavors may have little more pre-analytic plausibility than general doubt about whether promotion of critical attitudes in philosophy classes can promote critical attitudes elsewhere, say in considering speeches by politicians.

Moreover, even if the causal thesis is problematic across the board, the thesis of mutual reinforcement, as we have seen, has non-causal as well as causal interpretations. For one thing, the exhibition of such values in actual contests may illustrate, express and reveal values common to athletics and academics to a wider audience. Thus, a team in which players work together to improve after honestly analyzing team weaknesses can illustrate how critical analysis of one's skills, coupled with the desire to improve and a plan to do so, can lead to improvement.

In addition, cognitive and moral virtues critical to success in the mutual quest for excellence may function as standards that can be used to critically appraise behavior both within and outside of athletics. Thus, a professor can say to a student, "if the basketball team can keep trying to overcome its weaknesses in spite of repeated failures, you can keep trying to overcome your writing deficiencies as well." Or a professor can say to a student athlete, "in effect I'm your coach in this course and if your coach in athletics expects you to pay attention when you are told where and how to improve, I expect the same." Similarly, student-athletes can say to professors who may have negative stereotypes about them something like, "Look, I've worked hard to overcome obstacles in my athletic career and you shouldn't just dismiss my ability to improve in this course just because you assume football players aren't good students."

All this suggests that it is a mistake to regard academics and intercollegiate athletics as totally independent practices that most often must be in conflict. Rather, when properly conducted, these practices can be mutually reinforcing. While some conflicts may be unavoidable, e.g., traveling to a contest may take up time that can be used to prepare for an examination or may result in a missed class, there may be gains for both endeavors by emphasizing the parallel values that lead to success in each.

Three Criticisms

In this section, I will assess three critical reactions to the thesis that academics and athletics can and should be mutually reinforcing. The first criticism is that the point is trivial. The second, which is partly empirical in character, maintains that intercollegiate sport as actually practiced does not reinforce academic or moral values, and, baring drastic reform, is unlikely to do so. On one version of this criticism, critics express skepticism about whether values learned in sport are always good ones and, even if they are, about whether they transfer to other spheres of activity, such as academics. The third argues that whatever virtues athletes exhibit as individuals, a kind of culture of athletics harms the academic atmosphere at our most selective colleges and universities.

Triviality

Is the claim that competitors in athletics need to develop various intellectual and moral virtues, such as dedication, a reflectively critical attitude towards their performance and those of others, and respect for fellow competitors as facilitators, trivial? Is the corollary thesis that athletic competition often expresses and reveals such qualities to a wider audience also lacking in significance?

Critics argue that virtually any practice requires the same or similar sorts of virtues for successful performance. In fact, the same may be true at least in part of immoral practices! Imagine an association of pick-pockets who critique each other's performances and strive to get better and better at their nefarious activities. They too may need to be dedicated, honest about their strengths and weaknesses, and attempt to learn and grow in skill as a result of failures.

Moreover, many if not all of the virtues associated with athletics also are needed for academic success as well. Accordingly, athletics hardly are unique in involving the kinds of virtues specified since those are traits necessary for success in a wide variety of practices. Even more important for the present inquiry, they are already involved in the exercise of various academic enterprises. Accordingly, critics conclude, intercollegiate athletics are at best redundant in an academic setting and fill no special educational role within the university.

The critics surely are right on one point; namely, that any claim for the uniqueness of athletics with respect to intellectual and moral growth fails.[15] However, the case that athletics and academics are not only compatible but also can be and sometimes are mutually reinforcing does not presuppose any claim about uniqueness. Indeed, since the argument in part is that the character traits necessary for success in athletics are identical with or at least similar to those necessary for success in academics and scholarship itself is a rejection of the uniqueness thesis.

Moreover, the worry about immoral activities, illustrated by the example of the association of pick-pockets, also is misguided. Of course, it is true that almost any virtue can be misused; a murderer may show courage in risking capture, an honest person may tell the truth in a cruel or callous manner, and evildoers can be dedicated and committed in pursuing a misguided cause. But, in fact, such examples do not show that traits such as courage, honesty, and dedication are not virtues. Rather, they suggest that whether or not they are exercised properly depends on context; on what other principles, virtues or goals are involved in their exercise. When athletic competition is carried out as a voluntary activity, the primary purpose of which is to test oneself against challenge, with due regard to the status of fellow competitors as persons facilitating the challenge, it is carried out within moral boundaries requiring fairness and mutual respect. Thus, it surely is unlike stealing (the case of the pick-pockets); stealing is non-consensual and does not require respect for the "marks" as persons in their own right.

Moreover, while the uniqueness thesis must be discarded, there is a case that intercollegiate sport can (and, again, often does) play a special role in illustrating and expressing important values within an academic community. Thus, intercollegiate athletics is a public practice visible to an audience, sometimes a wide audience, extending well beyond the participants. Moreover, in our culture at least, there is widespread understanding of athletic competition and in the case of popular sports, (and unlike, say, nuclear physics, mathematics, or analytic philosophy) sophisticated understanding of their nuances on the part of wide audiences. Thus, intercollegiate sports are ideally placed to illustrate the values and principles that are required by the pursuit of excellence in meeting challenges. Indeed, as suggested earlier, contests (or even seasons of competition and perhaps athletic careers) are unscripted narratives so the story of successes and failures in meeting the challenges of the sport are visible for all to see.

Thus, while the critic of our argument is quite right to point out that athletics are not unique in presupposing certain values required for success, they still occupy a special place due to the moral framework in which they take place, their public role, and their widespread accessibility to audiences that go well beyond the participants actually involved. The triviality criticism, then, does not undermine the thesis that many of the values implicit in properly conducted intercollegiate athletic competition parallel and may reinforce those involved in academic enterprises.

Perhaps triviality creeps in through another route. Some writers do not deny that college athletes often possess some special virtues, such as a capacity for working with others as a team, but deny that such virtues arise from participation in college sports. Rather than sports promoting the development of such virtues, prior possession of those virtues is necessary for success at sports. For example, does participation in athletics promote teamwork or do those who already are team players tend to succeed in sports?[16]

However, we need to be careful of a double standard here when we dismiss claims about the less tangible educational benefits of participation in athletics as myths, but on the other hand accept the equally intangible benefits of a liberal arts education as unquestioned givens. For example, isn't it also plausible to use the pre-selection argument to dismiss the value of education at more selective colleges and universities? One can argue that their graduates do well only because these colleges and universities admit those already most likely to succeed in the first place. However, such a conjecture does not show that the model of self-selection applies fully either in academics or athletics; it remains plausible to think the causal arrow goes both ways. That is, both college athletes and many students at large are recruited/accepted because they already possess certain abilities valued by coaches and faculty, but surely coaches and faculty help enhance these abilities and sometimes help their charges to develop new ones as well.

In any case, the pre-selection and triviality arguments at best address only the causal versions of the thesis of mutual support. Even though I think they are open to question even at the causal level, they do not undermine either the claim that key values presupposed by the mutual quest for excellence in athletics can express, reveal, and reinforce the importance of similar values in academic inquiry, and can also serve as a basis for criticism of unworthy performances in both areas as well.

Ideals vs. Reality

A proponent of the second criticism might begin by noting my frequent use of qualifiers such as "in proper balance" and "properly conducted." According to this criticism, the idea of athletic competition as "a mutual quest for excellence through challenge" is a fine ideal and if actually applied just might justify the mutual reinforcement thesis. However, the criticism proceeds, this model has little to do with reality.

In fact, this criticism takes several forms. According to one, the actual practice of competitive sports, including intercollegiate athletics, does not teach or express the kind of positive values suggested. Peter French has presented several versions of this argument. According to one version, dominance by college coaches tends to produce athletes who do not think for themselves but who learn simply to obey commands of their coaches and follow strategies the coaches lay down in advance. French cites intercollegiate football as an example of a sport "where every play and virtually every move of every player is directed by the head coach and a vast array of assistant coaches for every aspect of the game. Players, at best, are learning to follow orders and, I suspect, the consequences of not doing so."[17] In other words, in the actual world of intercollegiate athletics players are trained to suppress critical or strategic thinking rather than engage in it.[18]

At best, this portrait of the role of the coach surely is overdrawn.[19] Although some coaches may fit French's account, he provides little if any support for the claim that "very few" take seriously their role as moral model. His description of coaching may seem to fit football best but even here questions can be raised. French sees coaches as replacing the players' autonomy by taking over the game and calling all the plays but football involves constant decisions by players even in the most controlled offense. Football coaches with whom I have talked, including two who have coached extensively at the Division I level, all mention the ability to make good decisions under pressure as among the most important assets a player can have.[20] While the issue is to some degree empirical, many coaches may have very different styles of teaching, even in football, and practices may vary as well between the athletically elite football institutions and say, small liberal arts colleges in Division III of the NCAA.

If the picture of the coach presented by French is questionable when applied to football, it can be made to fit other sports only with even greater difficulty. Individual sports such as tennis, golf, and squash require constant decision making by the player, as I believe French himself would acknowledge. Basketball, although a team sport, requires players to recognize defenses, see and quickly exploit weaknesses in the play of opponents, and make the best responses appropriate to specific game situations. Similar points can be made about other team sports such as soccer, softball, and baseball. Surely, one of the most important and satisfying tasks of the coach in such sports is to teach players how to think about the strategy of the game and to make appropriate decisions given the context in the athletic contest.

Thus, I doubt that any sharp contrast between the supposedly authoritarian coach and the autonomy minded faculty will stand critical scrutiny. Faculty use their authority to select texts, pick subjects for discussion, and organize their courses often without student input but are not thereby regarded as authoritarian. Some faculty, a small minority I hope, are sarcastic and sometimes demeaning to students and advisees. While coaches may sometimes yell or get angry at players, this often may be because they want the player to develop his or her potential to the fullest. While more extreme examples of such behavior should not be tolerated, many faculty may demonstrate the opposite vice of simply accepting mediocre work from some students. "It's not my job to motivate," I've heard a professor say, or "If my students are satisfied with a B-, I'm not happy but I can't force them to work." Perhaps a more demanding attitude by such faculty, more like that of coaches, would be better than the passive acceptance of mediocre academic work by students.

French also raises a second version of the objection that in actuality, college athletes do not internalize the kinds of values in sport that might reinforce similar or parallel values in academics. As he points out, this objection can take two forms. The first version acknowledges that athletes might internalize positive values through their participation in athletics but denies these transfer to behavior off the playing field. The second goes further by denying that athletes generally develop morally as a result of their participation in athletics and suggests that in fact sport hinders moral development or promotes moral regression. Thus, French cites the work of a number of social scientists on the effect of sport on moral development and cites, for example, the work of Jennifer Beller and Sharon Stoll who claim as a result of their empirical research that

> Non-athletes use a significantly more principled and less calloused approach to addressing moral issues both in the sports arena and in societal contexts . . . Forty years of research, conducted by more than 20 researchers studying tens of thousands of athletes and non-athletes from youth, high schools, collegiate and Olympic levels, simply does not support the notion of sport as a character-building activity, particularly as it applies to sportsmanship behaviors and moral reasoning ability.[21]

French himself expresses some sympathy for the idea that "there are certain morally good virtues and values in sports participation" but doubts whether they transfer to the behavior of athletes once they leave the playing field. Others offer more extreme claims, such as Peter Heinegg, who maintains that the actual "virtues" of athletic competition are the "perpetual masculine wish: a state of total war without death or serious injury."[22]

However, while it certainly seems plausible to think that under some actual conditions, participation in athletics can encourage bad behavior, it is doubtful whether the empirical research justifies broad conclusions about the role of sport and moral development. Surly, a great deal depends upon the way sports are approached, taught, and practiced.

Before turning to such issues, however, it is important to distinguish the thesis of this paper from the bald assertion that participation in sport, including intercollegiate athletics, builds desirable moral character. The latter is in part an empirical assertion about sport as a form of moral education. However, the mutual reinforcement thesis (the thesis that academic and athletic values are or can be mutually reinforcing) is more than a causal thesis about the effects of intercollegiate athletics on participants. In addition, we have seen that it can function critically as when appeal to the values or normative parallels of academics and athletics can serve as a basis for criticism of actual practice in each area. It also can function educationally as when values expressed in a contest suggest their worth in other areas including academics.

Having said that, the empirical research on the relationship of participation on athletics and moral development is of philosophical interest because of its relationship to normative issues of theoretical and practical concern. Much of that research is based on scoring (or evaluation) of responses of athletes and non-athletes to various moral problems, including issues arising in sport. While that literature is too extensive to be surveyed here, I can suggest that its methodology raises a number of contentious philosophical issues.

For example, might the researcher's own theory of what is ethical influence findings, sometimes in ways that might be controversial? For example, much of Stoll and Beller's findings are based on responses to questions on the Hahm-Beller Values Choice Inventory (HBVCI). The HBVCI poses moral questions to the respondents and assesses the responses. But consider the following sample question from the website of the Center for Ethics at the University of Idaho, where Beller and Stoll conduct their research.

> Certain basketball teams are coached to run plays that cause the opponents to foul. Players and coaches believe this is a clever strategy because the opponents may foul out of the game, giving their team an advantage. Because the coach orders this type of play, the players should follow his directions.[23]

However, just which response to this question is ethically justified is quite controversial. For example, it might be argued that the strategy is unethical or at least morally questionable since we should want to play against the best our opponents have to offer, as Duval suggests in the comment cited earlier about Tiger Woods. Clearly, according to this view, we are not playing against opponents at their best if their star has fouled out of the game. However, according to what I suggest is a more plausible view, strategic skills, such as knowing how to play intelligently, are part of the test constituted by a sport. In a sport such as basketball or soccer, strategic skills including knowing how to avoid fouling on defense are among the skills tested by the sport. These skills have a legitimate role in the game and help define what counts as meeting the test or challenge of the contest. On the latter view, the coaches' decision is just good strategy, much as in baseball when the manager sends in a left handed pitcher to face the opposition's best left handed batter rather than sticking with his right handed ace hurler in a tight situation.

In other words, just what counts as bad sportspersonship in meeting the test of excellence can itself be morally controversial, and athletes who sometimes give what is considered the morally less mature or sensitive answer may have a plausible moral argument supporting their conclusion, even if they do not always articulate it well.[24] Beller and Stoll are judicious scholars who are not hostile to the idea of athletic competition, and I take their views quite seriously. Nevertheless, it is arguable that the evaluation of responses to questions may include contestable moral assumptions that influence the scoring. Of course, consideration of just one example is not enough to support such a point but perhaps does raise an issue of concern that warrants further investigation and discussion.

Following suggestions of Kohlberg, researchers on moral development might reply that they do not assess the moral correctness of the answers (substance) but only the sophistication and maturity of the moral reasoning used to justify them (form). However, whether this can be done without begging important moral questions, and even whether the substance-form distinction is viable, is sure to be philosophically controversial. To give one example, whether teamwork is regarded as an important virtue may vary according to whether one is sympathetic to communitarian theory or whether one places more emphasis on the values emphasized by liberal political theory such as fairness, truthfulness, and individual rights. Of course, just because the investigators make normative judgments does not mean their findings are subjective or unscientific, but if the judgments are philosophically and morally controversial, the findings of the studies become debatable as well.

Related questions can be raised about some of the arguments of David Shields and Brenda Jo Bredemeier, who have conducted some of the most important and well thought out studies of the effects of athletics on moral development. Shields and Bredemeier are quite careful about what conclusions they draw from their data, recognize complexity in what that data indicates, and have shifted their own account of morality from a Kohlbergian perspective to a broader viewpoint that tries to accommodate some of the insights of other approaches. However, much of their work also may rest on philosophically controversial assumptions or presuppositions.

For example, in their book, *Character Development and Physical Activity*, Shields and Bredemeier investigate aggression in athletics. They are careful to theoretically distinguish aggressive behavior, in the sense of action intended to harm or injure, from assertive or hard play, that while it may involve physical contact involves no intent to harm.[25] However, as Robert Fullinwider has pointed out elsewhere, it is unclear that they always adhere to this distinction, as when they claim that male athletes tend to express and accept more aggression than females.[26] Does this mean male athletes actually intend to harm their opponents more frequently than females or rather that they are more accepting of hard body contact as permitted by the rules of the sport? (Indeed, even if an athlete goes beyond the rules in initiating hard contact and even cheats in order to win, that would not be "aggression" in the narrow sense of the term specified by Bredemeier and Shields unless there was actual intent to harm or injure, rather than merely gain a competitive advantage.)

If what counts as aggression can be complex and even controversial in many contexts, so too is the identification of moral maturity. Bredemeier and Shields recently have characterized moral maturity as involving balancing of common and mutual interests, in which each party considers the values and points of view of the others, in trying to reach harmony of or at least compromise of interests.[27] But here, as Fullinwider also has pointed out, we need to be careful about the level at which such reconciliation or harmonization takes place; that of each individual action or at the level of acceptance of the practice or activity within which the acts take place.[28] Thus, a hard tackle in football may not equally advance the interest of all the players but may be acceptable morally if all players have freely entered the game of football with the knowledge that hard tackles are part of the game.

Bredemeier and Shields sometimes characterize the moral regression of athletes as a retreat from the perspective of dialogue and equal respect for competing interests to some form of egocentric reasoning. But that athletes want to win and think of their own team first does not show their perspective is necessarily egocentric; rather they may consider themselves part of a mutually acceptable quest for excellence in which all parties voluntarily try their best so as to constitute a challenge to the other. The terms of the sporting social contract dictate trying to win within the rules and principles of good sport. The voluntary acceptance of such a goal indicates not egoism or narrowness of perspective, but conformity to norms that are mutually acceptable to reasonable participants.

In all fairness, note that Bredemeier and Shields recognize the complexity of the issues they discuss. In one recent article, while they report that comparing a sample of college basketball players to non-athletes, the moral reasoning of the non-athletes was significantly more mature than was that of the athletes, they also point out, as have Stoll and Beller, that the moral reasoning of females about sport was more mature than that of males.[29] To complicate things still further when intercollegiate swimmers were added to the study, the moral maturity of swimmers and non-athletes did not differ.

Accordingly, the moral maturity of athletes, as they understand it, may differ according to all sorts of variables, including gender, whether sports are individual or team oriented, and perhaps the philosophy of the coach and institution, and perhaps even the divisional level of the NCAA in which the sport is played.

Indeed, Bredemeier and Shields conclude, sensibly in my view, that "generalizations about sport involvement and moral character" are not warranted and, in another venue, that "The influence that sport has for its participants depends on a complex set of factors tied to the specific sport, and the social interactions that are present."[30] Indeed, as suggested by the work of Stoll and Beller, interventions can make a difference. How well academic institutions integrate athletics and academics may have a significant effect on the educational and social benefits athletes derive from their experience in intercollegiate athletics.

Finally, remember that intercollegiate sports as actually practiced may sometimes violate the ethic of good sports, just as some academic practices may violate academic ethics. Thus, the claim that critical academic inquiry should be open to evidence on different sides of issues and that one's critics should not be prevented from raising good criticisms is not falsified by the existence of some closed-minded or highly partisan professors who stifle dissent. Similarly, the claim that athletics as a mutual quest for excellence requires meeting the challenges of worthy opponents playing at their best is not undermined by coaches or players who try to win by illegitimately avoiding the challenge, for example, by attempting intentionally to injure the opponent's best player. Moreover, just as academic inquiry practiced well may produce critical students committed to reasoned inquiry, intercollegiate athletics when practiced well may play a significant role in promoting individuals committed to fair play, to respecting challenge, and to valuing competitors as fellow practitioners. Perhaps even more important, they may illustrate or exhibit such values and provide standards of criticism when actual practice merits it.

Academic Underperformance and the Culture of Athletics [31]

A different set of concerns about the relationship between academics and athletics are raised by James L. Shulman and William G. Bowen in *The Game of Life* and are developed in a subsequent study, *Reclaiming the Game*. Shulman, the Financial and Administrative Officer at the Andrew W. Mellon Foundation, and Bowen, current President of the Mellon Foundation and a former President of Princeton, tell us that intercollegiate athletics, even at the level of the Ivy League and the small highly selective co-ed liberal arts colleges, may be as pernicious in its own way as at the scandal prone athletically elite Division I sports powers. Because the smaller more academically selective schools tend to offer more intercollegiate sports than others, athletes constitute a high percentage of their student body, as much as 30% to 35%. In the late 1950s, athletes at the schools studied by Shulman and Bowen performed well academically, often better than their peers. This, they maintain, is no longer the case. Rather, they suggest that if athletes are given too great an admissions advantage and if they perform much worse academically than their classmates, they can drag down the academic atmosphere of the whole institution.

Shulman and Bowen draw upon an extensive database involving cohorts of graduates from the institutions they study from the years 1951, 1976, 1989 and some recent but less complete studies from the 1990s. These institutions include academically respected Division I universities such as Duke and Penn State, the Ivy League schools, selective women's colleges such as Smith, and small co-ed selective liberal arts colleges such as Williams, Swarthmore, Denison, and my own institution, Hamilton.[32]

While the highly selective schools studied may not be typical of the majority of institutions of higher education, these schools have an importance larger than their numbers would indicate. Not only are they widely regarded as academic standard bearers, but they also appear to have resisted the temptations inherent in major intercollegiate sports. Many observers will conclude that if intercollegiate sports are harmful even in such a context, there is no place in higher education where they can be a positive educational and ethical influence. If athletics and academics are not mutually reinforcing in such contexts, can they reasonably be expected to be mutually reinforcing anywhere?

The argument of *The Game of Life* largely is quantitative. Its tone is not polemical, and the questions raised are important ones that academic institutions would do well to examine seriously. The picture of intercollegiate athletics it presents is depressing, and calls into question the assumptions of even those of us who think athletics often plays a positive role at the type of institutions covered in the study.

Nevertheless, the argument of the book, while serious and clearly presented, is open to question at a number of key points. I will comment only briefly on the statistical argument here, except to raise some very brief questions for further consideration. However, I will raise critical points about the principal explanation Bowen and Shulman provide for the alleged weak academic performance of athletes, and indicate the relevance of these points to the case for mutual reinforcement.

The core of *The Game of Life* is the statistical argument demonstrating increasingly worse academic performance by student athletes at the institutions studied. My own evaluation of this statistical argument is that it does raise cause for concern but that it is not conclusive or decisive. This is as much for what it leaves out as for what it contains. For example, although *The Game of Life* maintains that the credentials for admission of accepted student athletes are lower than for students at large, it does not offer any extensive analysis of who might have been admitted if the recruited athletes had not been accepted. If an academically border-line quarterback is admitted instead of an academic superstar, that is one thing but if the quarterback replaces another applicant with somewhat higher SATs or GPA, that is quite another thing. The second sort of candidate might not have done that much better than the quarterback anyway.

In *Reclaiming the Game*, it is argued that the difference between admitted recruited athletes and rejected applicants will not infrequently be substantial, especially at the most selective institutions. Indeed, this would not be surprising since the qualifications for admission at such schools already are exceptionally stringent. Note, however, that admitted recruited athletes at such schools also are likely to be very highly qualified, that those rejected as a result of preference given to athletes presumably are not as strong candidates as more successful applicants, and that differences may not be as great in institutions that give preference to athletes but are not quite as highly selective as the very top tier institutions.[33]

The Game of Life also does not consider in depth whether outstanding students (athletes and non-athletes alike) might be attracted to an institution because of its athletic program. In order to get a true picture of the effect of athletics on academics, don't we need to count the excellent students who would not have attended an institution if not for athletics as well as weaker students admitted primarily because of their athletic abilities? This was brought home to me in a seminar a few years ago when, after I had described the thesis of *The Game of Life*, a female three-sport athlete and absolutely outstanding student remarked, "I never would have come here if I hadn't been a recruited student athlete."

To raise just one more question, the book also does not consider if many athletes mature academically during their four years at college. Perhaps they start out doing less well than other students but by the time they graduate, the gap may have diminished or vanished. If some athletes arrive on campus with the idea that they are there primarily to play a sport, this attitude may lead to weak performance in class during their first few semesters, and a lower class rank than other students. But perhaps many have grown academically by the time they are juniors and do just as well as others from that point. If so, although they may never quite catch up to their peers in terms of GPA or class rank, they may in fact be performing just as well in the classroom by the time they graduate.

Remember also that according to *The Game of Life*, female athletes perform just as well academically as female students who are not athletes (and in some institutions continue to perform better than others). So the major concern involves male athletes in high visibility sports, which of course are just those sports where the participants are likely to be more diverse socio-economically and perhaps ethnically and racially as well.[34]

Of course, none of these questions is sufficient to undermine the overall thesis of the book, that student athletes in the institutions studied do less well academically than students at large and even do less well than predicted (underperformance) prior to admission. However, they do suggest that the argument is less than complete and may well overstate the effect of the presence of a large proportion of student athletes in the student body.

Although a number of other serious questions can be raised about the statistical argument of the book, perhaps the explanation the authors offer for the weaker performance of student athletes at the schools studied is of greater interest. While Bowen and Shulman cite such cultural trends as early specialization of young athletes, as well as admissions practices that target specialists instead of well-rounded applicants, they attribute much of the fault to what they call a culture of athletics. This culture, while not precisely defined, involves a tendency to socialize mainly with other athletes, pursue certain majors in proportions different from the rest of the student population, accept more conservative values than other students, and be more focused on financial success after college than other students. This culture of athletics has been fostered by early specialization of youngsters into particular sports, recruiting policies by admissions officers that reward such specialization (the search for a well rounded class rather than well rounded individuals), and consequent estrangement of athletes from the academic mission of their institutions.[35]

This explanation is not implausible if presented as partial, but is it likely to be the whole story, or even the most significant part? Before we come to any firm conclusions, don't other possible explanations need to be considered? For example, do faculties that have increasingly become less and less involved with student life exhibit an increasing indifference to or even disdain for the athletic involvement of students? Does this in turn reinforce withdrawal by athletes into their own culture? Shulman and Bowen have found that athletes with faculty mentors outperform other athletes academically but are there institutional obstacles to the development of such a relationship?[36] If so, underperformance by athletes at the institutions studied might be in significant part a result of experiences of indifference or rejection (as well as other institutional factors that might need to be considered) rather than being due largely to lack of academic commitment on their own part.

To their credit, Shulman and Bowen briefly consider the possibility of faculty disdain for athletes or prejudice against athletes as a possible explanation for the relatively poor performance of student athletes but acknowledge they have no way to analyze possible effects statistically. In *Reclaiming the Game*, Bowen and his co-author Sarah A. Levin consider at somewhat more length what they call "stereotype threat." According to Stanford psychologist Claude Steele who originally proposed the idea, "Members of certain minority groups are prone to underperform academically because of an unconscious fear of living up to negative group stereotypes."[37]

Bowen and Levin acknowledge that "stereotyping (of athletes) can be real and it may well take a toll academically" but again acknowledge they have no way of assessing its impact. However, they suggest that it is unlikely to be as significant as for African-American students and that, in any case, instructors often are not able to identify all the athletes in their classes.[38] The first point surely is true but perhaps the second is doubtful. At my institution, and many others like it, coaches instruct their players to alert instructors at the start of the semester about possible absences due to scheduled contests so that no misunderstandings will arise later. So many instructors will know the identity of athletes in their classes, even those in low visibility sports.

However, I myself doubt if very many faculty, whatever their personal feelings, grade athletes unfairly. What may be more likely, however, is that some faculty express a kind of indifference to athletics that may discourage student athletes from coming to them for help at the first sign of academic trouble. For example, a few years ago at a college symposium on athletics, a well meaning colleague said something like the following; "I treat missed classes exactly the same for athletes and for others; if you miss a class because of a game or because you were out drinking the night before, it's one missed class on your attendance record." Although there is a surface appeal to equality here, I can sympathize with student athletes who miss a class with this instructor because of a game and then hesitate to come to this instructor for help about the missed work since they fear or resent being regarded as just like the student who was too drunk to come to class. In any case, it is possible that if enough faculty either exhibit outright disdain for intercollegiate athletics or are indifferent to the situation of athletes, athletes may sense this and may be more reluctant than other students to seek help from those faculty or be less likely to get into a mentoring relationship with them.

However, even if attitudes of some faculty toward athletes have relatively little effect on academic performance, other institutional factors may play as large a role as the culture of athletics. For example practices and games may conflict with review sessions and presentations by visiting lecturers. If instructors schedule office hours at times when practices usually are scheduled, athletes may have fewer opportunities to come for help than other students. In such cases, more thought by the faculty member and better communication with coaches may be helpful. In my experiences at a Division III institution, coaches I have contacted often will either rearrange their practice schedule or excuse a student-athlete from practice if contacted well in advance and the conflicting academic obligation is significant. Finally, there is the amount of time and energy which goes into athletic practices. (Bowen and Shulman point out that other students in time consuming extra-curricular activities, such as staff of college newspapers, tend to perform better than other students academically but do not demonstrate that the time commitment and degree of physical effort involved are comparable.)

All this suggests that even if the culture of athletics does play a role in explaining the academic performance gap between student athletes and other students at the institutions studied, other factors may be at least equally important. If so, attributing the gap largely to the attitudes or practices of the student athletes themselves may be unjustified.

Finally, it is important to note that not all aspects of the culture of athletes, as described by Bowen and Shulman, are negative. Why is it a bad thing if student athletes major disproportionately in some subjects or if they have more conservative values than other students? Indeed, the latter can be viewed as a contribution to intellectual diversity and might well enliven classroom discussion if instructors encouraged more conservative students to defend their positions in class.

The significance of this for the mutual reinforcement of academic and athletics is that if there is a significant gap in academic performance between (male) student athletes and students at large, institutional changes, such as giving more consideration to athletic schedules when posting office hours or holding review sessions, or enhancing communication between coaches and academic faculty may well improve the situation. Stronger forms of intervention, including reforms in athletic scheduling, particularly at athletically elite Division I institutions, as well, might improve things even further.

In any case, the argument of *The Game of Life*, while it does raise significant questions about whether athletics undermines academic values at very selective institutions, is open to question on a number of points and does not seem to me to be decisive. However, the book does raise issues of real concern that do suggest the need for critical reflection on the relationship of athletics and academics, even on the part of those institutions that do not offer athletic scholarships and regard athletics as in some way as adjuvant to what goes on in their classrooms. In view of that, let me conclude with some brief suggestions about how we might better integrate academics and athletics at many colleges and universities and take better advantage of the many parallels (or overlaps) among academic and athletic values that can enhance both enterprises alike.

Suggestions for Reconciliation

The main thesis of this paper has been that the practice of intercollegiate athletics, when properly conducted, presupposes and expresses or illustrates values congruent with and mutually reinforcing of many of the values involved in academic inquiry and study, properly conducted. This thesis has conceptual, justificatory, and causal interpretations. As we have seen, three kinds of objections to the thesis, that it is trivial, too ideal to apply to reality, and that it ignores the role of the culture of athletics in undermining academic values, have been considered and found to be at best inconclusive. Indeed, the third objection and versions of the second apply most strongly to the causal interpretation thesis and perhaps not at all to the others.

However, the causal thesis is important since actual practice is what most directly effects human lives. Given that the practice of intercollegiate sports is not going to vanish, and that it does promote important values ranging from entertainment to illustration of values such as teamwork and dedication, we should want to promote the integration of mutual reinforcement of academics and athletics.

The extent to which such integration and reinforcement presently exists surely differs from division to division of the NCAA, from conference to conference, and probably from institution to institution within conferences. In the case of athletically elite Division I universities, where athletics in high visibility sports serve the function of providing entertainment cited by French, the primary responsibility of educators and athletic administrators is to ensure that athletes on athletic scholarships have a reasonable opportunity to receive a solid education. Recent reforms instituted by the NCAA, including tying an institution's ability to give out athletic scholarships to graduation rates of athletes, are important steps in the right direction. I myself would like to see stronger restrictions on national travel and class time missed during seasons, as well as other reforms. However, I also think that athletics at this level provides many benefits to large communities and can be conducted in a way that is at least minimally compatible with academic values. However, it is true that men's basketball and football in particular raise significant problems at many athletically elite Division I schools and raise the greatest difficulties for mutual reinforcement at such institutions.

More, of course, can be expected of institutions that compete at a less elite level, especially those that explicitly view athletics as of educational value. Many such institutions in my experience are successful, although to varying degrees, in integrating their athletic and academic programs.

Let me briefly suggest some approaches that may help in such a process and that might apply not only to smaller colleges and conferences like the Ivy League but to a broader range of institutions, including large universities whose teams consistently vie for Division I national championships.

One is to more explicitly examine issues about athletics within the normal curriculum, or to provide special extra-curricular programs for athletes that discuss the ethical and educational issues that may arise with respect to intercollegiate athletics. For example, athletes, as well as students at large, might be encouraged to enroll in courses that discuss ethical, psychological, and sociological issues that arise within sports. Sports, including intercollegiate athletics, are prominent features of our culture, and should be subjected to critical scrutiny just as are medicine, law, and business. If courses are not available, informal discussion groups for athletes, sometimes including coaches, moderated by parties independent of departments of athletics, can discuss ethical issues in sports, such as how far to go in the pursuit of victory, coaching philosophies, and the values that should be promoted in intercollegiate athletics. Of course, it is important that such formal occasions be centers of genuine reasoned inquiry, rather than designed to instill a favored philosophy of athletics, and different points of view should be presented and engaged.[39]

Less formally, avenues for contact between faculty and coaches should be developed and utilized. I can attest that even in small institutions, misunderstandings and misperceptions of coaches by faculty and vice versa develop simply because of lack of contact. Miscommunication, and sometimes unfair stereotyping by one group or the other, can hardly be good for student athletes who sometimes get caught in the middle. Good communications and personal relationships can go a long way towards alleviating problems. Moreover mutual understanding of the problems facing both coaches and faculty can often lead to compromise, as when a scheduled contest conflicts with an examination or review session.

Moreover, if one accepts something like the idea of athletics as a mutual quest for excellence through challenge, more emphasis needs to be placed on the role of coach as educator. After all, on that account of athletic competition, the coach is teaching student athletes how to meet certain kinds of challenges and helping them to learn from both their successes and failures. While winning surely is important, and often signifies success at meeting the challenge of a sport, it is not everything and not always within the control of the coach. Coaches should be evaluated, then, on more than their record of wins and losses (although that record should not be ignored either). Perhaps one way of doing this is including faculty on committees that make recommendations on the reappointment of coaches, something already done at many institutions.

Finally, setting reasonable limits on the time that participants must devote to athletics is crucial. In particular, participants in many sports, even at the Division III level, are encouraged to participate during the off-season in such activities as strength training, summer camps, and unofficial scrimmages among players. I myself do not think all of this is wrong or undesirable; competitive athletes want to train hard to improve in the off-season. The trick is to reconcile the understandable and even admirable desire of the athletes to improve and be ready for next season with the demands of a rigorous academic schedule, all without unduly limiting the freedom of athletes to make their own choices about priorities.

Of course, all these issues need much more thorough exploration than can be provided here. Discussion of them may make all of us, participants, spectators and casual observers, better understand the connection between academic and athletics conceived of as a search for excellence through challenge.

Although the many failings of intercollegiate athletics, especially at the level of athletically elite Division I institutions, may have caused many observers to question their worth, I hope our discussion has shown that an important case can be made for the compatibility of and even mutual support of values implicit in academic and athletic practice. Athletics need not be regarded as hostile to academic inquiry but can and I suggest frequently does enhance the educational experience of athletes, express and celebrate important values, and contribute to enrichment of the academic community itself.

Notes

1. James L. Shulman and William G. Bowen, *The Game of Life* (Princeton: Princeton University Press, 2001).
2. A number of philosophers of sport have defended different versions of the idea that academic and athletic values can be mutually reinforcing. For example, see Peter Arnold, *Sport, Ethics, and Education* (London: Cassell, 1997) and Robert L. Simon, *Fair Play: The Ethics of Sport* (Boulder: Westview, 2004) especially Chapter 6. The present paper is an extension and development of some of the points made in that chapter.
3. Peter French, *Ethics and College Sports: Ethics, Sports, and the University* (Lanham, MD: Rowman and Littlefield, 2004), 115.
4. French, *Ethics and College Sports: Ethics, Sports, and the University*, 116.
5. A significant number of studies have raised doubts about whether many (or even any) Division I athletic programs actually generate a profit. For one discussion of this issue, see Chapter 11 of *The Game of Life*. What remains controversial, in my view, is how to correctly estimate both expenditures and income. For example, how should we count enhanced visibility of a university with highly ranked teams and the effects of such visibility, if any, on admission?

6. Myles Brand, "The Role and Value of Intercollegiate Athletics in Universities," *Journal of the Philosophy of Sport*, Vol. XXXIII (2006): 9-20.
7. Brand, "The Role and Value of Intercollegiate Athletics in Universities," 14.
8. Brand, "The Role and Value of Intercollegiate Athletics in Universities," 10.
9. Brand, "The Role and Value of Intercollegiate Athletics in Universities," 11.
10. For elaboration, see Simon, *Fair Play*, Chapters 2 and 3. For a similar view, see Jan Boxill, "The Ethics of Competition," in Jan Bixill, ed. *Sports Ethics: An Anthology* (Malden, MA: Blackwell, 2003), 107-115.
11. Bernard Suits, "The Elements of Sport," in Robert Osterhoud, ed., *The Philosophy of Sport: A Collection of Essays* (Springfield, IL: Charles C. Thomas), 48-64. This essay is widely reprinted, for example in William J. Morgan, ed., *Ethics in Sport* (Champaign, IL: Human Kinetics, 2007) 9-19. Interested readers would do themselves a favor by exploring Suits' brilliant and humorous but not widely known book, *The Grasshopper: Games, Life and Utopia* (Toronto: University of Toronto Press, 1978) reprinted by Broadview Press of Peterborough, Ontario in 2005.
12. Suits' fuller account includes the important element of the lusory attitude, or acceptance of the constraints set by the constitutive rules just to make the game possible. See the references in the previous note for discussion.
13. *The New York Times*, Feb 3, 1999: D4.
14. In particular, see Drew Hyland, *The Question of Play* (Lanham, MD: University Presses of America, 1984): 148-151.
15. J. S. Russell presents an acute case against uniqueness, and also points out some confusions in my own earlier discussions of the question, in his paper "Broad Internalism and the Moral Foundations of Sport" in William J. Morgan, ed., *Ethics in Sport* (Champaign, IL: Human Kinetics, 2007), 51-66.
16. The role of pre-selection is suggested, for example, in *The Game of Life*, 96-97.
17. French, *Ethics and College Sports*, 52.
18. In the remainder of this section, I draw extensively on material developed in my paper "Academics and Athletics: Athletics and Intellectual and Moral Growth," which was presented at the NCAA Convention in Nashville in January 2008. That paper appeared in the new *Journal of Intercollegiate Sports*, Vol. 1 No. 1 (2008): 40-58.
19. Some of the points made below were also developed in my review of French's book in *Theory and Research in Education*, Vol. 4 (2006): 361-369.
20. When I first arrived at Hamilton College as a young instructor in the late 1960s, I heard a story about the then football coach, Don Jones. The Hamilton team was losing at half-time to a physically superior opponent and when Jones walked into the locker room the players asked how they could possibly win the game. Jones replied, "You are supposed to be smart. Figure it out yourselves" and walked out. Hamilton won! While he may not have been the typical football coach, there may be many more like him at the majority of institutions that play college sports than there are coaches who resemble the tyrannical coach cited by French.
21. Sharon K. Stoll and Jennifer M. Beller, "Do Sports Build Character?," *Sports in School: The Future of an Institution* edited by John Gerdy (New York: Columbia University Press, 2000): 18-20 quoted by French in *Ethics and College Sports*, 54.
22. Peter Heinegg, "Philosopher in the Playground: Notes on the Meaning of Sport" in Jan Boxill, ed., *Sports Ethics* (Malden, MA: Blackwell, 2003) 54, quoted by French, *Ethics and College Sports*, 55.
23. Stoll and Beller discuss the HBVCI and provide sample questions on their website at www.educ.uidaho.edu/center_for_ethics.

24. I do not suggest this is true of every question on the HVBCI but perhaps it is not an isolated instance either. For example, another sample question on their website concerns the responsibility of athletes to call bad calls in their favor by the officials to the attention of officials. Now I agree that in many cases, players should not accept advantages that come from mistakes by officials. Perhaps Colorado's famous "victory" over Missouri in a crucial college football game played in 1990 when officials lost count of the downs and gave Colorado an extra (illegal) down on which to score is a case in point. However, it is not clear to me that when players say that, for the most part, it is the job of officials in refereed sports to make judgment calls, that the players are being morally callous. Just when players should refuse to accept the benefit of a bad call in their favor may well be a complex issue that can not easily be reduced to all or nothing answers. For example, if I think I fouled an opponent during a basketball game and the referee does not call it, is it because the official missed the foul, is it because the referee's interpretation of what counts as a foul is different from mine, is it because the referee thought I gained no advantage from the foul and hence it was trivial, or what? Is it morally callous of me to not say anything and just keep playing or am I respecting the referee's experience and competence by doing so?

25. David Lyle Light Shields and Brenda Jo Bredemeier, *Character Development and Physical Activity* (Champaign, IL: Human Kinetics, 1995), 184. See, for example, Bredemeier and Shields, "Athletic Aggression: An Issue of Contextual Morality," *Sociology of Sport Journal*, 3 (1986) where on p. 22 aggression is defined in terms of intent to injure.

26. Robert Fullinwider, "Sports, Youth and Character: A Critical Survey," Working Paper #44 by CIRCLE (Center for Information and Research on Civic Learning & Engagement), College Park, MD, February 2006. It is in pdf form but hasn't a distinct internet address; the closest link is http://www.civicyouth.org/?page_id=152 which brings up the list of CIRCLE working papers.

27. See, for example, Bredemeier and Shields, "Moral Growth Among Athletes and Nonathletes: A Comparative Analysis," *The Journal of Genetic Psychology*, 147 (2001): 15-16. See Fullinwider, "Sports, Youth and Character," 25-26 for citation of further sources where Bredemeier and Shields express similar views.

28. Fullinwider, "Sports, Youth and Character." See especially 25-27.

29. Bredemeier and Shields, "Moral Growth Among Athletes and Nonathletes: A Comparative Analysis," 7.

30. Bredemeier and Shields, "Moral Growth Among Athletes and Nonathletes: A Comparative Analysis," 15, and Bredemeier and Shields, *Character Development and Physical Activity*, 195.

31. This section draws upon and expands upon my comments in my review of *The Game of Life* in *The Journal of the Philosophy of Sport*, XXIX, (2002): 87-95.

32. The same data base was the basis for another widely discussed book, *The Shape of the River*, in which Bowen and former Harvard President Derek Bok defended affirmative action programs in the colleges and universities they studied.

33. Indeed, a colleague has suggested that preference for athletes at the most highly selective schools may improve the academic quality of the student body at very slightly less selective schools where the candidates rejected by the most selective schools due to preference for athletes may end up.

34. Thus, in the 1989 cohort at co-ed liberal arts colleges, only 59% of the male athletes in high visibility sports had fathers with a bachelors degree compared to 82% of students at large. While the total number of students involved may not be large, these students may have greater difficulty making the initial adjustment to college than those

from more privileged backgrounds, yet also make a small but perhaps significant contribution to the socio-economic and perhaps ethnic and racial diversity of the student body. See *The Game of Life*, 51.

35. Explanations for the academic performance of athletes, including an explanation based on the "culture of athletics," is found in *The Game of Life*, 68-83.

36. See *The Game of Life*, 71-72.

37. See *The Game of Life*, 73-74, and *Reclaiming the Game*, 235.

38. *Reclaiming the Game*, 236 (parentheses are my own).

39. One example of such an existing program is the MAAX Program at the University of Wisconsin. As described by the University, The Madison Academic and Athletic Exchange (MAAX) is a curriculum-based service-learning initiative in civic engagement. It brings first-year University of Wisconsin students, including but not restricted to intercollegiate athletes, together with local high school student-athletes for a collaborative inquiry in a course on the relationship between academic and athletic forms of "practice." I was fortunate enough to speak to these students in the spring of 2007 and was impressed by their engagement and reflection on issues of academics and athletics.

11. How to Duck Out of Teaching

Douglas Stalker

What's new on campus? Duping! It's all the rage with professors who are tired of giving lectures to the drifting youth of America. Duping is, quite simply, not doing. It is avoiding, evading, eluding, abstaining, dodging, and good old ducking. And it is now on display on almost every campus in the United States. Here are eight duping techniques that will work for any professor, tenured or untenured, in the time it takes to erase a moderate-size blackboard:

The Title Trick

Give the students honorary titles to make them feel special—and willing to take on new duties. It is easy to think of titles that sound great. For example, call everyone in class a peer editor. Then you can have the students pair up and take turns going over each other's term papers. Tell the students that you are going to selflessly give up some of your professorial power in order to empower them. When all is said and done, you won't have to raise your red pen even once.

You can also get students to record all the grades and sign the grade roster for you. Have a drawing (that is the democratic way, of course) to see who gets to have the title of peer executive officer for the day. Tell the students that this is an exercise in leadership and management ability. Remember to make a solemn display of handing over the official pen, grade book, and grade roster to the peer executive officer.

The Computer Razzle-Dazzle

If something is done with a computer, it must be educationally great. So set up a computer dupe: a computer-based course in which students have to send e-mail messages to each other a minimum of 10 times per day. To get them going, tell them psychological research has shown that first thoughts are always best thoughts, and that contact with your peers is essential to building and maintaining academic self-esteem. They will spend so much time on e-mail that they won't notice you haven't logged on for days.

You can add a personal touch by sending randomly generated e-mail messages to each student. Any high-school kid who likes computers can set the system up for you. You can easily create the messages by modifying the horoscopes in your daily newspaper. For example, one message might say: "You are doing well but have doubts about future endeavors like reading the next chapter. I know you have what it takes to overcome obstacles! Turn the pages of the textbook for yourself! Take responsibility for sharpening your own pencils! Your last fill-in-the-blank test showed great promise of things to come. Do not be surprised if I repeat this message to reinforce its meaning for you."

The Great Group Dupe

Tell the students that yours is a problem-based course with group learning, and have them divide up into groups. It doesn't matter whether any group actually solves the problems, what the problems are, or even if there are any problems at all. Everyone will be happy about working in a group because they will believe that things are getting done—even if nothing really happens. Like most people who can program a VCR, today's students are perfectly happy to confuse the process with the product.

It might be good to walk among them every few weeks, reminding everyone that the whole is greater than the sum of its parts, to discourage individual effort. You might want to walk around the room saying "Cohesion, think cohesion!" as you do some isometric push-pull exercises with your hands to make the point more vividly.

The Mea-Culpa Escape

Stand in front of your students and confess everything. Tell them that higher education has become an institutionalized fraud because it keeps the students passive, subjects them to lectures, coerces them to take notes, and makes them endure tests. All that is miles away from real, multidimensional learning that lasts a lifetime. You need to pull out all the stops as you wail about the sins of academic America. Draw a circle on the board and keep pointing to it—try pounding your fist on the board—as you mention the cycle of passivity and the economic consequences associated with stunted growth and sheltered lives.

Then, with a selfless gesture toward the exits, send the students out into the world to do experiential projects of their own devising, like running a lawn-care business for the semester. Make sure that they do your lawn on their rounds so that you can turn in some grades, and tell them not to come by too early in the morning. Word that instruction in terms of their being sensitive to the needs of others.

The Tick-tock of Pointless Talk

You have about 2,000 minutes to fill during a 14-week semester. Why not fill them with chitchat? Anyone who watches daytime TV simply loves pointless talk and, sooner or later, comes to believe that it has a point. If you have 2.5 hours of class time to fill per week and a class of 30 students, you have to get each student to speak for only five minutes a week. Following the three principles of chat satisfaction can make that relatively simple task a breeze.

Principle 1 is essential: There is no topic like no particular topic. Your students can have a good chat bouncing from the last episode of *Friends* to anything else they care to discuss—the popularity of sport-utility vehicles, the history of pizza, the price of body piercing, you name it.

Principle 2 follows directly from Principle 1: Sticking to the topic is for dorks. Coherence is irrelevant; indeed, relevance is irrelevant. Mental drift is in fashion, and it is fine to have a remark like "Burping should be a collegiate sport" followed by the statement "Cancún could be the 51st state."

Principle 3 is the basis of cognitive democracy: No one has to know what he or she is talking about. In the true marketplace of ideas, a marginal student can speak at length on everything from Sumerian poetry to soggy French fries.

The Yo-Yo Presentation

Why do professors have to stand in the front of the classroom—like truly alienated workers—trying to explain things? Why do they have to carry the load, day after day? You can redress that injustice with the best role reversal around: class presentations. You go from active to passive; your students go from passive to active.

The best topics, you should emphasize, are those with personal meaning to the presenter. Remind your students, in addition, that information is not learning. That is code for: No time in the library is required. Then just hand the students the formula: what _____ means to me. In class, they can say their talk is titled "A Personal Perspective on _____." Anything can go in the blank—the Yalta conference, the supply curve, Kant's categorical imperative, angular momentum.

Recitations are a dandy variation. They have another benefit: You can dispense with assigned readings because you have students read the books out loud in class. Plays are the paradigms here. You can have someone be Hamlet, someone else be Claudius, and so on. The students stand in front of the room and read their parts out loud to the rest of the class—no need for them to memorize anything beforehand. Other natural subjects for recitations are Plato's dialogues, Blake's poetry, and Faulkner's novels. Heck, it can work with anything that has sentences.

When reading paragraphs gets old, you might want to suggest that your students act out a page or two of text. Suppose, for instance, you are teaching an introductory biology course. Think about the improvisational possibilities inherent in the parts of the cell. Some students can play the cell wall; others can be structures in the cytoplasm. If they are honors students, they might even put together a little dance of cell division. (As for grading presentations, see my article titled "A Classroom Application of the Radio Shack Digital Sound-Level Meter.")

The Furniture Flimflam

Some of the best ideas are right under your nose—or your posterior. Rearrange the classroom each day. Have the students put the chairs in a different configuration—a circle, a triangle, a trapezoid. Any polygon or closed curve will do, but the best arrangements are those that take up to 10 minutes to complete. If you spend 10 minutes per class moving chairs, in two and a half years you will duck out of teaching the equivalent of an entire three-credit course. Over a 30-year career, that becomes a dozen courses. The furniture flimflam is actually a course-reduction measure.

Today's students are used to putting chairs in a circle, so most of them won't ask any dumb questions about why they are moving the furniture. If a few of them cop an attitude, just mumble something about the difference between confronting and communicating, or how a classroom should facilitate their transformation into a community of learners.

You can get students really motivated by mentioning scientific studies. Tell them about the research comparing people in hospital rooms with and without a view of the outside, which showed that the people with a view were discharged earlier and used fewer pain pills during their hospitalization. Who, then, would hesitate to arrange the chairs so that they face the windows? If you don't know of any relevant research, make some up.

Or you could go metaphysical and download for your class some New Age hooey from the Web, or material from the dozen or more sites devoted to feng shui. With a few Chinese terms, you can energize students to lay out the chairs in a hexagon contiguous with a rhomboid.

The Heavenly Remote

Any hermeneuticist knows that the medium is the message. And what is the medium for today's professor? Every plugged-in classroom in America has it: a

VCR. Bring in a video for class, dim the lights, push the play button on the remote, and you've done your academic work for the day.

You can use any video in any course. For openers, you have the presumption of relevance on your side: Everything that happens during class has something to do with the course. You can also rely on the dominant mental activity in higher-education circles, free association. With a little free association, your students will begin to believe that any video has something to do with the course. That is a logical point—everything freely associates with everything else; *ergo,* you're home free.

If rewinding and returning videos gets to be too much, start taping TV programs. You can spend class after class watching your homemade tapes of, say, daytime talk shows, reruns of sitcoms, detective shows, even the Weather Channel from time to time. For example, if you teach logic, tape Regis and that Kathie Lee impostor. When you show the tape in class, tell the students that you want them to spot the fallacious arguments that Regis tries to foist off on surrogate Kathie. If you teach ethics, tape Jerry Springer. For aesthetics, tape music videos from MTV. Marketing? Those Budweiser frogs are worth two or three upper-level courses. Physics? Professional beach volleyball on ESPN2. Criminal justice? Reruns of *Hawaii Five-O.*

It's a great time for a professor to be alive, isn't it? Unfortunately, it still takes some effort to record TV shows at home and bring the tapes to your campus. Why can't each classroom be hooked up to cable TV? Surely your college or university can get group rates from a cable company and find a TV manufacturer to donate the sets. Very few administrators seem to realize how much that could mean to the educational process, especially insofar as it would allow them to say things like "We've got cable in all the classrooms, but Harvard and Yale don't." Perhaps faculty members will have to get the ball rolling by contacting their AAUP representatives so that cable service can get on the table at the next contract negotiation, right there alongside the dental plan and the early-retirement options.

12. The Happy Immoralist

Christine Vitrano

In the lead article of a symposium featured in the *Journal of Social Philosophy,*[1] Steven Cahn claims that an immoral person can achieve happiness. As an illustration, he presents the fictitious example of Fred, a happy immoralist. Several philosophers have objected to Cahn's view, and after a brief presentation of it, I shall argue against those critics.

According to Cahn, Fred has achieved his three most important goals in life: fame, wealth and a reputation for probity. Nevertheless, he is "treacherous and dishonest."[2] He maintains his reputation for moral uprightness by keeping his immorality secret. Because he has succeeded in doing so, he is satisfied with his life. In short, he is happy.

Fred is not bothered that his happiness is caused by immorality. Although the thought that Fred is happy might anger some people, Cahn argues that the injustice in which Fred has enjoyed it does not give us reason to deny Fred's happiness. He is satisfied, though immoral, because being moral is not important to him. His only concern is appearing to be moral, and he has achieved that goal.

An immoralist like Fred can achieve happiness, because happiness and morality represent two separate dimensions from which to evaluate a person's life. Historically, many moral philosophers denied this distinction, viewing happiness and morality as inseparable. They saw virtue as necessary for happiness, and the moral saint was the paradigm towards which we were to strive if we wanted to live a happy life. Although some contemporary philosophers continue to deny the distinction between happiness and morality, I do not believe this view is plausible, for it fails to reflect the way in which the concept of happiness functions today. I shall now consider several arguments put forth by contemporary philosophers who wish to challenge Cahn's account of Fred's happiness.

John Kleinig views happiness as "a recognition that the various parts of one's life are functioning well in a coherent and stable fashion."[3] Kleinig refers to Fred's happiness as "epistemically unsound" because of the way Fred has achieved his goals, and he describes Fred's "path to success" in maintaining happiness as "an extremely perilous one."[4] Kleinig believes that for most of us, "happiness is bound up with living a life very different from Fred's."[5] Kleinig says that "real happiness" is intimately related to "a certain kind of social world" characterized by "trust, truthfulness and respect."[6] Given Fred's values, Kleinig concludes that, "at one important level his happiness is chimerical."[7]

Kleinig's objection to Fred's happiness is surprising, given Kleinig's own understanding of happiness. Kleinig identifies happiness with the recognition that "one's important goals are being accomplished, and that one is satisfied with how they are being accomplished."[8] Clearly Fred meets this condition, for Fred is achieving all his important goals and is exceedingly satisfied with the way his life is going. So why does Kleinig describe Fred's happiness as "epistemically unsound" and "chimerical"?

Kleinig is bothered by the "fragility of Fred's psychosocial world."[9] Fred's happiness is caused by deception and falsehood, but according to Kleinig, "real happiness" is bound up with virtues that Fred's life lacks. This approach introduces an element of objective value into Kleinig's account of happiness. He adds that, in addition to reaching our goals, we must have the right goals.

Jeffrie Murphy shares Kleinig's intuition about the instability of Fred's happiness, charging that Fred is attached to "temporal values that are vulnerable" particularly because they are "dependent on the responses of others."[10] According to Murphy, temporal desires leave one "vulnerable to the vicissitudes of fate and fortune and carry only temporary satisfaction," leading to a kind of happiness that is only momentary."[11] Murphy also suspects that Fred's happiness is diminished by the fear of its fragility, and that contemplation of future unhappiness would "at the very least pose a serious obstacle to his being fully happy now."[12] Murphy concludes, "When I think of the man described by Cahn, I find that I *pity* him . . . But why would I pity him if I thought he was truly happy?"[13]

Christopher Gowans also questions Fred's happiness, suspecting Fred is "not only lonely but anxious as well."[14] Although Gowans is willing to acknowledge some diversity among the causes of people's happiness, he believes that "human nature seems to impose some limits on this diversity."[15] Gowans believes that friendship is essential for happiness, and he wonders "whether Fred, while sitting alone watching himself praised on his wide-screen television, ever feels lonely."[16] Gowans suspects that Fred also suffers from anxiety over being exposed, and "since he has no friends, he has no one to whom to express this."[17] Gowans believes that Cahn's example "does not provide us with a convincing case of a happy immoralist," and he concludes that "perhaps Fred is happy in some respects, but we should be most engaged with the respects in which he is probably not."[18]

The first problem with these objections to Cahn's example is that they fail to accurately reflect the common understanding of happiness. Although the ancient Greeks had a tradition of conflating happiness with morality, denying that happiness was attainable by anyone who was not virtuous, I believe the word no longer retains that meaning today. When I say that someone is happy, I am referring to her state of mind. Being happy implies nothing about the value of a person's life independent of her own perceptions. A person's happiness is proportional to how positively she views her life; the more favorable her impression, the happier she will be.

Happiness is best characterized as a mental state of the subject, not as a state of affairs occurring in the world, and the concept has no necessary material conditions. We can describe someone without contradiction as "Poor, but happy," "Wicked, but happy," or even "Alone, but happy."

Happiness is not the primary or sole reason for action; it is merely one motivation among others. Some people act out of a sense of duty, or a desire for excellence, but these concerns may have nothing to do with happiness and provide no guarantee of it.

Fred views his life positively, because he is attaining those goals he deems valuable, yet all three objectors express skepticism over the value of those goals and share the view that Fred's blatant immorality precludes him from happiness. But focusing on what Fred's life lacks is irrelevant to the question whether he is happy, for if Fred is not bothered by what his life is missing, he need not be dissatisfied. That I would not be happy living your life is no reason you are not happy living it.

The connection posited by Kleinig between happiness and "a certain kind of social world" may apply to some people, but not to Fred. For people who value being moral, considerations of happiness clearly will be intertwined with morality, for their satisfaction will require living up to their ethical obligations. The mistake is to assume all people share these values. Gowans makes a similar error by assuming that Fred would benefit from genuine friendship. If I am content being alone, having more friends may not increase my happiness. Although friendships, family relationships and children are all sources of some people's happiness, to others they can become sources of misery.

Returning to the charge that Fred's happiness is unstable, I wonder whose happiness is ever "epistemically sound" or invulnerable to "the vicissitudes of fate and fortune"? I believe Fred's happiness is no less secure than anyone else's, for our moral values provide us with little protection against many sources of misery and unhappiness. For example, we can have strong attachments to other people whose health and safety are beyond our control. Likewise, we usually value our health and careers, but no matter how virtuous we are, one or both may fail. The happiness of all people is fragile, although most of us tend not to think about our situation, clinging instead to the false belief that virtue can guard us against evils. In reality, the immoralist's happiness, like the happiness of everyone else, is vulnerable to the vicissitudes of life.

Furthermore, I wonder why Gowans assumes that Fred does not have any friends; after all, Fred is supposed to be a *successful* immoralist, not an unsuccessful one. Although he is immoral, no one else knows. On the outside, Fred appears to be kind-hearted and caring; people believe he is a virtuous person. Surely then, Fred is respected by many who consider him a good friend. What distinguishes Fred is not that he has no friends but that he doesn't care whether he has any.

The same sort of misunderstanding leads Murphy to misdiagnose Fred's situation. You may pity Fred because you frown upon his lifestyle choices; *you* would prefer to be a more honorable (if less popular) person. Perhaps you are also skeptical about Fred's ability to keep up the charade. You may be worried that Fred's duplicity will be exposed; you may fear the repercussions if his immorality is revealed. But why assume Fred shares your values or anxieties? You might not want happiness that results from immorality, but someone else might. Your moral objection to Fred's lifestyle is a reflection of your own values and says little about the quality of Fred's life.

Thus, none of Cahn's critics presents a compelling argument that challenges Fred's happiness. Those tempted to deny it seek to keep morality and happiness closely tied, because once you recognize the independence, you open the door to the dreaded question, "Why be moral?" If you acknowledge that one's happiness can come into conflict with the duty to be moral, and you agree that it is rational to pursue one's own happiness, you are forced to acknowledge that behaving immorally could be rational.

Many moral philosophers try to avoid this conclusion by denying that morality and happiness can conflict. They presume that acknowledging reasons for action other than one's moral obligations will diminish the importance of morality, or encourage people to take their moral obligations less seriously. However, I believe the solution to the issue is not to deny the immoralist's happiness. The philosopher's attempt to steal back the word 'happiness' from the common lexicon and supply it with a "philosophical" definition is futile; it does little to improve the prospects for morality, and only deepens the chasm between philosophy and common sense.

In conclusion, philosophers should acknowledge that sometimes people have good reasons for acting immorally. Considerations of one's happiness may conflict with considerations of moral duty. In such challenging cases, I agree with Cahn that "How we decide tells us not only about morality and happiness but also about the sort of person we choose to be."[19]

Notes

1. Steven Cahn, "The Happy Immoralist." *Journal of Social Philosophy* 35 (2004): 1.
2. "Happy Immoralist," 1.
3. John Kleinig, "Happiness and Virtue." *Journal of Social Philosophy* 35 (2004): 2.
4. Kleinig, 2.
5. Kleinig, 2.
6. Kleinig, 2.
7. Kleinig, 2.
8. Kleinig, 2.
9. Kleinig, 2.

10. Jeffrie Murphy, "The Unhappy Immoralist." *Journal of Social Philosophy* 35 (2004): 12.
11. Murphy, 12.
12. Murphy, 12.
13. Murphy, 13.
14. Christopher Gowans, "Should Fred Elicit our Derision or Our Compassion?" *Journal of Social Philosophy* 35 (2004): 15.
15. Gowans, 15.
16. Gowans, 15.
17. Gowans, 15.
18. Gowans, 15.
19. Steven M. Cahn and Jeffrie G. Murphy, "Happiness and Immorality," in Steven M. Cahn and Christine Vitrano, eds., *Happiness: Classic and Contemporary Readings in Philosophy* (New York: Oxford University Press, 2008), 265.

13. Mentoring: Lessons from Steven Cahn

Robert B. Talisse and Maureen Eckert

It would be difficult to overstate the extent of Steven Cahn's academic accomplishment. His impact on professional philosophy has been far-reaching and multifaceted. Cahn has authored commanding essays on perennial topics such as free will, the existence of God, the problem of evil, social justice, and the nature of happiness; his intellectual purview extends across the areas of ethics, social and political philosophy, aesthetics, metaphysics, and philosophy of religion. His work in philosophy of education has proven especially influential; in fact, some graduate programs in philosophy require students preparing to teach their first courses to read Cahn's essays on teaching and grading, and many professors have improved their teaching by reflecting on Cahn's analyses. Yet this is only one of the ways in which Cahn has helped to shape how philosophy is taught. Through his careful and studious editorial work, Cahn has made available to the profession dozens of excellent textbooks covering nearly every area of philosophy.

Cahn's interest in philosophical questions concerning teaching and pedagogy brought him to topics beyond those typically discussed within professional philosophy. Throughout his career, Cahn has sought to clarify and defend a liberal and humanistic vision of the nature and purposes of the university. This endeavor has resulted in a series of books and articles focused on a wide array of concerns, including the liberal arts curriculum, affirmative action in the academy, the nature of academic excellence, the travails of college administration, and the moral responsibilities of professors.

Many of these issues are brought together in Cahn's most recent book, *From Student to Scholar: A Candid Guide to Becoming a Professor*. In this work, Cahn examines the long and often arduous road leading from a student's first year in graduate school, through the dissertation stage, and eventually to getting a full-time academic job. Cahn's good sense is manifest on every page.

In short, then, Steven Cahn seems to have covered all the bases, and for this the academy is in his debt. Yet there is one aspect of the academic life which Cahn has not addressed fully, namely, the process of *mentoring* students. In a way the lacuna is surprising since Cahn has on several occasions registered his deep appreciation for his own mentor, Richard Taylor. As recent graduates of the Ph. D. Program in Philosophy of the City University of New York who benefited greatly from Steve's guidance, perhaps we are especially well-positioned to devise an account of the ethics of mentoring students. Drawing upon the example Steve has set, we propose five principles of good mentoring.

Before proceeding, however, we should emphasize that we will mean by *mentoring* something quite broad. To be sure, the term is typically reserved for the process of directing a student's dissertation research and writing. But there is a range of activities professors engage in on behalf of their students—graduate and undergraduate—that is properly described as mentoring. For example, undergraduates who wish to continue on for graduate work often need to be mentored in order to complete an acceptable writing sample to accompany their applications. To take another example, even those undergraduates who do not intend to continue on to graduate school are often required to complete a senior thesis in their major and under the direction of a faculty member. And even with regard to graduate students, there are several occasions for mentoring outside of dissertation-writing. So, although what we will say below will apply most directly to the process of mentoring students as they work to complete a dissertation or a senior thesis, we hold that what we have to say is applicable, *mutatis mutandis*, to these other contexts.

One further clarification is in order. By *mentor* we will mean something more substantial than *supervisor*. Although it is a central responsibility of a mentor to supervise a student's dissertation or thesis, a supervisor is not necessarily a mentor. A dissertation can be successfully supervised with minimal interaction; a mentor necessarily plays a larger role in the research activities of the student. For example, a mentor will typically help the student select a dissertation topic and develop a research plan; mentors sometimes meet regularly with their students to discuss newly-published articles related to the topic of their work, and so on. In making the distinction between mentoring and supervising, we are in no way suggesting that the role of supervisor is necessarily deficient, only that mentoring is a different role.

1. Neither Master nor Cheerlead

First we must specify what the role of mentor involves, and here it will help to identify the aim or objective of the mentor. We believe it is uncontroversial to say that the mentor's primary aim is to facilitate the student's intellectual growth; in fact, it could be said that the mentor's objective is to manage the student's transition from student to professional. But in any case, if the aim is the student's intellectual growth, the mentor must be careful not to dominate or master the student. A faculty member dominates his students by insisting—subtly or overtly—that they reach his own favored conclusion or come to adopt his own position on the matter under investigation. Sometimes the result is achieved by browbeating students into conformity. In other cases, the faculty member tries to insulate the students from material that could cause them to appreciate a competing and disfavored view. In either case, the student emerges with a skewed view of the academic field to which he or she is now expected to contribute. A proper mentor avoids assuming the role of intellectual master.

There are at least two reasons why this often proves to be difficult. First, students often decide who among the faculty shall be their mentor on the basis of the faculty members' work; in other words, students often *seek out* a master. This is understandable because the task of completing a dissertation is intimidating. Second, one mentors students exploring the same area in which one works and thus has well-developed views. However, a proper mentor will not allow students simply to mimic his or her own work. Intellectual growth consists to a large degree in developing an independent mind, and in order to develop this kind of independence, the student must be challenged to think in new ways, to explore new lines of argument, to develop new positions.

If mentoring is aimed at philosophical growth, it must also be distinguished from the kind of non-judgmental encouragement we characterize as *cheerleading*. Students of course need and deserve encouragement, but the cheerleader provides encouragement at the cost of serious criticism and honest engagement. The cheerleader, that is, seeks primarily to nurture self-confidence in the student. Again, self-confidence is important. But proper self-confidence develops as a byproduct of genuine achievement; in other words, self-confidence that is incommensurate with achievement is misplaced. So the cheerleader has put the cart before the horse: it is by attending carefully to the quality of the student's work that a proper confidence in one's abilities can be instilled.

Thus both mastering and cheerleading undermine the objective of mentoring. The dominated student will be intellectually paralyzed, and the student of a cheerleader will be undisciplined. However, the mean between mastering and cheerleading should not be taken to be any sort of indifference or dispassion. It is, rather, more of a Socratic engagement with the student's work and progress. It is useful to note that a Socratic type of engagement is far from uninspired, but the very image of intellectual enthusiasm. Whether it is Euthyphro, Protagoras or Theaetetus to whom Socrates suggests they "return to the beginning" or test whether a seemingly well-formed proposition is "really so," Socrates remains resolute, dedicated to the pursuit of a sound argument. He is willing to continue working on a problem no matter how long it might take, and offers this energetic commitment to his interlocutors. Which interlocutors do and do not accept his offer is very telling. Of course, Socrates denies that he is a "teacher," especially in terms of peddling intellectual wares for the passive student to digest. Yet, there is arguably no better model of a mentor with respect to inspiring seriously committed students' pursuit of knowledge. Socrates' intellectual enthusiasm ideally models the mean between dogmatic mastering and ineffective cheerleading, while also reminding us about the nature of intellectual challenge at hand, and this leads us to our next principle.

2. Press the Merits of Opposing Views

A dissertation must make an original contribution to some area of scholarship. In philosophy, dissertations are often highly polemical: students take up and defend some view concerning a problem about which many other philosophers have written. The case for the *originality* of the dissertation is made by showing how most of the other philosophers who have written on the topic are wrong. Naturally enough, in the course of writing a dissertation, students can lose sight of the merits of the views they oppose. In the most extreme cases, they lose sight of the fact that there is an opposing view at all—they come to see their own position as the only contender for truth, and all opposition to be too radically confused to even count as competition. There are at least two reasons why a mentor must not allow this to happen.

The first, and more obvious, reason is prudential: There is no topic in philosophy that is both an appropriate focus for a dissertation and not the subject of debate among many intelligent and sincere philosophers. The student's view, even if it is every bit as correct as the student is inclined to think, is not the only view in currency among professional philosophers. When moving in professional circles at conferences and the like, the student will have to interact with those who hold opposing views. If the student is convinced that his or her view is really the only viable position, these interactions may prove less than satisfying.

The second reason is philosophical. In *On Liberty*, John Stuart Mill deftly observed that "he who knows only his own side of the case knows little of that."[1] Keeping sight of the merits of one's opposition is a crucial element in understanding the strengths of one's own position. It is when we become convinced that there is no intelligent response available to our critics that we are most prone to advance sloppy and imprecise version of our own views. To be clear, the point is not that a good mentor must try to prevent the student from becoming convinced of the truth of his or her thesis; rather, the idea is that a good mentor presses the student to anticipate the ways in which the opposition is likely to respond to his or her arguments. A well-mentored student is prepared to formulate a detailed answer to the question, "What are the strongest objections to your view?"

3. Promote Reasonable Ambitions from the Start

As we have already said, the dissertation process is intimidating even under the best of circumstances. This perhaps owes to the fact that a dissertation is by its very nature unlike any other writing project a student has encountered. Students will often approach the task with an inflated sense of what they must accomplish. It is often thought that the student with an over-ambitious dissertation project may simply be left to his or her own devices; in the process of pursuing the over-ambitious project, the student will eventually come to focus on something more manageable. Although this *laissez-faire* approach is easier for the mentor, it ultimately sets the student up for frustration and eventual defeat. It is far better for the student to begin from a reasonable conception of his or her task. A good mentor helps the student to begin with the appropriate level of ambitiousness.

Yet even with reasonable ambitions in place, a student may nevertheless discover obstacles during the dissertation project. A new article may appear, or organizational problems arise—a seemingly endless chapter mired in a micro-debate, or insufficiently defined and differentiated chapters, for instance. A mentor has the acumen to note these obstacles and determine a strategy for overcoming them. Being able to enhance or even change the dissertation writing plan productively in light of the many obstacles that arise is key to moving the student towards completion. In many ways, frustration and stalling tend to breed more frustrations and stalling. Less writing often leads to even less writing or none at all. The plain objective is to help the student remain productive. Sometimes it can be that the student is his or her own worst enemy, although just as frequently a student immersed in writing may fail to perceive alternative approaches to a problem at hand, feeling wedded to the prospectus in every detail. The mentor guides not only with respect to content, but also with respect to the student *qua* writer, seeing the forest and the trees. A mentor has the ability to keep that forest in sight, and clear the brush when necessary, pointing out a path when a student is busy running headlong repeatedly at an oak tree. This metaphor may seem light, yet the paralysis that can set in and draw any progress to halt is a serious problem encountered while writing dissertations.

4. Return Work Promptly

A mentor is responsible for reading and commenting on the student's work as it progresses from the earliest sketches to full drafts of chapters. Students rely on feedback from their mentor. The time taken between submitting work and receiving a response can become dangerously unproductive for the student, being time not writing at all or time writing on material that may stand in need of complete re-evaluation.

There are often clashes between professors and students with respect to time that *reflect an asymmetry that is worth considering*. On the one hand, a professor's time is valuable, as professors bear multiple professional demands that they must balance. On the other hand, students' time tends to be regarded as not especially valuable. They are often seen merely as students, despite the fact that they may be teaching courses as graduate assistants or adjuncts, attempting to publish, and often working other jobs to make ends meet. Students' time is not marked by the focus of the demands made on faculty members. It is, however, marked by diverse demands, lacking the focus of professional life while typically being anything but undemanding.

In this respect, an asymmetry between the value of a professor and a student's time is an earmark of a professional asymmetry, one between the professor *qua* professor and the student *qua* student. A professional asymmetry regards difference in specialized knowledge, achievements in a field, and carries with it differences in social and economic status. Yet the social and economic differences are precisely what come to fore when students' time is considered less important or altogether unimportant. This professional asymmetry does not take into account the time a student spends involved meeting the diverse demands upon him or her. While respecting a professor's valuable time it is important that students' time is not devalued altogether simply because they are not professors. Honest, adult coordination of the time frames and deadlines (respecting the professor's time with deadlines) should be reciprocated with equally honest, adult coordination of commentary on work submitted on time (respecting the student's time with deadlines). Likewise, when deadlines are failed on either side, honest, clear determinations of the causes need to be made, and new deadlines set (assuming no continual failures arise; continual failure rendering any work or mentoring a moot point).

This manner of respecting students' time establishes a pattern for professional practice with respect to creating and maintaining reasonable deadlines for one's own students and colleagues as well as meeting one's own deadlines. It is not unheard of that professional academics over-commit to projects and fail their deadlines. The issue then turns on how responsibly they handle such situations. The mentor models "best practices" for students prior to their becoming professional. This is not a matter of replicating professional asymmetries, but instantiating practices that will benefit students once they themselves join the profession.

5. Stay Connected

Although one is released from the institutional office of mentor at the moment the student's dissertation is successfully defended, the responsibilities of the mentor go beyond this institutional role. A mentor is responsible for helping the student to prepare for the job market. Minimally, this involves composing a carefully and honestly written letter of recommendation to accompany the student's job applications. More frequently, the mentor is expected to help the student prepare for the interview process, which in philosophy includes brief (usually 30 minute) interviews at the meetings of the Eastern Division of the American Philosophy Association, and more extended (usually two days) meetings on campus. The entire experience is exhausting at best, and demoralizing at worst. Graduate programs sometimes offer procedural preparation—mock interviews and job talks—while a mentor may be in a unique position with respect to seeing a student through this endurance test. Often the only advice students receive in situ comes from other job seekers and candidates. The war-stories shared between new Ph.D.s on the market may serve to lessen their worries or distribute them equally, but a mentor can do better and has more to offer. Interviews are notoriously difficult to interpret. Even the best-prepared candidate may be surprised by certain questions, or puzzled by the expressions and attitudes of interviewers. A mentor can provide the strongest debriefing, especially when the mentor focuses on the student and their answers and comportment, instead of becoming bogged down in decoding the possible decision. Interviewing is a learned skill. The more one does it, the better one can get at it, though only insofar as some feedback is provided. While it might be impossible to know for certain what was really said and expressed at the interview table, a mentor can help a protégée keep score. This means that if there is an emergent pattern or habitual tendency on the part of the student, the mentor is in a position to point it out. Once again, a mentor can be something more than a cheerleader.

Even after a student finds a job, the mentor should take an active interest in the student's career. This involves, at the very least, making oneself available for career-related conversations and advice. But good mentors go beyond this. They offer to read drafts of papers being prepared for journal submission, and write to their students frequently about grant or fellowship opportunities and other professional matters. In short, a good mentor stays connected with students well beyond graduate school.

There is a point of course at which a mentor ceases to be a mentor for a former student, a point at which they become colleagues who regard each other as equals in the profession. We suspect, however, that there is always a remainder, always a sense in which the mentor-student relationship endures. For those lucky enough to have worked with a proper mentor, there is always a person one thinks to call first and to keep updated through the ups and downs of professional life; and, perhaps, a person who comes to mind when, in talking with one's own students, one finds oneself giving advice that sounds very, very familiar.

Note

1. Mill, John Stuart, *On Liberty and Other Essays*. (Oxford University Press: Oxford: 1998), 42.

Afterword

Steven M. Cahn

Every contributor to this book has played a significant role in my academic life, and I am deeply grateful to each one for having devoted the time to preparing an essay for this collection.

The expectation might be that I would comment on the various papers, but I prefer to receive them in the spirit with which they were offered, and leave to others the challenge of engaging with the arguments and conclusions. I would note only that I find the quality of all the pieces to be remarkably high, just as I would have expected.

My special thanks to Maureen Eckert and Robert B. Talisse for planning the volume and bringing it to fruition. I can barely remember the days long ago when they sat in my classes, but I shall never forget their numerous subsequent kindnesses.

Most readers will value the individual articles to the extent that they provide philosophical and pedagogical insight. For me, however, the volume in its totality serves as a remembrance of those abiding friendships that have been the most treasured aspect of my many years in academia.

Bibliography of Steven M. Cahn

Books Authored

Fate, Logic, and Time
   Yale University Press, 1967
   Ridgeview Publishing Company, 1982
   Wipf and Stock Publishers, 2004

A New Introduction to Philosophy
   Harper & Row, 1971
   University Press of America, 1986
   Wipf and Stock Publishers, 2004

The Eclipse of Excellence: A Critique of American Higher Education
   (Foreword by Charles Frankel)
   Public Affairs Press, 1973
   Wipf and Stock Publishers, 2004

Education and the Democratic Ideal
   Nelson-Hall Company, 1979
   Wipf and Stock Publishers, 2004

Saints and Scamps: Ethics in Academia
   Rowman & Littlefield, 1986
   Revised Edition, 1994

Philosophical Explorations: Freedom, God, and Goodness
   Prometheus Books, 1989

Puzzles & Perplexities: Collected Essays
   Rowman & Littlefield, 2002
   Second Edition, Lexington Books, 2007

God, Reason, and Religion
   Thomson/Wadsworth, 2006

From Student to Scholar: A Candid Guide to Becoming a Professor
   (Foreword by Catharine R. Stimpson)
   Columbia University Press, 2008

Books Edited

Philosophy of Art and Aesthetics: From Plato to Wittgenstein
(with Frank A. Tilllman)
Harper & Row, 1969

The Philosophical Foundations of Education
Harper & Row, 1970

Philosophy of Religion
Harper & Row, 1970

Classics of Western Philosophy
Hackett Publishing Company, 1977
Second Edition, 1985
Third Edition, 1990
Fourth Edition, 1995
Fifth Edition, 1999
Sixth Edition, 2003
Seventh Edition, 2007

New Studies in the Philosophy of John Dewey
University Press of New England, 1977

Scholars Who Teach: The Art of College Teaching
Nelson-Hall Company, 1978
Wipf and Stock Publishers, 2004

Contemporary Philosophy of Religion
(with David Shatz)
Oxford University Press, 1982

Reason at Work: Introductory Readings in Philosophy
(with Patricia Kitcher and George Sher)
Harcourt Brace Jovanovich, 1984
Second Edition, 1990
Third Edition (also with Peter J. Markie), 1995

Morality, Responsibility, and the University: Studies in Academic Ethics
Temple University Press, 1990

Affirmative Action and the University: A Philosophical Inquiry
Temple University Press, 1993

Twentieth-Century Ethical Theory
  (with Joram G. Haber)
  Prentice Hall, 1995

The Affirmative Action Debate
  Routledge, 1995
  Second Edition, 2002

Classics of Modern Political Theory: Machiavelli to Mill
  Oxford University Press, 1997

Classic and Contemporary Readings in the Philosophy of Education
  McGraw-Hill, 1997

Ethics: History, Theory, and Contemporary Issues
  (with Peter Markie)
  Oxford University Press, 1998
  Second Edition, 2002
  Third Edition, 2006
  Fourth Edition, 2009

Exploring Philosophy: An Introductory Anthology
  Oxford University Press, 2000
  Second Edition, 2005
  Third Edition, 2009

Classics of Political and Moral Philosophy
  Oxford University Press, 2002

Question About God
  (with David Shatz)
  Oxford University Press, 2002

Morality and Public Policy
  (with Tziporah Kasachkoff)
  Prentice Hall, 2003

Knowledge and Reality
  (with Maureen Eckert and Robert Buckley)
  Prentice Hall, 2003

Philosophy for the 21st Century: A Comprehensive Reader
  Oxford University Press, 2003

Ten Essential Texts in the Philosophy of Religion
  Oxford University Press, 2005

Political Philosophy: The Essential Texts
    Oxford University Press, 2005

Philosophical Horizons: Introductory Readings
    (with Maureen Eckert)
    Thomson/Wadsworth, 2006

Aesthetics: A Comprehensive Anthology
    (with Aaron Meskin)
    Blackwell, 2008

Happiness: Classic and Contemporary Readings
    (with Christine Vitrano)
    Oxford University Press, 2008

The Meaning of Life, 3rd Edition: A Reader
    (with E. M. Klemke)
    Oxford University Press, 2008

Seven Masterpieces of Philosophy
    Pearson Longman, 2008

The Elements of Philosophy: Readings from Past and Present
    (with Tamar Szabó Gendler and Susanna Siegel)
    Oxford University Press, 2008

Exploring Philosophy of Religion: An Introductory Anthology
    Oxford University Press, 2009

Exploring Ethics: An Introductory Anthology
    Oxford University Press, 2009

Philosophy of Education: The Essential Texts
    Routledge, 2009

Index

Aeschylus, 70
Allen, W., 95
Aristotle, 1, 43, 70, 71, 80
Armstrong, D. M., 73
Austin, J. L., 71

Baier, K., 37
Barry, B., 19, 20
Baum, F. L., 94
Beller, J., 128-132
Berkeley, G., 85, 91, 102, 102-105
Bjorklund, F., 51
Bloom, A., 100, 101
Bowen, W. G., 132-136, 139
Brand, M., 118-121
Bredemeier, B. J., 130-132

Cahn, S., 2, 3, 11, 13, 14, 21, 33, 34, 40, 41, 61, 66, 93, 114, 149, 150, 152, 155
Carroll, L., 85, 87, 89, 91, 94, 105
Clemente, R., 94
Cottingham, J. 34

Da Vinci, L., 67
Darwall, S., 34
Darwin, C., 68
Descartes, R., 70, 72, 86, 90, 93, 95, 96, 97, 99, 100, 102
Dewey, J., 1, 2, 11, 70, 76, 77, 78, 79
Dodgson, C., 85
Dostoyevsky, F., 70
Duval, D., 122, 123, 129

Einstein, A., 67, 68
Euthyphro, 157

Faraday, M., 68
Frank, R., 9
French, P., 116-119, 127, 128, 137
Freud, S., 68
Fullinwider, R., 131

Gardner, M., 87, 91
Goodman, N., 75
Gopnic, A. 87, 92
Gowans, C., 150-151

Haidt, J. 44, 45, 48-55
Hall, J., 5
Heath, P., 87, 91
Hegel, G. W. F., 70, 77
Heidegger, M., 70
Heinegg, P., 129
Henry, P., 35
Hobbes, T., 70
Hook, S., 61, 64-66
Hume, D., 50, 72, 76, 77, 78, 80, 98, 99, 103

Ivester, D., 10

James, W., 88, 91

Kant, I., 43, 70, 76, 77, 80, 91, 96, 145
King., M. L., 100
Kleinig, J., 149-151

Lavoisier, A., 68
Leibniz, G., 94, 103
Levin, M., 95
Levin, S. A., 135
Lewis, D., 103
Loeb, L., 103

Matthews, G., 94, 95, 101

Mill, J. S., 72, 91, 158
Milton, J., 67
Morgenbesser, S., 101
Murphy, J., 149-151

Nagel, T., 17
Newton, I., 67, 68
Nietzsche, F., 70, 85
Nicklaus, J., 122

Picasso, P., 67
Plato, 26, 46, 72, 77, 80, 86, 146
Poincare, H., 68
Protagoras, 157

Quine., W. V. O., 99

Racine, J., 67
Rawls, J., 2, 18, 28
Renoir, J. 67
Rorty, R., 73-75
Russell, B., 93

Shakespeare, W., 38, 67, 70
Shields, D., 130-132

Shulman, J. L., 132-136
Simon, H., 9
Sisyphus, 33, 36, 39
Smart, J. J. C., 73
Socrates, 94, 157
Spaeman, R., 94
Spinoza, B., 71
Steele, C., 135
Stoll, S., 128-132
Suits, B., 121

Taylor, R., 39, 155
Theaetetus, 157
Thurber, J., 94

Vermeer, J., 67
Von Hirsch, A., 22

Waits, T., 155
Williamson, O., 4
Wittgenstein, L., 85, 98
Wolf, S., 33, 34, 35, 37, 39, 40, 41, 42
Wolff, R. P., 21
Woods, T., 122, 123, 129

www.ingramcontent.com/pod-product-compliance
Lightning Source LLC
Chambersburg PA
CBHW051058160426
43193CB00010B/1238